The Media in Transitional Democracies

Contemporary Political Communication

Robert M. Entman, *Scandal and Silence*

Max McCombs, R. Lance Holbert, Spiro Kiousis and Wayne Wanta, *The News and Public Opinion*

Craig Allen Smith, *Presidential Campaign Communication*

James Stanyer, *Intimate Politics*

Katrin Voltmer, *The Media in Transitional Democracies*

The Media in Transitional Democracies

Katrin Voltmer

polity

First published in 2013 by Polity Press

Polity Press
65 Bridge Street
Cambridge CB2 1UR, UK

Polity Press
350 Main Street
Malden, MA 02148, USA

ISBN-13: 978-0-7456-4458-5
ISBN-13: 978-0-7456-4459-2(pb)

A catalogue record for this book is available from the British Library.

Typeset in 10.5 on 12 pt Times Ten
by Toppan Best-set Premedia Limited
Printed and bound by the MPG Printgroup, UK

For further information on Polity, visit our website: www.politybooks.com

Contents

Detailed Contents

Introduction

> There you have it – reforms on unprepared ground, and copied from foreign institutions as well – nothing but harm!
>
> Dostoevsky, *The Brothers Karamazov*

The collapse of authoritarian regimes and the rise of democracy around the world over the past decades add up to one of the most significant developments in global politics which has changed the lives of millions of people. In all these transitions the media have played a pivotal role, not only by disseminating the images of change to a global audience, but also by becoming a force of change in their own right. When in 1989 the Berlin Wall came down, I was living in Berlin (the part of the city which was then called West Berlin). For months, since the first demonstrations took place in various cities of the then GDR, everybody in the city, and indeed around the world, was glued to the television screen, following the events as they unfolded at breathtaking speed across Central and Eastern Europe. Thirty years later, the uprisings in the Middle East that became known as the 'Arab Spring' captured the attention and imagination of people everywhere in the world like no other of the many transitions that had taken place since 1989. While I was working on the last chapters of this book, my postgraduate students were constantly searching the web, tweeting and chatting to stay abreast of the events in Tunisia, Egypt, Syria and elsewhere in the region. Some of these students were themselves from Arab countries, and while they probably felt that they were in the wrong place at this important moment in the history of their country, they were still able to take part in the uprisings as virtual participants thanks to the opportunities opened up by new media technologies.

People climbing over the Berlin Wall, the 'tank man' on Tiananmen Square, Colonel Gaddafi begging for his life: all are iconic images that will signify the joy, heroism and horrors of democratization for the years to come. Anti-regime protest and regime change have become global media events, forging a close link between democratization and modern mass communication. As a result of the crucial role that international broadcast media played during the events of 1989, the collapse of communism in Eastern Europe has been dubbed the first 'TV revolution' in history. And Egypt's struggle for democracy became known as the first 'Facebook revolution'. However, the assertion that the media have played a central role in the democratic transitions of the past couple of decades does not imply that they determined the success or failure of the many struggles for democracy, or even that they were responsible for their occurrence in the first place. But it is safe to say that in a media environment that offers fewer opportunities for mass mobilization and global information flows, all these events would have taken place in a different way and would probably have yielded different outcomes. It is this difference which this book sets out to explore.

The active involvement of the media and their strategic use by those fighting for (or against) democratic transition distinguish the transitions that have taken place since the late 1980s from earlier regime changes of the so-called 'third wave' of democratization (Huntington 1991) – for example, those in Southern Europe and Latin America in the mid-1970s. Since then, economic and technological advances of the media industry have fundamentally changed the dynamics of democratic transitions. News has become a global, highly competitive business driven by a constant hunger for breaking headlines and dramatic images. Satellite transmission and 24-hour news channels have accelerated the global flow of news. With regime change high on the agenda of Western foreign politics, political protests and upheavals have gained a high level of news value, which immediately catapults the events to the top of the international news agenda, thus expanding the scope of the event to global significance.

Yet the role of the media in transition processes is not confined to providing iconic images for the consumption of global audience spectators. They also affect the course of the events in various ways. The fact that the whole world is watching shapes the behaviour of the actors involved in the process and thus the dynamics and the eventual outcome of uprisings against authoritarian regimes. The availability of ever more sophisticated communication technologies has expanded the repertoire of strategic choices for both democracy activists and the ruling elites, who are trying to preserve their grip on power. Activists have quickly learned how to utilize, sometimes even manipulate, the media for their own purposes. And political leaders and governments have followed suit. At the beginning of the twenty-first century, the internet and mobile communication technologies have complemented traditional channels of mass communication and are about to reconfigure the strategic arena of political change yet again. In particular, the new ways of interaction, networking and information-sharing opened up by Web 2.0 have added a fresh dynamic to the interplay between democratic change and the media.

Furthermore, the importance of the media in transitions to democracy does not stop with the overthrow of the old regime. Even more important are the years that follow. Are the media able to take on a role that supports a viable democratic political process? or do they impede the consolidation of the emerging democracy? The fact that the media often play the role of midwife during regime change does not necessarily mean that they automatically slip into a democratic role once the old regime has ceased to exist. In fact, the recent wave of democratization not only witnessed the first TV and Facebook revolutions, but also the first attempts in history to build and consolidate democratic institutions in a media-saturated environment. In the established democracies of the West, the structures and methods of operation of key institutions, such as parliaments, elections and political parties, were developed before the media became a pervasive force in everyday and political life. In contrast, the new democracies of the late twentieth and early twenty-first century immediately leapfrog into what has been labelled 'media democracy' (Meyer 2002) – a notion that denotes a state of affairs where the media's rules of the game shape, to some extent even determine, the functioning (and dysfunctioning) of political institutions. Nowadays, professional media management and public relations have become an integral part of the political process and a precondition for political success, be it in elections, in intra-elite power struggles or in implementing policies and regulations. In the established democracies of the West, the increasing adaptation to the imperatives of the media has raised widespread concerns about the possible impact of media-centred politics on the quality and viability of democracy (for a political science perspective, see Patterson 1993; for a journalistic view, see Lloyd 2004). These concerns apply even more to young democracies. The complexities of modern 'media democracy' have caught most of the newly elected political leaders in transitional democracies largely unprepared, including those who spent years in opposition fighting for press freedom and freedom of expression. In modern 'media democracy' multi-channel competition, global news flows and the internet all create a highly unpredictable environment for political action. Moreover, once released from direct state control, the media in new democracies become part of a commercialized global market in which news decisions are largely governed more by profit rates and less by considerations about their possible consequences for the viability of the young democratic institutions.

It is against this backdrop that the transformation of the institutions of mass communication has become one of the most contested arenas of the transition process. Even though most journalists have been eager to take on a more professional and adversary role vis-à-vis political powerholders, the democratization of the media often remains incomplete and deficient – with far-reaching consequences for the democratization process as a whole. Many new democracies have seen fierce confrontations between governments and the media, quite tellingly dubbed 'media wars'. Most of these disputes revolve around recurrent disagreements over the degree to which elected political officials can claim privileged access to the media agenda, the principles and institutions of media regulation, the accepted norms and practices of journalism in a democratic society and the question whether – and if so in what way – the media should play an active part in the political, economic and social development of the country. With few exceptions, it took years for post-authoritarian governments to agree on new, or at least revised, media legislation, and in many cases the media are still operating in an insecure regulatory environment. Indeed, the democratization of the media seems to be a magnifying glass through which the achievements and drawbacks of democratization can be understood.

Experiences from many new democracies show that consolidating the new political order, including the media, is much more difficult than initially anticipated. Norms are more ambiguous than textbook knowledge would imply, changes take a long time to have any effect and frequently yield unintended consequences, and the situational constraints of domestic and international constellations often leave little room for implementing the ideals and hopes of the early years of the transition. Taking stock of what has been achieved so far, it becomes evident that different trajectories of transition from authoritarian to democratic rule have created a wide spectrum of shades of grey, making it difficult to judge how democratic the new democracies of the 'third wave' actually are. Some of them seem to be stuck in transition – no longer there, but not yet here. Indeed, there is growing scepticism among students of democratization and practitioners alike over the future prospect of many of the democratic newcomers. Some have even declared the end of the transition paradigm. For example, Carothers (2002) argues that we have to abandon the teleological thinking that has guided democratization research for the past decades. Like Dostoevsky, whose quote from *The Brothers Karamazov* heads this Introduction, these scholars doubt whether Western institutions and practices can work properly when implanted into a different political and cultural environment. We might even have to accept that some of the 'third wave' democracies are not heading towards the liberal model of the developed West. Instead, new hybrid forms of democracy, and with them hybrid forms of journalism, are emerging, the structures and processes of which we are only just beginning to understand (Voltmer 2012).

Evidently, neither the Western model of democracy nor the liberal model of independent media can be easily exported to other parts of the world, even though for many journalists, policymakers and citizens alike these models remain an ideal towards which to strive. In fact, the more that non-Western countries are adopting democratic forms of governance, the larger the divergence between the 'original product' and its local implementation becomes. At the same time, there is also growing scepticism among democracy activists in non-Western countries about the desirability of becoming like the West. In many countries of the developing world, in particular Africa and Asia, the implementation of democracy and media freedom is couched in a context of postcolonial sentiments. As societies struggle to free themselves from Western dominance, they also aim to find their own way into a democratic future. In a complex process of 'domestication', the norms and practices of democracy and democratic journalism are reinterpreted in the light of local cultures and experiences and adjusted to the needs and constraints of everyday life, which often differs dramatically from the relatively secure and wealthy circumstances in advanced Western democracies. To be sure, in many cases the call for 'going local' is nothing more than a justification of the persistence of authoritarian practices. But the experiences of the last two decades or so, when radical neoliberal economic reforms, premature elections and uncurbed media liberalization have frequently resulted in more inequality, violent intergroup conflicts and political polarization, are calling for a greater sensibility for the specific conditions under which transitions are taking place outside the Western world.

Following these observations, this book adopts Whitehead's notion of democracy and democratic journalism as 'floating, but anchored' concepts (2002: 6). The argument of the book is based on the assumption that the media have a role to play in the consolidation of emerging democracies that is not just a by-product of market activities, but an intentional objective of journalistic activities. Following from this, the norms of independent and diverse media serve as an anchor in the analysis of the interaction between mass communication and democratization. But these norms have to be contextualized within the cultural interpretations, historical trajectories and political and economic constraints of the particular situation in which they are put into practice.

Given the importance of the media in the transition process and the sharp conflicts surrounding their transformation between political actors and journalists, democratization scholars have paid surprisingly little attention to this crucial part of regime change from authoritarian to democratic rule. Since the beginning of the 'third wave' in the 1970s, an impressive body of literature has emerged that has helped to understand and explain the dynamics and prospects of new democracies. But in most of the standard works of the field one even does not find the media or mass communication listed in the index, not to mention dealt with systematically as part of the investigation. The few examples that incorporate the media in the analysis of the transition process include Haerpfer et al.'s (2009) textbook *Democratization* and a volume by Gunther and Mughan (2000) that compares the role of the media in established and new democracies. Most authors who do refer to the media usually do so from a general normative perspective that deals with them as part of the democratic principles of pluralism and liberal rights. The main point of reference here is Dahl's (1989) theory of procedural democracy, arguably the most influential conceptualization of liberal democracy, which incorporates freedom of the press, specified as institutional guarantees for 'freedom of expression' and 'alternative sources of information', into a set of criteria that together constitute democracy (ibid.: 220–2). Empirical democratization literature which is concerned with developing measurements of democracy and democratization frequently includes 'press freedom' and 'pluralism of the media' as indicators for the degree to which a country has adopted democratic institutions and procedures (for an overview, see Bernhagen 2009a). But there is no further analysis of the processes by which these standards are implemented in the course of institutional reforms, the relationship of the media with post-authoritarian elites, or the way in which the media actually perform their new democratic roles as watchdogs and forums for political debate.

Meanwhile, communication research has produced a growing body of knowledge about media in non-Western societies, many of which are emerging democracies. A heightened interest in what is going on in Asia, most notably China, and other parts of the developing world has led to a demand to 'de-Westernize' the theoretical and empirical concepts underpinning this research (see Curran and Park 2000b). Most of the research on media and communication focuses on particular geographical areas or individual countries with an emphasis on issues of media regulation and media industries (for Eastern Europe, see Dobek-Ostrowska and Glowacki 2011; Paletz and Jakubowicz 2003; for Latin America, see Fox and Waisbord 2002; Skidmore 2001; for Asia, see McCargo 2003; Willnat and Aw 2008; and for Africa, see Hyden et al. 2003; Nyamnjoh 2005). Thus, even though these studies have provided in-depth knowledge, they offer only few entry points for a more global, comparative perspective on the link between the media and democratic transitions.

About the book

This book aims to fill the gaps in the existing literature in three ways. First, it provides a synopsis of a large range of regional and case-specific research on media in transitional democracies, thereby enabling a comparative understanding of the similarities and differences in the relationship between media and democratization in different parts of the world. Second, by bringing together the divergent strands of political science democratization research and communication studies, the book offers new interdisciplinary perspectives on issues of political communication in processes of democratic transitions. And third, the book suggests a theoretical framework that allows us to explore the media–politics nexus in emerging democracies across time and across different national and cultural contexts. This differentiated view makes it possible to understand better the multitude of contextual opportunities and constraints that shape the way in which the media affect democratic change and the conflicts and problems that accompany the transformation of media institutions and journalism in the aftermath of regime change.

To this end the book is organized in three main parts. Part I outlines the normative foundations of democracy, democratization and the media. A central argument of the chapters of this section is that democracy and press freedom are both contested concepts that are socially constructed through public discourse. Chapter 1 is mainly concerned with the concept of democracy and democracy's various paradoxes of mutually dependent, but potentially contradicting, values. As a consequence, depending on the preferences of a given society at a given point in time, democratic institutions and practices can take on different forms, thus defying the notion of liberal democracy, as it has been established in the West, as a universally applicable manifestation of democracy. Chapter 2 turns to normative media theories and identifies independence and diversity as the two main dimensions of democratic media. Alternative forms of implementing these principles are discussed as are how cultural preferences and situational factors might together shape the understanding of the boundaries of press freedom.

Part II explores whether the media act as a force that promotes or inhibits transitions to democracy. Together the chapters of this section provide different perspectives on the media's role across time and specific pathways from authoritarianism to democracy. In a first step, Chapter 3 distinguishes two dimensions of the media – technologies and editorial content – to understand how the media can affect democratic change. Communication technologies provide structural conditions of distributing messages and building organizational ties that can be used by democracy activists, state agencies and individual citizens to pursue their goals. At the same time, the media actively take part in the political process by making editorial decisions that affect the knowledge that is publicly available and thus shapes the perceptions and decisions of both individual and collective actors. Chapter 4 then explores the impact of communication technologies and journalistic news decisions on democratization processes across time. Using the distinction between liberalization, transition and consolidation, the chapter shows that the role of the media in democratization takes on different forms depending on the particular stage of the process. Finally, Chapter 5 argues that the outcomes of media transformations differ depending on the role the media have played in the previous authoritarian regime. The path dependency of media democratization is exemplified with regard to four ideal-typical authoritarian regimes that precede current transitional democracies.

In Part III the focus of the analysis turns to the question of how the media themselves are affected by the transition process and how their institutions and practices are transformed in the course of rebuilding the political regime. In other words, besides being a force for change or stability the media are also subjected to transformation as the political, economic and social environment changes. Building on Hallin and Mancini's (2004) conceptual framework of comparative media systems, this part of the book focuses on four arenas of media transformation: the relationship between the media and the state (Chapter 6), media markets, commercialization and ownership (Chapter 7), political and societal parallelism (Chapter 8), and journalistic professionalism (Chapter 9). For each of these arenas selected issues are covered in 'Focus' sections to discuss specific problems involved in transforming the media into institutions that contribute to the viability and endurance of new democracies: the attempt to establish public service broadcasting in Central Eastern Europe illustrates how the persisting interferences of the state hamper the editorial autonomy of the broadcasters; the issue of political ownership, in particular in Russia and Latin America, highlights the fact that privatization and commercialization are not a guarantee for media independence as liberal theory would suggest; the problem of advocacy media in post-conflict societies serves to address issues of legitimate restrictions on press freedom; and finally, some light is shed on the 'dark side' of journalism – i.e., paid coverage and corruption in journalism.

The Conclusion brings together the main findings and the conclusions that can be drawn with regard to the media's role in democratic transitions.

As a final point, some explanations are needed about the terminology used throughout this book. As the title of the book implies, this study is concerned with 'transitional democracies'. This somewhat dubious species is also captured by terms such as 'new', 'young' or 'emerging' democracies. But what is 'new' and what is 'democracy'? As regards the former, I remember a conversation at a conference in Budapest in 2009 when a colleague from Poland exclaimed with a sigh of frustration: 'For how long are you going to call us "new"? We are now 20 years old and by any standard have reached adulthood.' This frustration is quite understandable, even though the growing literature on consolidation would not be able to answer this colleague's question. In this book, all countries that have turned away from authoritarian forms of government since the onset of the 'third wave' in the mid-1970s are regarded as 'new' or 'transitional' and thus fall into the realm of interest of this analysis. Many of them, like Portugal, Spain and Greece that marked the beginning of the 'third wave', are now regarded as consolidated democracies. Others, especially those that embarked on democratic politics during the 1990s, are still struggling with establishing sustainable democratic institutions and free media, and in some cases it is even questionable whether they will eventually succeed.

The term 'transition' is used throughout the book interchangeably with terms like 'democratization' or 'democratic transformation'. Thus, it is not confined to the short period immediately following the breakdown of the old regime, as suggested by O'Donnell and Schmitter (1986). Further, while Linz (2000) reserves the term 'authoritarian' for a particular non-democratic regime type as distinct from 'totalitarian' regimes, this book uses terms like 'authoritarian' or 'autocratic' in a general way to refer to any form of non-democratic regime regardless of its specific power structure.

Neither does the book subscribe to one particular definition of 'democracy'. Readers who want to learn more about the controversies surrounding different notions of democracy – from minimalist to maximalist positions – are referred to introductions to democratization (see, among others, Grugel 2002; Haerpfer et al. 2009; Morlino 2012; Potter et al. 1997). Instead, this investigation is mainly interested in the process rather than the outcome; that is to say, the focus of the analysis is on democratization rather than on 'democracy'. If we understand democratization as a process leading towards more participation and a more open public sphere, then democratization is open-ended with regard to both its beginning and its end point. Ultimately, democratization is an endeavour in which both new and old democracies are engaged. For even if a democracy is firmly established, its qualities are never securely owned. New events and developments – like, for example, the so-called 'war on terror' – can undermine democratic norms of transparency and even the rule of law, while the changing notions of citizenship demand a renewed relationship between the rulers and the ruled. In this respect, both old and new democracies are on the same journey. In fact, the global protests of the year 2011 – from Tunisia to Greece, from Russia to Syria, and from New York to Chile – made it all too clear that citizens around the world are striving for similar ideals of self-determination, free expression, human dignity and accountability of those in power, notwithstanding whether their country calls itself a democracy or not.

Part I

What Democracy? What Media?

The first part of this book is devoted to the values and norms that constitute our understanding of a 'good' democracy and the role the media are playing in democratic life. For many democracy activists struggling against an authoritarian regime, democracy is primarily defined by all those things which it is not: state violence and fear, restrictions on individuals' autonomy to lead the life they want to live, manipulative state propaganda, restrictions on free speech and, in many cases, economic decline. But once the dictator and his (rarely her) clique have been removed and crude censorship is abolished, a clearer vision of what democracy and free media actually mean is needed to build the new order.

The recent wave of democratization, which has brought democracy to more countries of the world than ever before, has revitalized scholarly debates about the standards of 'good' democracy and democratic media. Yet, at the same time, there seems to be a widening gap between the political and journalistic practices in the newly emerging democracies, on the one hand, and the sophistication of academic debate, on the other. Evidently, democracy on the ground is a fuzzy and contested concept that defies clear-cut definitions. A key argument of the two chapters that make up Part I of this book is therefore that the norms of democracy and free media have to be contextualized in the light of the specific historical, cultural and political circumstances in which a particular new democracy emerges. Alongside a core of indispensable principles, democratic practice has, as will be discussed in Chapter 1, to navigate through numerous normative paradoxes that cannot be resolved in a uniform, one-size-fits-all manner. It is therefore important to develop a better understanding of the particular cultural values and contextual constraints in which political actors and journalists in new democracies operate.

Chapter 2 engages in a more detailed discussion of two key principles of democratic media: independence and diversity. Like other democratic norms, these principles allow for a wide range of interpretations and practices. Not only emerging democracies, established democracies too have to address fundamental questions like: 'How free is a "free media"?' and 'What are the best ways of practising and fostering diversity?' These are difficult questions, and different circumstances will require different answers.

Following the reasoning of the philosopher Onora O'Neill, Chapter 2 argues that freedom of the press involves not only the rights of the speaker – i.e., the media and all those who seek to communicate their views through the media – but the communication process as a whole. Press freedom therefore comes with the responsibility to consider the consequences of journalistic outputs on the listeners. From this more holistic perspective, the ultimate goal of press freedom is to enable a robust and inclusive public debate, which is at the heart of a healthy and sustainable democracy. In new democracies, achieving this goal is a particular challenge. The volatility of the transition process, fragile institutions and the centrifugal forces frequently unleashed by the breakdown of dictatorial rule make it an extremely difficult task to find the right balance between freedom and openness, on the one hand, and responsibility and restraint, on the other.

The discussion of the diversity norm focuses on two different modes of representing different opinions, interests and identities that exist in society: internal and external diversity. While internal diversity, with its principle of neutral and balanced reporting, has become the standard of professional journalism, widely taught in journalistic textbooks and codified in codes of practice, it is argued that both forms of media diversity have their specific strengths and drawbacks. A particular point is made to emphasize the role that partisan and advocacy media can play in building political identities and mobilizing the citizens of new democracies to participate in public life. However, there is also the risk of external diversity being a source of destructive divisions and intolerance.

1

Democracy and Democratization: One Idea, Many Roads

There are probably few words in contemporary political public discourse that bear as much hope and aspiration as 'democracy'. Equally, there are probably few words that are as much overused. As democracy is becoming 'the only story in town' – to paraphrase Linz and Stepan's (1996: 5) famous definition of a consolidated democracy being 'the only game in town' – the boundaries of what it actually means are becoming increasingly blurred. The pervasiveness of a democracy discourse that was unleashed after the end of the Cold War and is constantly reinforced by global media has made it ever more difficult to distinguish between democratic and non-democratic politics. Under the cloak of democracy, political leaders have suppressed opposition and 'managed' election results to legitimize their power. Meanwhile, the 1993 invasion of Iraq by Western troops under the command of the US has equally been justified by its purportedly democratic mission: to end dictatorship and to bring democracy to the country. However, for many people, the Iraq War has given democracy a bad taste as something that is used as a Trojan horse to promote the neo-imperialist interests of the West.

With the unprecedented spread of democracy around the world in recent decades, the meaning of the term has become increasingly contested not only among scholars, but also amongst political factions and various groups of democracy activists. Is Russia a democracy? Is Turkey democratic enough to be allowed into the European Union? And is Britain becoming less democratic with the introduction of new security laws to fight terrorism? Depending on one's understanding of what democracy is, the answers will be different. In fact, the many struggles and popular protests that swept across the globe in 2011 were driven by an urge for democracy that encompassed citizens in established and emerging democracies as well as in dictatorships: protesters in the Arab world demanding freedom, justice and respect; the 'Occupy' movement in the US, Britain and many other Western democracies demonstrating against the unchecked power of financial markets; and Greek demonstrators defending their right to a decent living standard and their country's independence from external dictates.

This chapter explores how an idea with universal appeal – government by the people – is interpreted and practised in different ways at different times and in different places. Even though democracy is founded on a set of indispensable principles and values, this chapter argues that it is surprisingly elastic and adaptable to specific circumstances arising from the historical, cultural and political trajectories in which it is implemented. In fact, it is the openness of the democratic idea that has kept it alive over centuries and enables it to grow roots in places that have little in common with the countries where institutionalized democracy first developed. Because of the ambiguous boundaries of the concept, we would be mistaken to try to pin down the 'true' or 'best' form of democracy. Instead, the way in which democracy is practised is always a specific balance between local values and universally shared norms, thus giving way to a wide range of variations that challenge rigid definitions of what democracy should look like.

Lost in definitions: democracy and democratization

Democratization research is struggling with a conceptual uncertainty that lies at the very heart of its subject: the impossibility to agree on what exactly democracy is. This problem is becoming even more apparent as more countries with no, or only weak, cultural ties with the Western world abandon autocracy and embark on implementing democratic institutions of government. For most of the twentieth century, democratization was perceived as a process whereby emerging democracies set out to adopt Western models of democratic governance – most notably the American presidential system with extensive mechanisms of checks and balances, or the British Westminster model of parliamentary democracy. However, the outcomes of transitions, especially in Asia and sub-Saharan Africa, frequently defy this expectation. Even the democracies in Central Eastern Europe, a region that regards itself as part of the historical and cultural heritage of the West, seem to function in somewhat different ways from their proclaimed role models.

One of the conceptual problems with democracy is that any definition always involves both ideals of what is regarded as 'good' democracy and empirical descriptions of how democracy works in actual existing democratic countries. Since democracy was not invented at the 'green table', but emerged as a product of specific historical circumstances,[1] the concept and institutional arrangements of modern democracy are bound to be ambiguous and in some cases even contradictory. Democracy developed in an iterative, sometimes arbitrary, way, or – as Dahl (2000: 25) puts it: 'Democracy, it appears, is a bit chancy.' Hence, the outcomes of this process could well have been different from what is known as democracy today. The contextual nature of democracy applies as much to its ancient Athenian form, which is now – rightly or wrongly – regarded as the origin of modern democratic governance, as to liberal democracy of our time. As Dahl (1989: 24–33) shows, it was only by combining the idea of equal votes as a mechanism of decision-making (*isonomia*) and the non-, or predemocratic practice of representation inherited from medieval institutions, that democracy was made fit for politics in modern territorial nation-states. The conclusion from this observation is that if democracy is the product of specific historically contingent political and intellectual developments, then different forms of democratic governance could be possible.

So, what then is democracy as we know it? The key idea is encapsulated in the Greek words of which the term 'democracy' is composed – *demos*: people; *kratos*: power or rule – describing a form of government whereby the ultimate power lies with the people. Since in modern representative democracy 'rule by the people' is mainly exercised through elections, one way of determining whether or not a country is a democracy is by finding out if it conducts elections to select its political leaders. However, as countless rigged elections with results of almost 100 per cent of votes in favour of the incumbent highlight, more is necessary to qualify a country as democratic. Elections have to be fair and free, open to all citizens and conducted periodically. For a country emerging from autocracy, organizing elections that meet these requirements is an enormous achievement. The so-called minimalist school of thinking in democratization research therefore regards holding free and fair elections a sufficient definition of democracy (Przeworski et al. 1995).

Other scholars have challenged this reduction of democracy to elections, arguing that elections alone do not make for a 'good' democracy (for an overview of various notions of the prerequisites of democracy, see Bernhagen 2009a). To start with, elections are only meaningful if there exist real alternatives between which voters can choose. Viable pluralism not only involves a substantial range of oppositional groups, but also a free press through which divergent views can be expressed and debated in public. Further, to prevent democracy from being taken hostage by autocrats after the election has been won, a system of checks and balances has to be in place that ensures 'horizontal accountability' of the ruling elites (O'Donnell 2003). Central to this system of accountability are the rule of law and an independent judiciary, together with a press that acts as a watchdog, monitoring the actions of public figures on behalf of the citizens. A further layer of requirements is added by scholars who emphasize the importance of an active and competent citizenry for the viability of democracy. After all, it is the citizens who are the sovereign of the democratic process, and without their constant engagement, democratic politics would soon be left to a small circle of elites.

What can be observed here is that the definition of what democracy is – and should be – tends to expand its boundaries very quickly once one starts thinking about how the key idea of 'government by the people' can be achieved in practice. There is a noticeable danger of conceptual overstretching as layers of criteria and sub-criteria are added to the key definition of democracy. Paradoxically, the conceptual expansion is both realistic, because based on the empirical observation of democracy's complexities when enacted in real life, and idealistic, in the sense that no real existing society is able to achieve all the conditions stated by theorists of a maximalist school of democratic scholarship.

One of the weaknesses of mainstream definitions of democracy is that most of them take a rather essentialist approach. Whether by reduction or by expansion of the conceptual scope, the unspoken assumption seems to be that eventually the true nature of democracy can be grasped by observing its features in existing, apparently functioning democracies. As a consequence, the empirical manifestation of the established democracies and their media systems in Europe and North America serve, often inadvertently, as normative standards for a 'good' democracy. However, this Euro- and US-centric approach underestimates the degree to which democracy is reinterpreted and enacted by the people who live in a particular democracy, no matter how consolidated the system is. Abstract concepts, like freedom, representation or justice, as well as practices, like voting, running for office or joining an online discussion forum, mean different things in different cultural and political contexts. Thus, the meaning and practices of democracy are constantly reconstructed and renegotiated in

the light of the experiences and beliefs of the people who participate in the democratic enterprise. Deep history that may date back over centuries can be as important as actual situational factors in shaping the interpretations of democracy. It is for this reason that democratization scholar Laurence Whitehead (2002: 187) proposes an 'interpretavist' approach to democratization, in which the meaning and practices of democratic politics are achieved in a process of social construction. Instead of having a fixed meaning that can be applied universally, an 'interpretavist' definition of democracy is embedded in broader cultural, historical and political discourses that together shape the outcome of the transition process. Even established democracies periodically go through times of interpretative uncertainty and self-reflection, for example in the event of high-profile political scandals or national disasters. However, they can rely on an accumulated set of previous agreements, laid down in official documents (court decisions, committee reports, etc.) or stored in collective memory, that serve as a point of reference in the actual debate. Citizens and policymakers in emerging democracies operate on far less solid ground.

However, challenging the conceptual purity of democracy and acknowledging its cultural determinants raise new problems and questions. Does this mean that we have reached a postmodern age of democracy where 'anything goes'? Is, for example, Putin's vision of a 'sovereign democracy' (see Okara 2007) with restricted rule of law and the absence of media freedom in broadcasting just one of many variants of democracy? Obviously, the concept of democracy has to maintain its core of shared values, otherwise it would lose its meaning altogether. Whitehead (2002) is concerned about this possible conclusion that could be drawn from his notion of an 'interpretavist' approach to democracy. He suggests the notion of a 'floating but anchored' (ibid.: 6) conception of democracy and its key values, where the core meaning is grounded, but more peripheral concepts are open to debate and interpretation.

Democratic paradoxes

As discussed above, the principles and institutions of 'government by the people' and the conditions that guarantee effective popular participation form the indispensable foundation of democracy. These are complemented by broader value orientations and peripheral concepts that are believed to support and enable democratic rule. Pluralism, competition and individualism are taken as examples here because they are not only central to the variations of democracies across cultures, but also of crucial importance for how the role of the media is perceived in these contexts, as will be discussed in more detail in Chapter 2. Unfortunately, these – as numerous other – democratic values do not solve the ambiguity problem of democracy. On the contrary. Rather than being distinct and clear-cut categories, these concepts are part of value dimensions; i.e., they comprise opposing, yet interdependent, preferences. The point is that, for a functioning democracy, both aspects of these value dimensions are vital, and the expansion of one usually happens at the expense of the other. In other words, democracy is built on normative paradoxes that require constant reinterpretation and readjustment in response to changing circumstances. Western democracy discourses tend to emphasize one pole of these value dimensions, thereby making the opposing end of the dimension less salient, even less legitimate. However, even within Western democracies there exists a considerable variation of value preferences.[2] But the scope of possible shades and the normative ambiguity involved have become more visible with the emergence of new democracies outside the Western world. The following discussion illustrates the 'multivalence' (Paley 2002: 477) of democratic value orientations with regard to the three exemplary value dimensions mentioned above.

Pluralism versus unity

The toleration of difference – in lifestyles, political views or cultural identities – is one of the defining aspects that distinguishes democracies from non-democratic regimes, which tend to impose homogeneity on their societies, if necessary even with means of suppression and physical violence. Pluralism allows individuals and communities to express and practise their uniqueness. With increased social and geographical mobility in modern societies and the global flow of ideas, the need to accommodate difference has become even more imperative. At the same time, societies – or, as political communities, polities – need a sense of unity that integrates the plurality of individual and group endeavours. Modern societies are becoming acutely aware of the centrifugal forces of diversity. As a response, in many countries discourses of unity have emerged, like, for example, the discussion about 'Britishness' initiated in 2006 by the then Chancellor Gordon Brown. It is probably indicative for the multiculturalism of British society that these ideas have not been widely followed up. In many new democracies the urgency to solve the pluralism versus unity dilemma is much more pressing. In contexts where nation-building is incomplete, where the central power has only limited reach and where a multitude of ethnicities compete for domination, unity and integration are a matter of survival. Under these circumstances, national media are frequently used as a means to limit pluralism and to promote a unifying national narrative. Not surprisingly, this instrumentalization of the media regularly triggers criticism from international media development groups. But in societies that are at risk of disintegration or even sectarian violence, a stricter control on who is saying what in the public sphere might be the lesser evil.[3]

Conflict versus consensus

Conflict and competition are regarded as the engine of the democratic process. From Mill's (1972/1859) notion of a 'marketplace of ideas', to Schumpeter's (1954) understanding of democracy as elite competition, to Dahl's 'polyarchy' (1971), democratic theory emphasizes conflict not only as an unavoidable side-effect of pluralism, but as a virtue. Mill, for example, believes that the confrontation of conflicting ideas eventually brings about 'truth'. In opposition to an understanding of democracy as a competitive power balance, and based on Habermas's (1984) notion of the 'ideal speech situation', theorists of deliberative democracy have recently pushed the emphasis towards the other end of the dimension by focusing on consensus as a desired outcome of public communication (see Gutmann and Thompson 1996). The acceptance of conflict varies not only across individuals, but also across cultures. Asian societies, especially those with a strong Confucian tradition, tend to avoid open conflict, which is often – rather mistakenly – regarded as an impediment to the development of a democratic culture (Fukuyama 1991). Even though consensus and social harmony are often used by political authorities as a pretext for oppressing oppositional voices, the ability to build bridges and to minimize divisions can be seen as an important resource for navigating through the turmoil and uncertainties of transition.

Individualism versus collectivism

Democracy and its principle of 'government by the people' is based on the autonomy and dignity of the individual. The rule of 'one wo-man, one vote' implies that every citizen, regardless of his or her social background, ethnicity or sex, has the right and the ability to participate in democratic decision-making. In fact, this acknowledgement of the dignity and uniqueness of the individual contributes much to the appeal of democracy in societies where rigid hierarchies, poverty and social exclusion dominate political life. It is therefore not by accident that women fought in large numbers at the frontline of Egypt's democratic revolution in 2011 – and that they feel themselves to be the main losers, as the military and conservative religious groups secure their grip on post-Mubarak Egypt. At the same time, it is the individualism of the West that triggers widespread resistance to democracy in many non-Western societies. Here, Western-style individualism is often regarded as aggressive and destructive because it is perceived as being acted out without regard to the needs and feelings of others and to the detriment of the cohesion of the community. Most non-Western cultures prefer a position on the individualism–collectivism continuum that emphasizes group needs more than their Western counterparts, sometimes at the expense of individual self-determination. Like with consensus-oriented cultural values, community bonds can be an obstacle to developing democracy, but can also be employed as a resource for strengthening involvement and participation. As Putnam (2000) shows, democratic participation is essentially collective rather than individual action, and requires social capital that creates mutual trust and the willingness to cooperate for a common goal. In fact, it is the loss of communal life and a culture of doing things together that, according to Putnam, are responsible for the present decline of American democracy.

Depending on how democracies – both emerging and established ones – position themselves on these and other value dimensions, which cannot be covered in detail in the present context, the resulting practices and institutions will be significantly different. With the growing 'divergence of democracy' (Diamond and Plattner 2001), it is important to acknowledge that different routes of democratization do not necessarily lead to a deviant or even deficient outcome of the transition. Instead, the hybridity of norms will bring about 'multiple democracies' (Blokker 2009), as they negotiate their way through the complexities of transition. Ultimately, the universality of democracy derives not only from the ability of different cultures to adapt to the norms of democratic governance, but also from the ability of democracy to adapt to the divergent cultural frameworks of both Western and non-Western societies.

Exporting democracy

The cultural embeddedness of democracy is one of the main reasons why democracy – as practised in the West – cannot be easily exported. This is not to say that some countries are less fit for democracy than others. Rather, when evaluating the quality of the new democracies of the 'third wave' we have to keep in mind that democracy cannot be adopted in a one-to-one fashion. The meanings of the institutions of government (Sartori 2001) and of the institutions of public communication (Voltmer 2012) change as they travel from one place to another. Moreover, the direction of 'democracy trade' has been changing in recent years. No longer is the West, in particular the US and Britain, the only standard-bearer of what 'good' democracy is. Equally important are emerging role models that are perceived as culturally closer and therefore more useful for solving the problems of democratic transition. For example, Turkey has become an attractive alternative to Western-style democracy for aspiring democrats in the Middle East. The reason is not only Turkey's booming economy and successful modernization path, but probably more importantly the way in which religion has been brought back into public life, which appeals to all those citizens who feel uneasy with the strict secularism of most Western countries. Similarly, Africa's emerging democracies are looking as much towards South Africa or Ghana as they look to the US or Britain when seeking inspiration for how to do democracy – and how not to do it.

Recent attempts at exporting democracy without due consideration of the local context and the situational constellation of political and cultural factors illustrate the pitfalls of a mechanistic understanding of how democracy works. Premature introduction of elections or badly planned privatization, not to mention attempts at initiating 'regime change' by military force, are but the most dramatic instances where exporting democracy has gone badly wrong, leaving behind a traumatized and disillusioned population (Collier 2009). One of the reasons for the failure of democracy in some places can be seen in its insufficient integration into the local customs and existing interpretations of cultural ideas. Therefore, Owusu (1997), an anthropologist who was involved in drafting Ghana's new constitution in the early 1990s, calls for a 'domestication' of democracy. By this, he means a process by which democratic institutions are adapted to local value systems and customs, thereby instilling a sense of familiarity and ownership in ordinary citizens. It is through this hybridization, the fusion of exogenous and endogenous elements of institutions and the localization of abstract principles, that democracy can get a chance to consolidate in different contexts and gain long-term legitimacy. As an example of the domestication of democracy Owusu points to the resurgence and even reinstitutionalization of traditional leaders in a number of African countries (for example Botswana, Ghana and Zambia) that have established a 'House of Chiefs' as a second chamber to represent community interests and provide recommendations regarding tribal affairs. Of course, this measure is not immune to misuse and exploitation for particularistic ethnic agendas; but it provides a possible road of reconciling traditional forms of self-governance with modern democratic institutions. Those who frown at this mixture of pre-modern and pre-democratic elements with contemporary institutions of liberal democracy might be reminded of the British House of Lords, which is a relic from medieval times and whose members are not democratically elected but are appointed by various bodies or even hold their seats on the grounds of hereditary privilege.

Contributions by anthropologists to the study of democratization (for an overview, see Paley 2002; for media and politics in Russia, see Roudakova 2008) or scholars interested in language and political discourses (for post-communist countries, see Dryzek and Holmes 2002; for Senegal, see Schaffer 1998) have deepened our understanding of the cultural contingency of democracy and the diversity of routes that transition to democracy can take. These studies have not brought us any closer to a clear definition of democracy, but they have heightened our sensitivity for the processes that link institutions and values. For institutions do not work independently of the sense that people are making of them and the interpretative concepts they use to evaluate their performance.

2

Democratic Media: A Question of Means and Ends

It is almost a truism to say that the media are an indispensable part of a viable democracy. In fact, it is impossible to think of a democracy without a free press and the right to express one's view freely in public. Conversely, a dictatorship that tolerates the unrestrained flow of ideas in the public realm seems a contradiction in itself and one would assume that sooner or later the lack of control over thoughts and words will undermine the very foundations of that regime. However, the media are not democratic by nature. They serve dictatorships as happily as they flourish in democracies. It is not the media as a means of communication that makes them a democratic force, but particular norms of their institutional structure and the quality of their performance that establish them as a cornerstone of democracy. This chapter is about the normative ideas that link the media and democracy. The main emphasis will be on journalistic media – i.e., the traditional means of mass communication press and broadcasting, and, especially, on how the news media have taken on the form of political institutions that are organized and regulated in a particular way to codify their relationship with other political institutions – e.g., governments and political parties (Cook 2006; Schudson 2002). Most of the normative debates about communication values have so far evolved around press and broadcasting. In this respect, the internet is presently going through an interesting transitory state from an unlimited and largely unregulated space to one that is increasingly incorporated into existing economic and political power structures. Because of the convergence of different forms and channels of communication made possible by digitalization, the internet encompasses journalistic forms of mass communication (online media, websites of established offline outlets), interpersonal communication (social media, discussion forums) as well as new hybrid forms like blogs. Most of the normative principles discussed in this chapter also apply to the internet, even though many internet activists who reject any regulation or notions of responsibility as censorship would probably oppose this view.

In the process of transforming the media from an instrument of authoritarian power into a democratic political institution, policymakers and any stakeholders involved in the process are faced with a number of fundamental choices. Whatever choices are made in the course of the transition, they are deeply rooted in, and influenced by, normative questions such as: What is the role of the media in democratic life? Do the media have particular responsibilities, specifically during transition? Or is the very notion of a responsible press a violation of press freedom that should be rejected in the first place? How can the plurality of interests and identities be best represented by the media? Or does too much diversity exacerbate disintegration in volatile transitional societies? As the answers to these questions differ according to the normative presumptions of the actors involved and the wider cultural environment in which they operate, the outcomes of the transition process will differ too.

This chapter argues that the norms of public communication are far more ambiguous than textbook knowledge might imply. Even in contexts where most people would agree on 'democracy' and 'press freedom' as first principles, the boundaries of these values and the way in which they are put into practice remain contested among media scholars and policymakers alike. These debates are by no means confined to new democracies where consensus about basic principles might not yet have been achieved. Established democracies are also frequently going through often bitter disputes over the role of the media in political life, indicating the volatility of media standards and their openness to change. Following the notion of the social construction of institutions, as outlined in the previous chapter, any discussion of the role of the media in democratic life has to be aware of the negotiated nature of the norms that guide the organization and performance of the media. However, the challenge remains – as Whitehead (2002: 19) puts it – to distinguish between the 'floating' and the 'anchored' elements of these norms, i.e., those aspects that are negotiable and those that are indispensable in order for democracy to preserve its distinct meaning.

This chapter starts off with a discussion of how philosophers and normative media theorists have justified press freedom as a key principle of democracy. It then moves on to look more closely at two basic standards that guide media regulation and media performance: independence and diversity. Alternative conceptions of these standards are discussed and how they affect policymaking and journalistic practice. To prevent this discussion from becoming too esoteric, examples will be given from both established and transitional democracies to illustrate the implications of normative preferences and the dilemmas when putting them into practice.

Means and ends

The view that the media are fulfilling certain functions for democracy (and society at large) has become commonplace in normative media theory (McQuail 1992). However, this has far-reaching implications. It means that media freedom is essentially seen as a means to an end, an instrument to bring about public goods rather than an end in itself. In other words, media freedom comes with certain expectations and responsibilities that ultimately restrict the media in the way in which they use their freedom (Blumler 1992; McQuail 2003; Voltmer 2010). In this respect, the philosophical justification of press freedom differs from that of freedom of expression, which comes without preconditions because expressing ideas and sharing them with others are a natural part of being human (Barendt 2005; Lichtenberg 1990a).

Given the extent to which governments (and any other actors in the political arena) depend on the mass media as a channel to communicate to the wider public, it does not come as a surprise that the questions as to what exactly the media's responsibilities are and who is entitled to stipulate them are highly contested between the media and those who demand access. Indeed, the inability to achieve consensus on these issues is the main reason why the democratization of the media has turned out to be one of the most disputed and unresolved areas of transitional politics. The dangers and pitfalls of a teleological, or consequentialist, view of media freedom have led many journalists to reject it altogether. In contrast to the responsibility model of press freedom, liberalist views aim to keep to a minimum external definitions of how the media should perform their role to serve democracy (see Siebert et al. 1956). However, the liberalist position of non-responsibility is not without risks either, as it has made the media vulnerable to the detrimental consequences of commercialization and the imperatives of market demands. Critics of a teleological view of press freedom often overlook the fact that responsibilities not only pose limitations on press freedom, but also serve as a protective shield against the domination of particularistic interests, whether political, economic or religious. This book is based on the proposition that the media do have a democratic role to play and that it is legitimate to expect them to meet certain normative standards, even though the particular way in which these expectations are put into practice is open to debate and will vary across cultures and times.

Communication scholars have suggested various lists of functions the media are expected to fulfil – some longer, some shorter, often mixing normative assertions of what the media ought to do with empirical observations of what they are actually doing (see McQuail 1994: 79; for the context of new democracies, see Norris and Odugbemi 2009). The following set of three is confined to the political functions of the media in view of what we expect the media to do in and for democracy:

- to hold government officials to account by acting as a 'watchdog' that brings misuses of power or policy failures to the knowledge of the public;
- to provide citizens with the information they need to participate in the democratic process in a meaningful and effective manner;
- to serve as a forum for different voices, both official and alternative, to mobilize public support for their cause.

The idea of the media serving as a '*watchdog*' that monitors state power is closely linked to one of the central arguments that inspired the struggle for press freedom in Western Europe over the past two centuries. First articulated in the philosophical writings of seventeenth- and eighteenth-century enlightenment thinkers (most notably John Milton and Immanuel Kant), then further developed by the theorists of liberalism (among others John Locke and John Stuart Mill), freedom of expression and freedom of the press were part of a movement that put the individual and his autonomy and dignity at the centre of social and political life (Keane 1991; Levy 1985). In an age of absolute power and strict censorship the state was seen as the main adversary of individual rights and freedoms, and the public expression and dissemination of ideas, especially critical ones that challenged the existing order, were part of the struggle for democracy and individual self-determination. From this point of view, press freedom is understood as freedom from and against the state. In a similar line of thinking, probably going back to Edmund Burke, the press is seen as a 'fourth estate' and hence part of a system of checks and balances that prevents any single power – executive, parliament or judiciary – from dominating public affairs.

The availability of reliable *information* beyond the small circles of elites is a crucial precondition for the workings of democratic politics. With the expansion of mass suffrage, the question of citizens' competence, knowledge and judgement has emerged as a paramount issue of democratic politics. Without a basic understanding of the political choices at hand, popular elections would become meaningless, even normatively questionable. In particular, the legitimacy of majority rule depends on the shared belief that voting decisions have been made on the basis of sound reasons and in good faith, even if people hold different views on the issues at hand. Indeed, it would be hard for the losing minority to accept the elected government if the outcome of the election was based on manipulated information and ignorance. In his influential theory of liberal democracy, Dahl (1989: 111) therefore stipulates 'enlightened understanding' – that is, the citizens' capability of making informed judgements – as one of the prerequisites of pluralist democracy. In addition, he finds it necessary to complement this standard with what he calls 'enlightened sympathy' (ibid.: 181), denoting people's willingness and ability to consider the needs of fellow-citizens. Both forms of 'enlightenment' require high-quality information. To enable citizens to make intelligent choices in their own interest, the media should provide sufficient information about the programmatic positions and the competence and integrity of candidates and political parties who are running for office. Moreover, this information has to be presented in a fair manner, allowing citizens to develop tolerance and respect for those with whom they might not agree and who might have different interests and value priorities. Even though the media are not the only source of information on political matters, they are undoubtedly the most accessible and the most universal. Thus, failure of the media to provide the kind of information that fosters informed popular participation poses a serious risk to the viability of democracy.

In some respects the *forum* function is like the flipside of the media's information function. While the latter focuses on the perspective of the citizens and their information needs, the former argues from the perspective of political actors and their need to communicate to their constituencies and the wider public. The idea of the media serving as a forum for public debate is often regarded as a modern embodiment of the *agora* in ancient Athens. During the city's democratic centuries (between the sixth and third century BC, though interrupted by intermittent tyrannies), the *agora* served as a public space where citizens of the *polis* came together to discuss and decide on public matters (Arblaster 1994: 13–24; Held 1996: 13–25). In modern nation-state democracies, with their large populations and vast territories, individual and simultaneous participation in the public debate is no longer possible. There is no physical space that could accommodate all citizens, and even in Athens, where the assembly did not exceed some 6,000 people, it was already impossible for everybody to make active use of their right to speak. Therefore, the media represent, and speak on behalf of, the citizens by giving voice to all views, interests and groups. For participation to be effective and inclusive, it is therefore of crucial importance that all relevant voices have access to the forum of the media: the government as well as its opponents, parties from different segments of the political spectrum, social groups and alternative movements.

Watchdog, information and forum functions might read like a shopping list, with each item being equally important as they developed in response to changing historical circumstances. However, there are hidden trade-offs between them, making it difficult, sometimes impossible, to maximize one without limiting the others. This tension becomes apparent when regulatory arrangements and journalistic professional codes of practice are to be set up to support these functions. As with the paradoxes of democracy, which have been discussed in Chapter 1, there is no universally applicable standard of how the different roles and norms of democratic media should be performed. Instead, the particular constraints, priorities and needs that emerge as a democracy develops will require recurrent processes of rethinking and renegotiation of the desired balance of these norms in an open and inclusive public debate.

Since the watchdog function aims at keeping state power at bay, this role requires a high degree of independence from the very power the media are supposed to control. A minimum of regulation and a maximum of rights and privileges allow journalists to take on a proactive, adversarial role vis-à-vis political officials. Freedom of information legislation, which provides the right to access official documents, and the protection of journalistic sources of information are examples of regulatory provisions that enable investigative journalism and support the media's watchdog role. In contrast, the forum function implies a more passive journalistic role that focuses on providing the platform on which political actors can present their proposals. Securing fair and equal access requires regulation and supervision, which in effect limit the media's discretionary power to select who and what they want to cover. This is particularly important during election campaigns. Many countries therefore have specific regulatory arrangements in place to ensure fair access for all parties and candidates to the media agenda. Finally, the implications of the information function sit somewhere in between. Providing information that matters requires proactive journalism and professional presentation skills. This cannot be achieved without the freedom to seek out and publicize information, but it also requires rules and norms to safeguard quality standards and to ensure that the interests of the public are not overturned by the media's own economic or political interests. Journalistic codes of ethics and press councils are regulatory instruments employed to specify, monitor and – if necessary – enforce media accountability (see McQuail 2003). Since quality issues affect the content of media reporting directly, they are usually left to self-regulation rather than state regulation, which inevitably bears the risk of censorship and political interference.

Even though most media perform all three functions to varying degrees, policymakers have to set priorities as to how to deal with the potential trade-offs between the policy implications involved. Kelley and Donway (1990: 97) approach the issue from a classical liberalist perspective by arguing that 'for advocates of limited government, the first [i.e. the watchdog function] is by far the more important. It is set by the end of government, the protection of rights, and would be required regardless of whether or not such a government employed democratic means of operation.' The authors go on to contend that since any form of regulation makes the media vulnerable to political pressure, strengthening the information function at the expense of the watchdog function cannot be justified. In the same volume, Lichtenberg (1990b) argues to the contrary. In her view, there is no guarantee that a free press left to its own devices would fulfil its democratic function of providing valuable information. In fact, 'editorial autonomy can inhibit the multiplicity of voices' (ibid.: 121). This holds for various reasons: corporate ownership is likely to exclude views that contradict its interests; further, the media's own constraints of production tend to result in a particular selection of issues; and journalists' reliance on authoritative sources gives elite voices a much higher chance of being heard than alternative views from groups outside the established circles of power. From this Lichtenberg concludes that some kind of regulation is necessary to ensure a satisfactory quality of information and fair and wide-ranging access to the means of public communication.

Valid as these arguments are, the decision as to which of the media's democratic functions ought to prevail cannot be answered on the basis of pure philosophical argument alone. The emphasis on a particular aspect also depends on the specific political and social context in which policy decisions are made and how a society interprets and evaluates the key concepts of democracy and the role of the media therein. Here, the understanding of the state is of crucial importance. A political culture that views the state as the prime enemy of individual freedom, a Hobbesian 'Leviathan' who would quickly expand dictatorial powers if not held at bay, will tend to emphasize the watchdog function of the media. In contrast, there is usually a higher degree of tolerance of, even demand for, more extensive regulation where the state is seen as a benevolent and integrating force. Priorities about the media's role are further shaped by implicit or explicit views of a 'good' democracy. From a 'minimalist' perspective that views democracy primarily as a mechanism to select political leaders through regular elections, the demands for information quality will be fairly modest. Basic information about the relevant alternatives (political leaders, parties) is regarded as sufficient for ensuring an acceptable degree of rationality of electoral decision-making. However, if democracy is believed to go beyond simple voting to also include continuous public involvement and participation at all levels of political affairs, then the demands for high-quality information exceed what mainstream journalism is usually able to deliver without regulatory benchmarks (Strömbäck 2005).

Setting priorities can pose a particular dilemma in new democracies. After years of dictatorship, which often involved massive human rights violations and the waste of public wealth, curbing state power and implementing mechanisms of state accountability are undoubtedly of utmost importance. Strengthening the watchdog capacities of the media is therefore an important part of the democratization process and will help to increase responsive and responsible government. Watchdog media might also get involved in coming to terms with the past by finding out who was responsible for the misdeeds of the old regime. At the same time, the attempt of many dictatorships to depoliticize society puts revitalizing active and competent citizenship high up on the post-authoritarian agenda, which shifts the emphasis to responsible and professional journalism that provides citizens with mobilizing information and in-depth analysis. An additional complication is that many new democracies are deeply divided societies in which the preceding authoritarian regime allowed a particular group, often a minority, to dominate the political institutions and to control the resources of the country. In these cases, providing an all-inclusive forum for the many voices might be a priority when it comes to helping integration and fair representation.

Besides the normative dilemmas that arise from the particular situational constraints of transition, the meaning of the key concepts of freedom, power and pluralism often changes when Western discourses of democracy are interpreted through the lens of a country's own cultural preconceptions. Discussion of the media's democratic functions as outlined in the previous paragraphs draws on the arguments that developed in the political and intellectual environment of eighteenth- and nineteenth-century Europe. While virtually all cultures have developed a conception of freedom, discourses in non-European contexts have often taken different routes, resulting in divergent interpretations of the idea. For example, in Asian and African cultures freedom has a more ambivalent meaning than in modern Western cultures, often bearing connotations of selfishness and disregard of collective interests.[1] In Indian philosophical tradition the idea of freedom has often been related to spiritual freedom, which is achieved through self-control rather than through overcoming external restraints (see Taylor 2002). So far we know very little about how the reconstruction of key principles like freedom of the press in different cultural contexts affects the way in which the media are fulfilling their role.

Another example of how concepts are translated and integrated into local traditions of thought is the rhetoric of the media acting as a 'fourth estate'. As Albuquerque (2005) shows for Brazil, the concept of division of power, which in European political philosophy is regarded as a bulwark against absolutist state power, is met with deep-rooted scepticism. The dissolution of the state into three separate branches is seen as a source of instability and political deadlock. In this context, the idea of the press acting as a 'fourth estate' takes on a very different meaning. Instead of controlling power, the press in Brazil claims to act as an arbitrator that moderates disputes between the three constitutional branches. Other institutions, most notably the military, have also been known to present themselves as a moderating 'fourth estate'. But by adopting free press rhetoric from Western media theories, Brazilian journalists have successfully claimed this role for themselves, albeit with a surprising twist.

In the following sections, two of the main standards of democratic media – independence and diversity – will be discussed in more detail. Different, often conflicting interpretations of these standards will be explored as well as the dilemmas this might raise and how alternative views have shaped the debate about media transformation in new democracies.

Independence

Independence of the media raises the obvious question: what from? But it also raises questions about its scope. Are there legitimate reasons to restrict the media's freedom to cover what they wish? Do requirements to provide particular content impair the media's independence? The following pages deal with these key issues surrounding the implementation and practice of an independent press.

Press freedom and power

The high value attributed to the media's watchdog role explains why media independence is mainly understood as independence from the state. The most prominent example is the First Amendment of the American constitution: 'Congress shall make no law . . . abridging the freedom of speech, or the press' (Schwartz 1971: 1148–9). This statement, which has inspired campaigners for media freedom and democracy around the world, reflects the view that freedom of speech and freedom of the press have to be protected from political powers and their attempts to constrain the public communication of ideas. Evidently, independence from state interference is the precondition that allows the media to investigate malpractice of political officials and hold governments to account for their actions. In this role the media are believed to act on behalf of citizens who do not have the resources to dig into information that is difficult to access, often even deliberately withheld or manipulated. The Watergate scandal is often seen as a paradigmatic case of an independent press acting as a powerful watchdog and has gained almost cult status in the journalistic profession. As the scandal unfolded, *Washington Post* reporters Bob Woodward and Carl Bernstein played a crucial role in exposing the incredible degree of criminal activities, including fraud and corruption, employed by the Republican Party in the run-up to the 1972 election, which eventually forced President Nixon to resign from office.

But the media's watchdog role goes beyond spectacular cases of 'regicide'. Equally, or even more, important is the media's day-to-day reporting on government policies. As economist and Nobel Prize-winner Joseph Stiglitz (2002: 28) puts it: 'Free speech and a free press not only make abuses of governmental powers less likely, they also enhance the likelihood that people's basic needs will be met.' Stiglitz uses the concept of 'information asymmetries' to highlight the crucial role of the media in keeping political officials accountable and responsive to those who elected them to office. In politics, as in any other social relationship, knowledge is power. Therefore, government officials tend to control and monopolize information in order to gain advantage over their opponents. By disseminating information to a wider public, the media help to level the playing field between those in power and ordinary citizens. Since public knowledge is shared knowledge, it has the potential to result in collective action. For example, if people realize that their own problems are not just individual misfortune, but that they share these problems with many others, they will be more inclined to demand government action to improve their situation. Because of the potential dynamics of public information, media coverage – even anticipated media coverage – is an effective way of exerting pressure on governments to deliver policies that meet the needs of the electorate.

However, the relationship between the media and the state is more ambivalent than normative ideals imply. Even though most journalists see themselves as the watchdogs of political power, they are tied into production routines that have the potential to undermine their independence and ability to balance the information asymmetry between the government and citizens. Not only does investigative journalism require an overproportional amount of resources (time, money, skills), it can even be counterproductive to effective news reporting. The primary sources of routine news are government officials and other political elites who are in a position to provide journalists with the raw material of their stories: information about ongoing government activities, sound bites, leaks and background information. Maintaining good relationships with their sources is therefore of paramount importance for journalists, whereas the disclosure of damaging material bears the risk of disrupting this relationship. Politicians often react to negative news coverage with some form of punishment, such as limiting or interrupting contact with the journalists who were involved in the affair, thus leaving them cut off from the daily stream of news and quotes that keeps the news wheel going. Especially in immature democracies, where respect for the independence of the press is still superficial, these 'soft' sanctions are frequently extended to direct pressures and even threats. Brants and Van Kempen (2002) talk about the 'ambivalent watchdog' who is torn between the normative ideals of adversarialism, on the one hand, and the constraints of news production, on the other. Blumler and Gurevitch (1995: 25–44) even regard the watchdog role of the media as an inadequate concept for understanding political communication. They argue that the normative idea of an adversarial relationship between the media and political power disguises the fact that for most of the time the interaction between politicians and journalists is characterized by a culture of cooperation and mutual interdependency. This does not exclude occasional conflicts over the rules and norms of interactions, but both sides are well aware of the mutual long-term benefits of avoiding confrontations.

The close, at times even symbiotic, relationship between journalists and political officials is presently undergoing dramatic changes in response to increased commercialization of the media market and the widespread use of new communication technologies (Blumler and Kavanagh 1999). With more media competing for breaking news, individuals within the political system who seek to disclose facts without being named will easily find a journalist to pick up the leaked information – often without the necessary checks of its credibility. Furthermore, digitalization is fundamentally undermining governments' control over the flow of information because it makes it much easier for journalists to find and link together stories that can be held against individual politicians or political organizations.

For all these reasons, journalists in new democracies enter a field that is marked by normative ambiguities as well as dramatic changes (LaMay 2009). The tensions between the ideal of watchdog journalism and the constraints of news production, between a culture of censorship and the promises of newly won freedoms, makes it extremely difficult for them to find their place in the political game. Quite understandably, many of them might be inclined to 'indulge' in adversarialism after having been muzzled under the old authoritarian regime, while their counterparts (governments, political leaders and political parties) are reluctant to accept the loss of control that comes with democratic rule and an independent press. Things are even more confusing, as the transition process itself frequently raises normative dilemmas that make it difficult to stick to first principles. The volatility of the transitional situation might raise the question as to how conducive an adversarial press is for the consolidation of the new regime. In some situations a more cooperative relationship can provide the newly elected government with much-needed breathing space to manage the complexities of transition without the pressure of an excess of public criticism. An interesting example is Spain between Franco's death in 1975 and the approval of the new democratic constitution in 1978. During these three years of transition the political situation was highly fragile, with persisting opposition to the new democratic regime within the military (which later erupted in an unsuccessful *coup d'état* in 1981) and separatist movements in several regions of the country. In these circumstances the media decided to support the political course of the government, especially with regard to its stance towards national unity and a general amnesty for political crimes as part of a pact between old and new elites. Barrera and Zugasti (2006: 39) describe the relationship between the new government and the media as characterized by 'a high level of mutual understanding and even complicity', with both sides being committed to stabilizing the democratization process regardless of partisan differences or professional norms of journalism. By doing so, the media became part of the elite pact that made the Spanish case almost a role model of successful transition (Karl and Schmitter 1991). As democracy grew roots and consolidated, the media took on a more adversarial and critical role. Moving away from a journalism of national unity then paved the way for strong partisanship and political divisions, which still characterize the Spanish press today. It is important to note that the media's abstinence from criticizing the post-Franco government was voluntary and temporary. Since cooperation was not imposed by the government, the media were able to preserve – and regain – their independence after they began to opt out of the transitional elite consensus. Moreover, the strategy of elite cooperation across parties and between government and the media was made public and gained the support of the vast majority of the Spanish people.

Compare the Spanish case with the 1996 presidential election in Russia, where Yeltsin was in the running for re-election, even though at the beginning of the campaign he was far behind his contenders, most notably the communist candidate Zyuganov. In this situation the media had the proverbial choice between Scylla and Charybdis – the two dangerous sea monsters of antic mythology between which Odysseus had to navigate. Both options were deadly, and avoiding one risk meant coming too close to the other. In the Russian case, Yeltsin presented himself as the democratic choice, even though the chaotic economic reforms and spiralling corruption that took place under his leadership made many Russians doubt the virtues of democracy and capitalism. Meanwhile, Zyuganov left no one in doubt that he was against democracy and a free press. The media – especially the commercial television channel NTV, which by that time had a track record of independent reporting – decided to back Yeltsin at all costs. Not only was Zyuganov almost entirely excluded from access to the media; the media also suppressed important information about Yeltsin that would have weakened his electoral prospects. At the time of election Yeltsin's health was already seriously ailing and he had recently suffered a heart attack. None of this was mentioned in the media. In the end he won the election. Did this manoeuvre save democracy? Unlike in the Spanish example, voters were deliberately misled by the media, which withheld crucial information that would have allowed the Russian people to participate in a meaningful way. Oates and Roselle (2000) regard the strategy of the media during this campaign as a missed opportunity to consolidate democracy and to open up public debate in Russia (see also De Smaele 2006). The long-term consequences were a growing dependency of the media on powerful political actors and an acute cynicism of Russian audiences who have lost any trust in the credibility and honesty of the media (Mickiewicz 2008).

The examples illustrate the complexity of the media's role vis-à-vis the government during periods of transition. There might be good reasons for a tame watchdog in some situations; yet other circumstances might require not only a barking, but even a biting, watchdog. One factor is the particular point in time during the transition process. The period immediately following the breakdown of the old regime is characterized, in particular, by high volatility and uncertainty. In this situation building and stabilizing the new democratic institutions and protecting them against potential enemies are of the highest priority and might justify a more restrained role of the media. Another aspect is the type of elites that come into power after the change. Is the new government mainly composed of old elites who emerged as the victorious faction from in-fights within the old power elite, or are they genuinely committed to building a democratic polity? The survival of old elites should ring all alarm bells, whereas democratic novices in government might deserve a moratorium from a hostile media environment.

However, in a world of globalized markets and growing ownership concentration in the media industry, the state is by no means the main enemy of media independence. Corporate power might be less tangible than written laws and regulations. Yet the constraints of market competition and even direct interference by media owners into editorial decision-making systematically affect the way in which the media cover particular issues and – sometimes more importantly – what is omitted from the news (Baker 2007; Picard 1989). This is most obvious when it comes to issues that directly affect the economic interests of media owners or the industry in general – for example, coverage of issues of media regulation or in-house industrial conflicts. At the same time, uncovering scandals of misconduct of political powerholders can be a circulation booster for commercial media, who are therefore often at the forefront of muckraking and investigative journalism.[2]

Another force that has been gaining influence recently is religion. Many new democracies are deeply religious societies, some of them still struggling with establishing an effective line between political and religious affairs. In post-communist countries, democratization has opened up new spaces for religion to establish itself in public life, bringing to an end a period of suppression where religious expression was pushed to the margins of society in the best case, and subjected to persecution in the worst. However, institutionalized religion is frequently becoming a challenge to the consolidation of the new democratic order. This is not to say that religion does not have an important role to play in a democratic society. On the contrary, religious organizations contribute important alternative views and often constructive criticism on moral issues and the social fall-outs of an increasingly competitive and exploitative world economic system. However, religious influence becomes problematic – and a case for the watchdog role of the media – when religious values claim absolute validity and supremacy over the norms and rules that govern political or judicial institutions. Christian churches and Islam have been particularly successful in increasing their influence on policymakers and in some cases in effectively curbing the freedom of the press. One example is Poland, where the Roman Catholic Church frequently interferes in politics to an extent that clearly contradicts the principle of separation of state and religion. During the communist regime the church played a key role in supporting the opposition and protecting those who suffered state persecution. However, its relationship with the democracy that emerged after the demise of communism remains ambiguous at best. The church openly criticizes the secularism, liberalism, individualism and materialism of Western democracy, and has frequently ignored democratic institutions and procedures in pursuit of its own interests (Eberts 1998). The reference to 'respect for Christian values' in the 1992 radio and television broadcasting law in Poland is an indication for the church's power to impose its own norms on public discourse. This clause has been instrumental in removing programmes that did not find the approval of the church and even to withdraw licences (Press Reference 2010). But it may well be that the church has overestimated its authority in Polish society. As democracy in Poland gains maturity and self-confidence, a growing number of citizens are no longer willing to tolerate the influence of the church in public affairs and many simply ignore the directives issued by clerics on political matters.

How free is free?

Even those who want to see media regulation kept to a minimum would concede that press freedom is not absolute and that under certain circumstances restrictions on the media might be necessary. While establishing an open and inclusive media space is one of the prime objectives in processes of democratization policymakers, media activists and journalists are struggling with the complexity of press freedom, which frequently leads to contradictions, sometimes with adverse consequences. As Cohen-Almagor (2006) points out, freedom of expression and freedom of the press are costly, often even damaging. Hence, decisions have to be made as to who is bearing these costs and where the boundaries of toleration are to be drawn. In new democracies the transformation of the media is a particularly controversial and complex process because it involves both opening up freedom and regulating it at the same time. On the one hand, press freedom is still a vulnerable value that needs to be protected and nurtured in order to grow roots in the political culture of a country. On the other, the costs of unrestricted public speech can be dangerously high in volatile situations of uncertain transitions, unfinished nation-building and societal divisions.

Different types of values are frequently found in conflict with communication freedoms. First of all – and probably surprisingly – is democracy itself. As stated at the beginning of this chapter, it is impossible for democracy to flourish without an independent and vigilant press. But the content of public speech, whether expressed in the mass media, by individuals or on the internet, is not always in favour of democracy. This raises the question whether and to what extent democracy should tolerate public speech that openly challenges democratic rule and propagates a non-democratic alternative. In other words, should anti-democrats enjoy the very freedoms they aim to destroy? The possible tension between free speech and the sustainability of democracy is one of the many 'democratic paradoxes' – i.e., frictions and inconsistencies emerging from contradicting, yet equally valued, principles. Most established democracies will be confident enough to tolerate radical opposition and will ideally engage in an open and robust dialogue with the arguments of their enemies. However, new democracies might struggle to win this battle, especially when anti-democratic voices can rely on considerable backing amongst parts of the political elites; or when the hardships and repercussions of the transition process are seriously testing popular beliefs in democracy. Given the insecurities caused by radical political and economic change, it does not come as a surprise that extremist propaganda is able to attract a significant following, especially in the largely uncontrolled spaces of the internet. Neither prohibition nor laissez-faire-style toleration can solve this problem. What is needed in this situation, but is rarely available, is strong moral (not necessarily political) leadership to shape and civilize the public debate.

Another frequent justification for restricting press freedom is the national interest and state security. While most journalists would accept the fact that details about an ongoing military operation or the country's defence system should not be published, governments often use arguments of security and national interest to evade public scrutiny and to fence off investigative journalists. This is by no means confined to new democracies. For example, Britain's Official Secrets

Act, which excludes official documents from publication if this is deemed to be in the national interest, has bred a culture of secrecy that allows the British government a high degree of control over potentially damaging information (Curran and Seaton 1997). Even after Britain signed up to the Freedom of Information Act in 2000, a large number of laws still restrict public scrutiny in many areas. The global spread of terrorism has further heightened state secrecy in many countries, and journalists find it increasingly difficult to get access to sensitive information that would allow them to pursue their watchdog role (for the UK, see Article 19: Global Campaign for Free Expression 2006; for Russia, see Simons and Strovsky 2006; for a global view, see Puddington et al. 2010).

In South Africa the conflict over the media's commitment to the national interest illustrates the close interrelationship between power and normative issues (Wasserman and De Beer 2006). When President Mbeki called for support for his government in the name of the national interest, it was all too clear that this plea was aimed at debunking widespread media criticism of his policies, especially on HIV/AIDS and his dealings with Zimbabwe. The media defended themselves by claiming to act in the public interest, which in their view expands beyond, and sometimes even overrides, the national interest. However, Mbeki's references to the national interest also evoked notions of national unity and inclusiveness against the backdrop of the deep divisions left behind by the apartheid regime. In this respect, his criticism touched upon a vulnerable point of post-apartheid media, which were slow to respond to the new political and social circumstances. Debating the meaning of normative ideas – national versus public interest – and negotiating the boundaries between independence and responsibility played, and still do, an important part in South Africa's attempt to construct and reinvent its own vision of democracy in a non-Western context.

A third reason that might justify restrictions on press freedom concerns social cohesion and integration, which relate to one of democracy's paradoxes discussed in Chapter 1 – namely, while democracy celebrates diversity and conflict, it also depends on a shared understanding of core values to ensure mutual trust and social coherence across social groups. For societies to avoid anomie or even civil war, they need to reach an agreement on what the rules and norms are that govern public life. In other words, democratic conflict and competition are based on consensus over fundamental issues, including the rules and norms of public communication, which involves a shared understanding of what it is acceptable to say in public, and how. Any speech that challenges the social bonds of the political community or the rules of peaceful resolution of conflicts is therefore regarded as a potential threat to social cohesion and provokes a decision about the boundaries of what a particular society at a particular point in time is able and willing to tolerate.

Many new democracies are deeply divided societies emerging from bitter ethnic, religious or ideological conflicts, and the danger of the return of the monsters of the past remains present for a long while. In these transitions, democracy-building and nation-building take place at the same time, creating a highly complex and fragile situation. More often than not, the measures that are necessary to cope with each of these parallel processes are difficult, sometimes impossible, to reconcile (Linz and Stepan 1996: 16–37). Several countries that have emerged from civil war have taken measures to restrict public speech that could contribute to intercommunity hostilities.[3] Sometimes this moratorium on media freedom has helped to create a space where the wounds of the past could heal. But ultimately a society has to find ways of addressing the trauma and to find a language to describe the experiences which is both truthful and inclusive. Throughout this process, vigilance is needed to prevent powerholders from using intergroup tensions as a pretext for censorship of potentially oppositional opinions.

Finally, considerations of the sensibilities of individuals or a particular group can be a legitimate reason for restrictions on media coverage. Proponents of this view argue that members of a group targeted by offensive speech can suffer severe and lasting damage that is comparable to physical injury (Cohen-Almagor 2006). Violations of group sensibilities are probably one of the most frequent complaints against the press, but they are also one of the most problematic, because it is often difficult to draw the line between legitimate claims for respect and dignity and the unwillingness of group members to tolerate criticism. Depending on the ability of a group to voice protest against the way in which it is portrayed in the media, subsequent restrictions on media reporting can lead to idiosyncrasies that pose a serious threat to an open public debate. Stronger arguments are needed to demonstrate that the damage caused by the exercise of press freedom is greater than the damage caused by the limitations of this right. One such case is racist speech, which not only violates the dignity of the targeted group, but also the constitutional principles of democracy that guarantee equality of all persons regardless of their race, gender, age or other biological characteristics. Racist speech challenges the democratic principle of equality by depicting a group as inferior and hence denying it equal status in a political community of equals. However, as the perception of what kinds of statements are regarded as racist has changed over time and differs across countries, there is no clear-cut answer as to what constitutes the 'right' balance between free public speech, on the one hand, and the rights of individuals and groups, on the other. While, for example, the US exercises a relatively high level of tolerance of public expressions of offensive views, and has even seen a proliferation of hate speech channels over recent years, other countries, like France, have imposed stricter rules on the dissemination of racial prejudice in public communication (Bird 2000). In some new democracies waves of intolerance and ethnic hatred have sprung up after the abolition of censorship, posing a serious threat to the values on which democracy is built. Racists and extreme nationalists demand the rights of freedom of expression and the press to disseminate their views in public, often with considerable success. For example, the results of the 2010 general election in Hungary sent shockwaves across the region when the neo-fascist party Jobbik won 17 per cent of the vote, coming third after the winning centre-right party Fidesz and the socialists. Jobbik had been campaigning on an aggressive anti-Semitic and anti-Roma agenda, creating a climate of fear and violence amongst minority groups in the country. Hate speech and conspiracy theories were allowed to appear on the cover pages of Hungarian magazines thereby further reinforcing a rising trend of xenophobic sentiments in the population, while the established political parties tried to ride, rather than tame, the populist wave (Mayr 2010).

The re-emergence of religion as a powerful force in public life has opened up another fault line between different sets of values that do not sit easily together. On the one hand, religious groups depend on, and make use of, open and free media channels to express their views and mobilize support. On the other, the plurality of competing worldviews expressed in the public sphere tends to undermine the absolute truth claims of religious belief systems. As a consequence, religious groups often experience democratization as a hostile, rather than a protective, force and frequently campaign for strict limitations of public communication in traditional media and the internet. The question as to the extent to which religious sensibilities justify restrictions on press freedom can only be answered in the context of a particular society at a particular point in time. It also depends on the disputed content of public speech. The disclosure and critique of religious vested interests and their striving for domination is part of the media's watchdog role and essential for the viability of democracy. But ridiculing and devaluing the religious feelings of believers can reinforce prejudices and stereotypes that impede rather than promote enlightened debate amongst citizens.

O'Neill (1990) reflects on the scope of press freedom from a perspective that avoids the usual antagonism between the press, on the one hand, and other interests – state, society, groups, individuals – on the other. She points out that the principle of press freedom protects not only the expression of opinions but also – and even more importantly – communication as a process that includes both speakers and audiences. In other words, the freedom to express one's opinions entails the obligation to consider how this might affect the listener and, eventually, the communication process itself. If the ultimate objective of press freedom is to promote open dialogue between citizens, then expression of opinions that exclude some individuals by denying them equal status (for example, through racist speech) would contradict the purpose of this right. Thus, restricting the freedom to express racist views would actually expand the scope of a free and open public sphere. Understanding press freedom as a right that encompasses the entire communication process also emphasizes the obligations of the audience to maintain a communication culture that enables public dialogue. Press freedom promotes – and requires – toleration, i.e., the ability of both speaker and listener to accept disagreement and to acknowledge the rationality and honesty of other participants regardless of whether or not one shares their views. The complex relationship of press freedom with other democratic norms makes it a 'deeply deceptive first principle', as Corner (2004: 893) puts it, because it entails restraints as well as rights. Moreover, it is a hugely demanding principle because it requires a communication culture that enables the exchange of ideas in increasingly diverse societies.

Diversity

If press freedom is a 'deceptive first principle', then diversity is an 'elusive' one that includes 'multiple dimensions, means of assessment, and underlying assumptions' (Napoli 1999a: 8). Alongside freedom, diversity is one of the pillars of normative media theory. And like freedom, diversity is a teleological principle that, even though it is often treated as an end in itself, actually serves broader purposes both for individual citizens and society at large.

Diversity, the truth and the market

Liberal democracy has established processes and institutions that reflect the idea of pluralism as a system where different groups and interests compete with each other for influence over the public definition of political issues and, ultimately, the outcomes of political decision-making (Dahl 1971). In contrast, non-democratic regimes from eighteenth-century absolutism in Europe to modern-day dictatorships aim to reduce diversity by imposing a dominant way of thinking on their populations. This is not to say that autocratic regimes are monolithic. Under the surface of the official rhetoric, they are often divided along numerous frictions and differences. But any publicly expressed form of diversity in authoritarian systems is usually a concession of the ruler, or the ruling class, to pressures either from within the elites or from below, which otherwise cannot be kept under control.

Why then is diversity deemed so central to democracy? The nineteenth-century political philosopher John Stuart Mill (1972/1859) provides three compelling arguments for the virtues of diversity emerging from uninhibited public speech, which still influence our understanding of the role of journalism and the media in democratic society. Mill's thinking is concerned with the question of how the general good can be achieved through the self-development of individuals and their quest for happiness. In his essay 'On Liberty', Mill examines how 'truth' emerges from the free exchange of ideas. It has to be borne in mind that 'truth' in this context does not denote some kind of metaphysical truth about the essence of existence as it is, for example, addressed in religious doctrine. On the contrary, Mill's argument is based on the conviction that no such 'eternal' truth can ever be established. Hence, his use of the term 'truth' can be understood as an accepted proposition to solve problems that are of public concern at a given point in time. This 'truth', Mill argues, can best be discovered and tested through different ideas competing with each other for recognition in an open marketplace of ideas. The first of his three arguments that link diversity and truth stipulates that 'if any opinion is compelled to silence, that opinion may . . . be true' (1974/1859: 115–16). This argument emphasizes the fallibility of the human mind and how ignorance and prejudice prevent us from improving our lives. Mill refers to various examples from the past where religious or state censorship have suppressed opinions that later on turned out to be true. Thus, expanding the range of opinions is an effective mechanism to prevent, or at least minimize the possibility of, making errors and wrong decisions.

In fact, the lack of diversity and the resulting absence of alternative problem-solving options lead to one of the main reasons for the inherent instability of autocratic regimes. The suppression of criticism and alternative views prevents decision-makers from identifying emerging problems at an early stage and consequently leads to frequent policy failures. President Gorbachev was acutely aware of the problems caused by the restrictions on public debate when, in the late 1980s, he launched his policy of *glasnost*, or 'openness'. By inviting the general public and the media to participate in a public discussion of the problems facing the Soviet regime, he hoped to stabilize the system and to find a way out of the looming economic disaster. He was bound to fail, though, because the system had exhausted its capabilities to manage social and economic change. Ultimately, the dynamic unleashed by more pluralism and openness actually contributed to the dissolution of the Soviet system, as competing factions of the political elite started to play out their power struggles in the media, which further reduced the scope of possible compromise between the pro-democracy forces and those who wanted to preserve the old system by any means (Gibbs 2000; Lampert 1988).

Returning to Mill's defence of free public speech, we find that he moves on to argue that '[s]econdly, though the silenced opinion be an error, it may . . . contain a portion of truth' (1972/1859: 116). This point emphasizes again the relativity of knowledge. Nobody is in possession of the whole truth, and rarely does an opinion contain anything that would not be worth considering. Hence, diversity that even includes 'wrong' opinions enhances the possibility of finding the best possible solutions. Obviously, Mill is pushing the boundaries of free speech far beyond what was acceptable in his time. And indeed, as discussed in the previous section, singling out the kind of 'wrong' opinions that, rather than contributing to the advancement of knowledge and understanding, actually undermine public dialogue and, thus, truth-finding, remains one of the most challenging decisions to be made. Mill provides us with a powerful reminder of the risks of premature judgements about the exclusion of 'wrong' opinions (e.g., incitement to hatred or violence) from the public debate.

Mill's final, and third, argument states that 'even if the received opinion be . . . the whole truth, unless it is suffered to be . . . vigorously and earnestly contested, it will . . . be held in the manner of a prejudice, with little comprehension or feeling of its rational grounds' (1972/1859: 116). Undoubtedly, keeping even accepted 'truths' open to hard questioning puts high demands on those who are taking part in public communication – the media, political leaders and ordinary citizens. It requires the willingness to reflect continuously on the meaning and purpose of the very first principles on which our society is built. Otherwise, even values like 'democracy' or 'freedom' can become vacuous convictions that are used in a rather thoughtless way ('It's a free country and I can say what I want!').

In fact, Mill's defence of diversity and the notion of a 'marketplace of ideas' have themselves become a 'truth' that is rarely questioned any more. However, some critical remarks on the underlying assumptions are necessary. For a start, even though the metaphor likens the exchange of ideas to the exchange of goods on an open market, the conclusion that market forces are the best means to bring about the desired public debate of different views does not necessarily follow. Like the *agora* in Athenian democracy, the marketplace stands for a public space where people meet to talk about issues of the day as well as engage in trading goods. The *agora* was actually primarily a place where the citizens of Athens met to make decisions on public matters. Thus, historically both forms of exchange often occurred side by side, but each can be performed independently of the other. The market might be a suitable instrument to enhance diversity, but it often fails to do so. Even so, the 'marketplace of ideas' metaphor remains a potent cue for policymakers and has guided their decisions to the effect that preference has been given to market mechanisms over other possible alternatives when regulating media diversity (Entman and Wildman 1992; Gordon 1997; Napoli 1999b).[4]

Another argument that is implied by the 'marketplace of ideas' metaphor, but seldom questioned, is the assumption that it is through competition between different ideas that the truth eventually emerges. Mill probably adopted this argument from the economists of his time, most notably Adam Smith, whose theory of a free market suggests an 'invisible hand' is at work, which ensures that the best products prevail at low prices, whereas products of lesser quality disappear from the market. Applied to public communication, this would mean that the confrontation of different ideas helps to identify the view that represents the 'truth' – or comes closest to it – while disqualifying false propositions. Theorists of deliberative democracy have questioned the virtue of competition as a truth-finding mechanism. In his discussion of diversity in democratic communication, Bohman (2007) criticizes an understanding that reduces diversity to the confrontation of opposing views, as it is reflected in Mill's writing. Instead, he argues that the value of diversity is 'due to the distributed character of social knowledge and experience in modern societies across perspectives' (ibid.: 350). In other words, the aim of diversity in public deliberation is to expand knowledge and to overcome biases. In this kind of dialogical, rather than competitive, dialogue, it is unlikely that one view 'wins' over another. Instead, the (ideal) outcome would be a more comprehensive and more robust view of an issue.

The virtues and perils of internal and external diversity

Having established diversity as an epistemic device to advance 'enlightened understanding' amongst citizens (Dahl 1989) and to improve decision-making, it is now time to turn to the different patterns of diversity that can be observed in today's media systems. Britain's media may serve as a useful point of departure to illustrate different forms of diversity. For outside observers, the BBC is usually regarded as representing the quality of British media. It stands for balance, objectivity and high-quality reporting. Indeed, the BBC has become a global brand that serves as a role model for journalists around the world. The BBC has also been used as a blueprint for policymakers in new democracies who are involved in the reconstruction of the broadcast institutions of their country.[5] But there is another side to the British media: the printed press is markedly divided along ideological lines, with most of the newspapers positioning themselves on the political spectrum between left-wing and right-wing politics. These divisions characterize both high-brow and tabloid papers. In the British media landscape, the BBC stands for a model of diversity which is referred to in the literature as 'internal diversity', while the ideological divisions of the printed press represent the model of 'external diversity' (McQuail 1992: 145–7).

Internal diversity describes a situation in which all relevant viewpoints are represented within one media outlet. This can either be a single medium, like a public broadcaster, or all outlets in a media system. No particular views or groups are excluded, but they cannot expect particularly favourable treatment either. Consequently, internally diverse media are able to attract wide audiences with different backgrounds and beliefs. In contrast, the notion of external diversity refers to individual media outlets covering only a limited range of viewpoints because they have aligned themselves with a particular cause, group or party. Comprehensive diversity is then expected to be achieved across the entirety of divergent media. The journalistic role model underlying external diversity is that of a partisan or advocate. In fact, externally diverse media often compensate for the structural barriers of mainstream media that have become part of an elite-dominated hegemony of public discourse by giving voice to groups who are largely ignored or misrepresented in standard news reporting. External diversity creates fragmented audiences where particular groups who share the same beliefs or concerns gather around 'their' media. Structurally, the two forms of diversity differ in that internal diversity provides full representation at the level of individual media, whereas external diversity achieves this objective at the aggregated level of the media system as a whole.

How do both forms of diversity feature when judged against the democratic norms of public debate and deliberation? Obviously, internal diversity comes closest to the ideas underlying the 'market-place of ideas', or to what theorists of deliberative democracy have in mind when outlining the ideals and conditions of a democratic public sphere (Bohman and Rehg 1997; Habermas 1984). The open forum of balanced media provides an arena in which different views are expressed side by side and have to respond to each other. Without the need to take possible counterarguments into account, advocates would feel less inclined to think through their proposals and to correct possible weaknesses. Moreover, the exchange of different viewpoints might eventually result in a broader understanding of the problems at hand, opening up the chances for consensus across the lines of difference, be they ideological, religious, ethnic or regional. From the perspective of the citizens, internal diversity provides a kind of information that enables them to make considered decisions and to participate in an informed way. Learning about the views of others is also a crucial precondition for 'enlightened understanding' – i.e., the ability to respect fellow-citizens and to take their demands and needs into account, even if one disagrees with them (Mutz and Martin 2001; Voltmer and Lalljee 2007).

On all these accounts external diversity appears to fare less well. Speakers expressing their views in media that are aligned with a particular cause or ideology rarely encounter opposition, nor do they need to fear the probing questioning of adversarial journalists. Since they are preaching to the converted, they do not need to sharpen their argument in an attempt to make it more convincing to a wider audience. As for the citizens who obtain their information from externally diverse media, they get only a rather one-sided, if not distorted, view of the political debate. They will mainly find information that reinforces the opinions they already hold, and what they learn about other opinions might be presented in a dismissive tone that hardly encourages tolerance and 'enlightened sympathy'. In an externally diverse media system, individuals would have to read or watch several media outlets to get the full picture of the ongoing political debate, which only few have the resources to do. Hence, opinion-building in the context of external diversity seems bound to be less rational and more prone to errors than in internally diverse media systems.

However, the praise of internal diversity and balanced journalism, as contrasted with external diversity and partisanship, is often rather sterile and detached from how people actually use political news in their daily lives. Real citizens hardly resemble Margolis's (1979) – ironically exaggerated – portrait of 'good citizen Brown', who is busy collecting information about all parties and their manifestoes before making his carefully considered choice. Instead, normal citizens are busy with their ordinary lives, in which politics plays only a marginal role. They therefore seek out cognitive shortcuts that help them to come to a satisfactory decision without investing too much time and effort into information-gathering. For this purpose, biased information is of immense value. It comes with clear evaluative labels on it and thus provides reliable guidance in an increasingly complex and rapidly changing world. Research has shown that this kind of 'low salience learning' is surprisingly effective in helping citizens to participate in politics while getting on with work, family and social life (Neuman 1986). In contrast, for many consumers, the standard format of balanced news reporting that just confronts the claims of the main political opponents ('A said x, and B said y') tends to generate little more than grey noise. Internal diversity does not automatically result in better coverage, as journalists often resort to a rather mechanistic strategy of 'pairing truth claims' (Tuchman 1972) without exploring the reasons behind these claims. Frequently, neutrality simply becomes a disguise for adhering to the official line of the power elites while shying away from covering more 'risky' marginal positions.

Another reason why partisan media have their place in democratic life is the nature of politics. It's not just about 'finding the best solution' in an objective, almost technocratic manner. Politics has its roots in visions of the 'good society', beliefs about human nature and the proper relationship between the individual and the collective. And these ideas evoke passions that are only inadequately captured by detached accounts of opposing viewpoints. In *Hearing the Other Side* (2006), Mutz provides evidence that people who regularly take in a diverse diet of media information and who are engaged in conversations with people who do not share their own political views show higher than average levels of political knowledge and are more tolerant towards minority groups (see also Mutz 2002). Yet these 'enlightened' citizens are also less active than people who discuss politics with like-minded others. Obviously, getting engaged in politics is not simply an individual decision made after screening all relevant information. It is embedded in social contexts and a biased information environment that encourages participation and that links people with people who share their concerns and enthusiasm for a particular cause.

All these considerations are based on the experience and practice in established democracies. Do they apply in a similar way to new democracies? What kind of diversity would be best for countries that are in the process of building and consolidating democratic institutions? Again, there is no clear-cut answer and the best way of restructuring public communication depends on the particular circumstances and trajectories of the society in which it takes place. After years of dictatorship, when diversity was suppressed, often by draconian means, groups and individuals are keen to seize the opportunity of press freedom to finally launch their own outlets to promote and advocate their cause. Indeed, in many new democracies there is a flurry of new newspapers, radio stations, even television stations immediately after the demise of the old regime. Advocacy media and external diversity can help to strengthen political identities and foster the emergence of a vocal civil society and a functioning party system that is rooted in sustainable electoral support.

However, there are also great risks involved, as external diversity might further destabilize an already volatile post-transition situation. It is one thing to campaign for an idea or cause, but it is another to disseminate hatred and intolerance towards other groups. The situation can easily get out of control when the political elites are unable, or even unwilling, to call for moderation, or when there are no institutional procedures to reconcile political and social divisions.

To conclude: the meaning, practice and perception of an independent and diverse press cannot be judged without taking into account the particular social and political context in which public communication takes place. The nature and intensity of conflicts differ, as well as the institutional capacity to accommodate divergent interests and ideologies. Media diversity and democracy need and reinforce each other: while the public expression of a broad range of diverse opinions fosters openness and tolerance in society, tolerance and the willingness to accept opposing, even offensive opinions are fundamental prerequisites for diversity to function and in order to bring about its assumed benefits.

Part II

The Media and Political Change Across Time and Space

Unlike earlier regime changes from authoritarian to democratic rule, the 'third wave' of democratization has taken place in a media-saturated environment, which has fundamentally altered both the process and the outcomes of recent transitions. This part of the book investigates the way in which the media affect democratic regime change, what the conditions and consequences are for the media's involvement and how the interplay of politics and the media is shaped by broader historical and contextual factors.

The three chapters of this part introduce a set of key concepts that help to develop a more differentiated understanding of these questions. Chapter 3 draws on a long-standing debate in the social sciences: the relationship between structure and agency. The term 'media' encompasses both elements, each of which results in very different consequences at different times. The structural dimension of media refers to communication technologies that provide specific opportunities for controlling the production of, and access to, information. Transborder broadcasting, the internet and the recent convergence of hitherto separate communication platforms are examples of the dynamic development of communication technologies in past decades. Political actors make use of communication technologies to promote their own goals, be it pushing for more openings and freedom or stabilizing the existing power structure and upholding its legitimacy. In this respect, the internet has proved to be a double-edged sword, as it functions as a 'technology of liberation' as well as an instrument of control and surveillance. Even though communication technologies are tools in the hands of political actors, they often develop their own dynamic, leading to consequences that lie beyond the intentions of those who employ them.

The dimension of agency denotes the editorial activities of the media. As organizations, editors or individual journalists play an active part in constructing social reality by setting the agenda of public discourse and by providing narratives that endow meaning to events and social conditions. Evidently, the extent to which the media can take on the role of purposeful agents depends on the opportunities and constraints of the environment in which they operate. Elite constellations, the vibrancy of civil society, economic constraints and general public opinion are all factors that affect the degree to which the media can play an active role in the political process.

Chapter 4 uses the notion of stages of democratization to demonstrate how the media, in terms of (technological) structures and as purposeful agents, have affected the transition processes over time. Liberalization within the authoritarian regime, the dramatic phase of regime collapse and the long period of consolidation that follows mark specific contextual environments during which the media take on different roles. Even if there is little space for journalistic agency, media technologies have frequently limited the control of authoritarian elites over political dissent. The examples of *samizdat* literature in Eastern Europe and social network sites like Facebook during the 2011 uprisings in the Arab world demonstrate the power (but also the limitations) of media technologies for the mobilization of political opposition. Even though in these events the media, especially broadcasting and the internet, have been hailed as a democratic force, their impact on the consolidation of newly established democracies seems more dubious. While critical reporting and investigative journalism contribute to good governance, accountability and citizen empowerment, the growing trend of mediatization of politics often obstructs the establishment of viable political parties, fosters the rise of populism and might even nurture political cynicism among citizens.

The last chapter of Part II argues that the interplay between political change and the media is not uniform across different contexts. The legacies of the authoritarian power structure cast long shadows on how the new democracy works and what role the media are playing in the political process. The concept of path dependency helps to understand the lasting 'footprints' of the previous institutions and the behavioural pattern they established. The chapter distinguishes four authoritarian regime types: (i) military dictatorship, (ii) communist one-party rule, (iii) one-party rule in contexts of statism and (iv) personalized one-party rule in contexts of weak state institutions; these have dominated, respectively, Latin America, Eastern Europe,

East Asia and sub-Saharan Africa. Each of these regime types has generated distinct relationships between politics and the media, which to some extent continue to shape the role of the media even after the old order has been overthrown.

Taken together, the chapters of Part II argue that in order to understand the role of the media in democratic transitions, we have to distinguish their dual nature as communication technologies and journalistic agency. Moreover, we have to take into account the specific contexts across time and space that shape the way in which the media play their part in the process of change.

3

Communication Technologies and Journalistic Agency: Mass Media and Political Change

Undoubtedly, the media have been centre-stage in the transitions of the 'third wave', especially those that have taken place since the late 1980s. From the iconic images of the fall of the Berlin Wall in 1989 to the grainy pictures of Syrian protests in 2011 taken with mobile phones, the media have not only shaped our understanding of these events, but have themselves been a driving force of change. This chapter explores the media's impact on processes of democratization by taking a closer look at what we actually mean by the general term 'media'. Picking up on the distinction between structure and agency, it is argued that communication technologies as well as structural conditions and journalistic agency exercised by editorial decisions on news content constitute different, albeit closely interrelated, modes of influence. Even though most of the literature on media influences focuses on Western, specifically Anglo-Saxon, countries, tentative assumptions can be made about the significance of the media in non-democratic and democratizing contexts.

Structure and agency

Democracy sometimes seems to take root in unlikely places, like Mongolia, and even explodes in areas that have been largely missing on the mental map of democratization research, such as the Arab countries of the Middle East and North Africa. But there are also stubborn pockets of resistance where democracy does not seem to have much of a chance, like in Belarus, dubbed 'Europe's last dictatorship', North Korea or Singapore. Moreover, while some young democracies have made good progress towards consolidating the new regime, others are backsliding into authoritarian practices. Democratization scholars are divided over the factors that make transition to a sustainable democracy more likely in some countries than in others. Two main schools of thinking can be distinguished, one focusing on structural preconditions of democratization and the other on agency, i.e., political actors and the choices they make at crucial moments of the development. Theorists of structural explanations of democratization have identified a wide range of factors that are regarded as determinants of regime change towards democratic rule. These factors include – to name but the most important ones – economic development and capitalist markets (Lipset 1959), the existence of a sizeable middle class (Moore 1966), decentralization of a society's power resources (Vanhanen 1997), a political culture that empowers individuals to make use of their own capabilities and freedoms (Welzel and Inglehart 2008), and an enabling international environment (Pridham 1991). Most of these approaches have their intellectual roots in modernization theory that understands democracy itself as a central part of modernity, as it allows for more rational and effective decision-making based on universally recognized values. In several of these approaches to democratization, the media are included as one of the structural conditions that make democratization more likely to take off in a particular country. According to Vanhanen (1997), widespread access to the mass media ensures a more even distribution of one of the main power resources of modern societies: knowledge. Early modernization theorists believed that the media would pull underdeveloped countries out of their backwardness by broadening people's worldview from a parochial to a more cosmopolitan perspective. The ability to see beyond one's own small realm of daily life would ultimately create the psychological preconditions for the acceptance of change – from new techniques of agriculture to democratic governance (Lerner 1958; Pye 1963).

Structural conceptions of democratization have not remained unchallenged. The attempt to predict democratization by a set of structural variables appears too deterministic to capture the puzzling variety of pathways and outcomes that make democratization processes so unpredictable. The complex interaction between political, economic, social and cultural factors, together with simple luck and the proverbial 'window of opportunity' that may, or may not, open at the right time, constitute a constellation that is unique to each country. In addition, attempts at explaining democratization by structural preconditions suffer from the notorious chicken-and-egg problem: in the end it is impossible to distinguish between what are the causes and what the effects. For example, economic development is as much the result as the cause of democratic governance. On the one hand, people in relatively wealthy societies are more inclined to demand more participation rights in the political process; on the other, democratic governments are more pressured to be responsive to the demands and needs of the population than non-democratic governments (see Sen 2001). A similar causality problem applies to the media's role in social change. Access to information exposes people to new ideas and develops their cognitive competences and involvement in public affairs. But the media can only provide this kind of mobilizing information in a liberal environment that protects freedom of speech. It has to be kept in mind, though, that the mere access to the means of mass communication does not necessarily bring people in contact with new ideas. Where the authoritarian state is able to control the flow of information, the media are little more than instruments of propaganda and stagnation. Thus, the extent to which the media can promote ideas that challenge the existing non-democratic order depends on the degree to which the ability of the state to control the dissemination of divergent views is weakened.

Actor-based approaches of democratization recognize the crucial role of political elites in the transition process. Over decades, the resilience and charisma of political figures like Lech Walesa in Poland or Nelson Mandela in South Africa embodied their population's craving for change and helped to mobilize and maintain mass opposition in spite of violent suppression. The decisive moment of agency, though, arises when, for whatever reasons, regime change is possible. Scholars who analyse democratization within the agency paradigm understand the outcome of transitions as the result of the choices made by political elites, both established and dissident ones. The media can be part of the constellation of actors who actively shape the outcome of transition processes. The decision of the media in post-Franco Spain to join a cross-party elite pact in support of the juvenile democracy can serve as an example (see Chapter 2). Di Palma's book *To Craft Democracies* (1990) captures the agency-centred approach to democratization very well, suggesting that democracy is possible if the right people want it and make the correct decisions. Meanwhile, a look at the democracies that have emerged over past decades makes it all too clear that they differ – often dramatically – from what those who were involved in the initial transition had intended to create. Obviously, there are more constraints than anticipated that limit the range and effectiveness of the decisions that political actors can make.

The two strands of scholarship in democratization research echo a long-standing debate in the social sciences on the relationship between structure and agency. Having established the impossibility of empirically separating the two dimensions, Giddens (1984) suggests the concept of 'structuration' to explain how structure and agency are interrelated. According to this theory, social structures emerge from human action either as an intentional creation or through an accumulation of accidental iterations. Once institutions and the rules and norms that underpin them have been established, they constitute a framework of objective conditions that constrain individual choices and behaviour. However, even though established social structures develop a high level of stability and durability, they can be changed by the intentional choices of actors, resulting again in a reconfigured structural environment that offers new opportunities and constraints for those who are acting within this framework. Working along similar lines of argument, democratization research has abandoned the somewhat artificial divisions between structural and agency-centred approaches of earlier years. Regime changes are understood as a highly complex interactive process in which existing institutions, cultural norms and historical legacies affect the choices individual actors can make, but where individuals and groups are intentionally driving – or obstructing – political change (see Potter et al. 1997: 10–24).[1]

The concept of structuration can also be applied to the interactive processes between technologies and social processes. Technologies often appear like 'natural' objects, closer to the physical world than to society, and therefore outside the realm of negotiation. However, this view disguises the extent to which technologies are themselves shaped by social processes. They reflect the power structure and interests of the society in which they are created as well as the cognitive paradigms that shape the way in which a society understands itself and its environment. Like institutions, technologies take on the appearance of objective conditions whose structure and functionalities prescribe certain uses and outcomes while precluding others.

Applying these arguments to the media, it becomes evident that they impact on social processes both as structure and as agency. As technologies, they constitute structures that enable their users to communicate with others in a way that would not be possible without them, while at the same time creating constraints on what can be communicated and how. Media technologies often appear like objective facts, but like any other technologies, they reflect the social relations and needs of the society in which they are used. For example, mobile phones serve the needs of a highly individualized and mobile society; and social media like Facebook and Twitter have been created with the specific needs of a young generation in mind that organizes its social life in flexible and transient networks. As agency, the media participate in the social process as communicators in their own right. Media organizations have developed their own rules and routines of communication which are shaped both by the constraints of the technologies they employ and by the social structures in which they operate, such as markets and power hierarchies. Within this framework, journalists and editors are constantly making choices as to what topics to cover, when and how, thereby creating a cognitive environment that shapes the way in which people perceive social reality and, consequently, how they respond to it. Obviously, for the media to participate in social processes as communicators in their own right, a minimum of independence is required that endows them with a certain degree of discretionary power to make choices about the content that is disseminated. If excessive controls and censorship leave the media with little room for their own choices, they would be reduced to mere instruments in the hands of other agents.

In sum, to understand the role of the media in processes of democratization both as an enabling and a constraining force, we have to distinguish between structural and agency-related sources of influence, between the media as technologies and the media as participating communicators.

The contingent power of the media

The question how to conceptualize and measure media influence has been occupying communication studies from its very beginnings in the early twentieth century. Much of this research has been concerned with the micro level of influence, i.e., whether and how the media change individual attitudes and behaviour. While this has already proved to be difficult, influences on macro-level processes, which cut across individuals and institutions, large territories and long periods of time, are even more of a challenge to understand. Whether on an individual or a societal level, media influences can never be the only explanation for the changes under observation. Rather, media influences interact with, and are moderated by, other trends in society, sometimes acting as catalysts through which events or developments are set in motion, sometimes acting as amplifiers of already existing forces, sometimes reinforcing the status quo. Further, the direction of media influences is often difficult, if not impossible, to identify. For example, there is strong evidence for the media having the capability to change the perceptions and preferences of individuals who are exposed to them. But to ensure economic viability, the media are also keen to respond to the preferences and tastes of their audience. Hence, the attitudes and tastes of the audience are as much the cause as the effect of media coverage.

Media technologies

One strand of scholarship studying the influence of the media in modern society focuses on their technological features, rather than the specific content they convey, as factors that drive social and individual change. The approach is often referred to as 'medium theory', an expression that emerged from McLuhan's (1964) claim, 'the medium is the message'. The underlying assumption of this approach is that different media are not just neutral storage devices or transmitters. Rather, the structural features of specific media technologies shape the meaning of the messages they convey as well as the patterns of interaction of those who are consuming them. Most importantly, different media – print, audiovisual, digital – have in various forms and to varying degrees reordered the social organization of time and space (Thompson 1995: 31–6). By enabling people to communicate with distant others, the media have dramatically broadened the range of experience beyond the immediacy of face-to-face communication. It is safe to say that without the mediation of politics and the circulation of political ideas through all segments of society, regardless of geographical and social boundaries, mass participation and, ultimately, democracy would be impossible.

In a similar vein, theorists of the internet regard the unique technological features of this new medium as the main factor responsible for the impact it has had on human relationships, and in particular on the relationship between citizens and political power (Rheingold 1995). The unprecedented capacity to store and retrieve information, together with the possibility of creating links between different sets of information, have made it possible to bring together knowledge that has previously remained dispersed and disconnected. This new information environment makes it much more difficult for political powerholders to keep the lid of secrecy on potentially damaging information. The shockwaves sent out by the publication of some 80,000 classified documents on the investigative website Wikileaks in July 2010 would not have been possible without the huge storage capacity of the internet and its universal access facilities.

The technological potential of the internet has been further boosted by the digital convergence of different types of information, be it text, sound or images, into one code system that can be easily transferred between different platforms. As a consequence, the boundaries between hitherto separate media have been blurred. Before the digital revolution changed our information environment forever, different media were defined by distinct technologies: broadcasting, newspaper, telephone. Since these could clearly be categorized into a one-to-many model of mass communication on the one hand, and a one-to-one model of individual communication on the other, different regulatory regimes could be applied to each of these technologies. Such distinctions can no longer be made, and the internet is the global platform where these different models of communication merge. Audiovisual content produced by newspapers and broadcasters can be downloaded anywhere and at any time; individuals and groups can communicate with each other; and messages can be uploaded from individual devices like mobile phones to make them available to large audiences (Baldwin et al. 1996; Jenkins 2006). Moreover, convergence across different media platforms has helped to break down hierarchical controls over the flow of communication, thus making the communication environment more unpredictable and diverse.

What is most central to the technological argument about the social influence of the internet, though, is its non-hierarchical network structure. This feature enables citizens to express their views and to communicate with each other in the public sphere without the editorial interference of traditional mass media and beyond the restrictions of traditional one-to-one communication technologies. By allowing for horizontal many-to-many flows of information, the internet has become a mass medium that is no longer restricted to one-to-many communication, dominated by media or political elites. For the first time in the history of communication technologies, individual users can be both receivers and producers of messages on the same platform and at the same time.

With the internet, the emergence of 'imagined communities' is no longer a technological side-effect of the medium, as suggested by Anderson's (1983) analysis of the printed press in the nineteenth century. Rather, the technological structure of the medium itself empowers individual users to create these communities with whomsoever they wish to join for a shared cause (Van Dijk 2006). This has led many authors to proclaim the internet as an inherently democratic medium, pointing at the apparently perfect goodness-of-fit between its technological structure and the very ideas of democracy; the internet is perceived as having the potential to create a new era of democratic citizenship with a more open and inclusive sphere of public involvement where the production and distribution of knowledge are horizontally shared rather than controlled by top-down hierarchies (Coleman and Blumler 2009; Hacker and Van Dijk 2001; Hague and Loader 1999). Given the technological features of the internet, it comes as no surprise that its global rise has prompted widespread optimism among students and activists of democratization alike, who praise it as 'liberation technology' (Diamond 2010) that, unlike the traditional media of press and broadcasting, is believed to resist the attempts of control and instrumentalization by authoritarian rulers.

However, authors cherishing the democratizing power of the internet are not always successful in avoiding the trap of technological determinism. In its crude form, technological determinism draws a direct causal link between technology and social response, the assumption being that the effects of a medium mirror its inherent technological features. However, even though the make-up of a medium carries specific biases that make some uses more likely than others, this does not mean that people actually use the medium in the way implied by its structural features. This is not only so because of the *eigensinn* of individuals, but also because of the ambiguous nature of technology itself. For example, the internet allows citizens to connect freely with others regardless of their cultural background, beliefs or social class. At the same time, the internet allows for a much higher level of individual selectivity than any other medium. When people can choose their sources of information, they usually prefer those that confirm their beliefs. Likewise, they tend to socialize with individuals who are like them, socially, politically, culturally or otherwise. This tendency to avoid cognitive dissonance (Festinger 1962) and to form homogenous groups (Huckfeldt and Sprague 1987) has been found in many studies of information processing and social interaction. And it seems that these tendencies are even reinforced in the online world. As a consequence, the public sphere of the internet resembles more a patchwork of tribes than the utopian global *agora* where different views and opinions are exchanged and discussed. Sunstein (2001) therefore takes a more sceptical view of the democratic potential of the internet. In fact, he is concerned about an internet-induced 'balkanization' of society where, rather than opening their mind to new ideas, people only communicate with like-minded others. Moreover, the structure of a technology does not determine the content that is transmitted through its means. In fact, the internet has become a breeding ground for anti-democratic and racist ideas as much as for resistance to autocratic power and exploitation. The anonymity and the loose network structure of the internet have also played into the hands of terror groups who have turned decentralized action to their advantage (see Conway 2006; Nacos 2002; Tsfati 2002).

While it is beyond doubt that the internet has liberated and connected citizens, it has also become an instrument of unprecedented surveillance. As with traditional media, the internet is not a democratic force by nature, but can be used to great effect by authoritarian governments as well as by democracy activists. While democratization movements have developed their ability to mobilize resistance, governments – both democratic and non-democratic ones – have become more sophisticated in using the internet for controlling citizens and public speech. As Deibert and Rohozinski (2010) point out, the policy of openness and transparency practised by civil society groups even increases their vulnerability to state control and persecution. The authors therefore call for a more nuanced understanding of the power of the internet, emphasizing that 'linking technological properties to a single social outcome such as liberation or control is a highly dubious exercise' (ibid.: 55).

While media technologies connect distant people, they also create new problems of coordination. The compression of time and space has put new pressures on political decision-makers by merging the international and the national arena of policymaking and by shrinking the time frame within which political decisions have to be made. The 'CNN-effect' hypothesis addresses the question how media technologies have changed foreign policy. Similar observations can be made with regard to domestic politics, where governments are increasingly under pressure to deliver quick and visible solutions. Students of international communication suppose that since the early 1990s international crises like the first Gulf War in 1991, the American engagement in Somalia in 1992 and the decision of NATO to intervene in Bosnia in 1995 were significantly affected by new communication technologies and the information environment they have created. Global communication networks and 24-hour real-time reporting, as first provided on a global scale by the American news channel CNN, circulated the horrors of war around the world, thereby mobilizing global public opinion that was difficult to ignore without risking major political damage. Since then, digitalization and the internet have further accelerated the speed with which information reaches both ordinary citizens and policymakers around the globe. This leaves only little time for complicated diplomatic negotiations, careful gathering of evidence and consultations with experts and affected parties. In a media-saturated environment, political decisions have to be made immediately when a problem hits public attention (Gilboa 2005; Livingston and Eachus 1995; Robinson 2002).

A similar dynamic interplay between communication technologies and social processes can be observed during transitions to democracy. Huntington (1991) was the first transition scholar to acknowledge the crucial role played by communication networks during the spread of the 'third wave'. He suggests 'demonstration effects' at work whereby media users in one country observe political changes in another, either through cross-border broadcasting during the transitions that took place in the 1980s or, more recently, increasingly via the internet. Observing successful transitions elsewhere encourages opposition movements to intensify pressure on their own government in the hope that the international attention created by global information flows raises the costs for authoritarian leaders to resist the demands for change. Democracy activists have therefore developed sophisticated media strategies as part of their action repertoire, including the creation of spectacular events that attract the attention of international media and hence guarantee global attention.

Equally as important as receiving information *from* the outside world is the ability of democracy movements to communicate *to* the outside world with details about conditions within the country, especially when foreign correspondents have only limited access, or none at all. The importance of transborder communication going in both directions became particularly evident during the course of the so-called Arab Spring in 2010–11. The mobilizing power of information about the successful uprisings in Tunisia and Egypt that ignited similar street protests across the Arab world illustrates the significance of demonstration effects in processes of democratization. However, during the early stages of the uprising in Syria, getting information out of the country became even more important as their government sealed off the borders to outside observers. For months, user-generated images about the horrors of what gradually developed into a fully fledged civil war were the only pieces of information available to international news organizations. Even though traditional media struggled with how to deal with this unauthenticated material, the ability to distribute a narrative of the events that countered the agenda-setting of the Syrian regime became an important part of the struggle of the anti-Assad movement.

Another consequence of the demonstration effects of the media is the creation of a recognizable visual frame of democratization that affects the way in which protests are organized. People dancing on the Berlin Wall, the 'tank man' on Tiananmen Square in Beijing, the toppling of the statues of dictators (from Lenin to Saddam Hussein) and the recent 'colour revolutions': all have become visual icons of the 'third wave' of democratization. These images serve as role models for would-be democratizers and are increasingly shaping their strategies. Knowing that the media are looking out for mass demonstrations with visual appeal that captures the attention of their audience, democracy movements have become savvy public relations managers, providing the media with the expected images in order to gain international attention – even in cases where negotiations might be the better route to achieve change.

However, demonstration effects can also have negative effects on the prospects of democratization. Witnessing the social disintegration and economic disaster that followed the demise of the Soviet Union in the 1990s, authoritarian governments in other parts of the world might have felt encouraged to prevent further democratic developments in their own countries. For example, in hindsight the Chinese government will undoubtedly believe that suppression of the protests in 1989 was justified given the dramatic economic decline in Russia and the equally dramatic economic success of China in recent years (Voltmer and Rawnsley 2009: 236–8). And watching Gaddafi being massacred by Libyan rebels or seeing Mubarak appear at court in a cage will certainly have sent shivers of panic down the spine of other dictators in the region. It is easily possible that these images have contributed to hardening Syria's Bashar al-Assad's determination to crack down on the demonstrations at all costs.

Media content

Turning to agency as the second dimension of the media's impact on social and political choice shifts the attention to the editorial choices that news organizations make when they decide on which messages to communicate and how to present them in daily news coverage. Even though the media are dependent on the input they obtain from their sources – political leaders, experts and, increasingly, material provided by ordinary citizens – this does not mean that they simply transmit the messages of others. Rather, news is a cultural product that provides an interpretation of social reality through the 'grammar' of journalism, i.e., the norms, routines and aesthetic judgements news people apply when processing their raw material and transforming it into a text that is widely recognized as news. As a result, the image of the social world created by the news (and other media genres as well) constitutes an account of reality in its own right – a 'media reality' that defines social reality rather than simply reflects it (Parenti

1993; Schlesinger 1978). Thus, news is a social construct that, through its narratives, provides meaning to events that would otherwise be beyond the grasp of the majority of citizens. As Wahl-Jorgensen and Hanitzsch (2009: 3) put it, news is the 'primary sense-making practice of modernity' that constructs and maintains shared realities in a mediatized world.

Communication scholars have identified agenda-setting and framing as the most prominent and important ways in which the media construct reality and ultimately influence social processes. Agenda-setting denotes the choices the media make when selecting the material for the daily news from a potentially unlimited amount of information. Research on the implications of media agenda-setting suggests that the outcome of decisions – of voters, policymakers, business people, etc. – is, to an important degree, determined by the information that is available at the time of the decision. In other words, individuals might have come to a different conclusion with different pieces of information at hand (Iyengar and Kinder 1987; McCombs et al. 1997). It is for this reason that control over the public agenda is a key instrument of power. Political leaders in democratic and non-democratic contexts alike try by every available means – propaganda, manipulation, threats, bribes – to ensure the salience of those issues that benefit them and, more importantly, suppress those that are potentially dangerous.

Yet the media's power goes beyond agenda-setting. The media also interpret and evaluate the issues they are covering. The most obvious sign of the evaluative dimension of media content is ideological bias. However, there are more subtle – and, indeed, more pervasive – forms of interpretation of reality in the news. Research into framing has shed light on the way in which news texts imply the causes of an actual condition, the relevant values that are affected and possible ways of solving the problem (Entman 1993; Johnson-Cartee 2005). By linking a particular issue to more general beliefs, framing becomes an indispensable cognitive tool that gives meaning to facts and events that would otherwise be somewhat dubious and incomprehensible to the majority of news consumers. Gamson and Modigliani (1989) describe frames as 'interpretative packages' that, like agenda-setting, affect the attitudes and choices not only of the general public but also of policy decision-makers. President George W. Bush's rhetoric of 'war on terror' is an example of a powerful frame that encapsulates the interpretation of the 9/11 terror attacks as acts of war that, consequently, had to be responded to by military means. The 'war on terror' frame was part of a concerted strategy to legitimize the invasion of Iraq, accompanied by other rhetorical weapons, such as comparing Saddam Hussein to Hitler (see Entman 2004).

Media frames are more than cognitive tools to structure preferences in the policy debates of the day. They are also part of the grand narratives of a society, which the media employ, reinforce and modify. Iconic images and dramatic stories give life to key events, which become part of the collective memory of a society. Even though news is about current events, news reports frequently make reference to previous events as a means of framing what is happening now. For example, anniversaries are symbolic events which carry a high level of news value. They are used as occasions to rehearse and reconfirm the collective interpretation of these events (Dayan and Katz 1992; Ryfe 2001). News stories employ stereotypical narratives and characterizations by using us–them and friend–enemy dichotomies to reaffirm identities. The myth of Serb supremacy, the Hutus' narrative of century-long suppression by the Tutsis, the struggle for independence from colonial powers, the belief in the superiority of communism over capitalism that survived decades of shortages and even famines: all are examples of powerful frames that mobilized loyalty for authoritarian regimes and even hatred and violence against other groups.

News stories in Western countries have adopted what has been labelled 'strategy frames' (Cappella and Jamieson 1997; Lawrence 2000), denoting a narrative that describes how politicians driven by strategic calculations rather than by a particular vision or ideology are able to gain an advantage over their opponents. Compare this with news coverage from North Korea – admittedly an extreme case – which depicts the actions of the 'beloved' party leader Kim Jong Il as being driven by his desire to lead his country to happiness and wealth. One of the reasons why the strategy frame has gained predominance in Western news reporting is the increasing importance of the watchdog role in the professional self-perception of journalists, which has replaced a more subservient attitude towards political authority. In a news story composed around a strategy frame, the journalist is the invisible hero trying to find out what is behind it all, implying that it is he or she – rather than the politicians with their hidden agendas – who is really acting in the public interest.

However, the media are not the sole origin of a frame that dominates public discourse. Frames emerge from a multitude of discourses involving political and cultural elites, advocacy groups and political entrepreneurs, as well as interpersonal conversations among ordinary citizens, all of which accumulate into a sometimes diffuse, sometimes unanimous climate of public opinion. But it is the media who are able to condense these different strands of discourse into a simplified (often simplistic) package that is collectively shared. Once a particular frame has established itself in the public discourse, it is very difficult to change it, and it often requires key events to replace it with an alternative view of the problem.

Given the power of agenda-setting and framing, one of the main objectives of democracy activists and dissident journalists is therefore to push the boundaries of the range of issues that can be discussed in the public realm and to change the frames of reference of how people think and speak about their society. Often this means breaking the silence about what has been unspeakable for years: the 'disappearance' of dissidents under military rule in Latin America, the Gulags in the Soviet Union, or the luxuriant lifestyles of African leaders amidst poverty. Bringing in new issues usually means shifting the emphasis from the official discourse of success to areas of neglected problems and government failure. The nervous, often draconian reaction of authoritarian leaders to attempts at expanding the public agenda is an indication of the threat that emanates from losing control over the cognitive environment that shapes hearts and minds.

Conditions of media impact

Even though research has demonstrated how communication technologies and the media's agenda-setting power affect politics, it has proved difficult, if not impossible, to draw generalized conclusions about the relationship between media and social change, not to mention to predict the outcome of events as a result of media involvement. Evidently, the media's impact on social processes is contingent on a complex constellation of factors, which is unique to every single case. How then do modern communication technologies and the media's agenda-setting power affect social change? Evidence suggests that the media's impact on complex social processes is contingent on a multitude of external factors that are difficult to predict. For example, instances where 'demonstration effects' helped to bring an authoritarian regime to its end can easily be countered by other instances where this has not been the case. China's response to the mass protests in 1989 has already been mentioned. At the beginning of the twenty-first century several mass movements that have dominated the television screens and internet websites of an international audience for weeks have eventually failed in spite of their high visibility. The regimes in Burma and Iran have successfully sustained the condemnation of international public opinion when cracking down on protests, the regimes in Bahrain and Syria shot at protesters, while in neighbouring countries governments had no choice but to step down under pressure from those on the street. Likewise, the 'CNN-effect' hypothesis has been proved wrong by a number of crises when Western governments did not respond to the pressures of global media coverage in the predicted way – for example, they did not intervene in Rwanda in spite of horrific atrocities, or refrain from invading Iraq in spite of global public opinion turning against the intervention. Communication scholars have sought to develop a more differentiated understanding of the conditions under which, in some cases, the media are able to change the course of events, whereas in others policymakers remain unaffected even in the face of massive public opposition.

One crucial condition for media influence is policy uncertainty and divisions within the political elites. In other words, if the majority of decision-makers share a clear political vision, the decision taken is unlikely to be affected by whatever pressure is exerted by national or international media coverage. In contrast, if the course of policy is unclear and disputed among political elites, the media are able to direct the course of action that is finally taken (Koch-Baumgarten and Voltmer 2010). While research on the media–policy nexus has been exclusively conducted in the context of established Western democracies, evidence suggests that similar dynamics are at work in non-democratic contexts. In authoritarian regimes the constellation of elites has proved to be a crucial factor that determines whether or not the ruling elites have to give in to rising public dissatisfaction and street protests. During those crises, already existing splits between reformers and hardliners tend to break up to an open conflict about how to respond to the demands for change, which will quickly attract the interest not only of international media, but also of less controlled domestic outlets. Media that already sympathized with the opposition, but did take the risk of expressing this view, might feel encouraged to take sides for the reformers within the government, thereby further deepening the divisions.

Osa and Corduneanu-Huci (2003) come to similar conclusions, identifying media access and social networks as crucial factors that, in conjunction with divided elites, might lead to the erosion of authoritarian regimes. Media coverage can hardly exert any pressure if large parts of the population do not have access to it, either because of insufficient technological infrastructure or because of illiteracy and poverty that exclude people from participating in public communication. Without the resonance of public opinion and the potential risk of the loss of popular support, those in power can afford to ignore even harsh criticism from the media. For example, in contemporary Russia critical voices on internet forums and blogs are generally left in peace by state censorship, while traditional media are subjected to extensive control. But since internet penetration is relatively low, online dissent hardly reaches beyond a core group of activists and thus remains without significant political consequences (Fossato et al. 2008). However, the massive street protests that swept across Russia in 2011–12 demonstrate once more that it is impossible to predict when the relationship between elite discourse and alternative framing shifts to break up the acquiescence that had characterized Russian public life for years.

In addition to the spread of oppositional ideas through the media – traditional or digital – social networks are important for the diffusion of ideas through society. Research on the relationship between mediated and social communication shows that for media messages to become influential they have to be adopted by communication in personal encounters in everyday life. Mediated communication and interpersonal communication are closely interrelated and complement each other. Although people obtain most of their information about political affairs from the media, they turn to trusted others in their immediate social environment to develop a shared understanding of the meaning of this information (Chaffee and Mutz 1988). Hence, information from the media provides the raw material for making sense of the world and building arguments for political action. But it is in social groups that collective action is born and maintained. Huckfeldt and Sprague (1987) emphasize the importance of the structure of social networks for the location of opinions and their spread throughout society. Social networks are particularly important in contexts where the environment is hostile. For dissidents in authoritarian regimes, social ties provide security, emotional support and reassurance that are vital for enduring the threat of persecution and social isolation. However, while close social networks provide a sense of belonging and mutual trust, they can also be an obstacle to the spread of oppositional ideas. Granovetter's (1973) notion of 'weak ties' suggests that individuals at the boundaries of a group play an important role in enabling social change because they bridge in-group and out-group communication. Hence, for dissident movements to be successful they need both close-knit links with like-minded others and open communication channels to potential supporters outside the inner circles of groups.

To sum up, the media's role in processes of democratization can be linked to their dual nature as (technological) structures and agents of public communication. By transcending the limitations of time and space, they are instrumental in linking distant individuals and groups; they accelerate social and political processes; they construct social reality by setting the agenda of public discourse and by providing a narrative that endows meaning to events and social conditions. Media influences cannot be understood in isolation from their environment. Since they are embedded in the cultural norms, political hierarchies and social practices of their surroundings, they are often a force that stabilizes the status quo. But they are also attracted to the unusual, unexpected and sensational, thus acting – intentionally or not – as a catalyst for change. Dissident journalists can contribute to the erosion of an authoritarian regime by expanding the agenda of public discourse and by challenging dominant narratives that legitimize existing power structures.

4

Complex Transitions and Uncertain Outcomes: The Media and Democratization Over Time

Whether the media are a force that drives political change or an instrument of maintaining the status quo; whether it is mainly communication technology that shapes the course of events or journalistic agency; and ultimately whether the media are enhancing or inhibiting the quality and sustainability of newly established democracies – these questions cannot be answered without taking into account a country's position on its journey between authoritarianism and democracy. This chapter explores how the media's role in democratic transitions changes over time. The chapter employs a developmental view of democratization by arguing that, depending on the particular stage of the transition process, the media affect the course of events in different ways. As the constellation of power relations changes, political actors – both ruling elites and oppositional groups – adjust their media strategies in order to secure their control over public opinion. At the same time, the media also reposition themselves in response to the constraints and opportunities that arise from the changing circumstances. While reconstructing the role of the media across the course of democratization, the chapter considers how communication technologies and editorial agency – a distinction that was introduced in the previous chapter – affect political change at different points in time. Examples from various political contexts suggest an ambivalent role of the media in democratic transitions. Even though the media are an indispensable precondition of freedom and democratic accountability, they often hinder the consolidation of newly established institutions.

Stages of democratization: always moving forward?

Democratization is a process that stretches between two ideal-typical points: closed autocracy at one end and open and mature democracy at the other. To understand the process that connects these two points students of democratization have tried to identify patterns and regularities of transition. Knowing what comes first and what follows would be of great benefit in making predictions about the future course of a country's development and in providing the best possible support at any point in the process. A developmental theory of democratization assumes that the process evolves in steps that logically build on each other. The most widely used procedure distinguishes between three main stages: liberalization within the old regime and its eventual decay; transition to democratic rule; and, finally, consolidation and maturation of the newly established democratic order (O'Donnell and Schmitter 1986).

Liberalization refers to a gradual opening up of the old regime, a process which in some cases might go on over decades; in others it happens with an abrupt change of policy. Faced with increasing costs of suppression, authoritarian elites often see themselves forced to loosen their grip over society and to grant more freedoms to their citizens. Relaxing censorship of public communication is an important part of this policy. Liberalization is usually driven by the fear that without these concessions internal unrest amongst large sections of the population may lead to the destabilization of the regime. Violent clamp-downs on protest, draconian punishments for dissident activities and an expansive apparatus of surveillance not only undermine a country's reputation internationally, with a resulting loss of bargaining power and influence; such responses also bear the risk of deepening divisions between different factions of the ruling elites. Thus, allowing for some degree of liberalization can be understood as a strategic decision of the ruling elites in order to maintain the power structures of the regime. Rarely is this policy change intended to transform the country into a democracy. Yet liberalization is not without risks either. In some cases fewer controls and more space for critical debate might pacify discontent, but in others liberalization only invites opposition groups to intensify their struggle to bring down the autocratic regime once and for all.

Next, the *transition* stage includes the breakdown of the old regime and the subsequent construction of new institutions. The transition stage is an extremely dramatic and volatile period, sometimes involving hitherto unseen mass protests, which can quickly turn into bloodshed when police forces try to clear the streets of protesters in an attempt to restore public order. As the old regime crumbles, different parts of the elite begin to rethink their position within the power structure, with some – the so-called hardliners – trying to maintain the foundations of the existing regime, and others – the so-called softliners – pushing for change (O'Donnell and Schmitter 1986). As it seems no longer opportune to support the old leader, some parts of the elite might even decide to defect to the opposition camp. Depending on the remaining power resources of the old ruling class, hardliners and softliners might come to a power-sharing agreement that allows the old elite to maintain some of its privileges in exchange for giving way to free and competitive elections. Karl and Schmitter (1991) regard transitions that are based on this kind of elite pact as more likely to result in a stable democracy than other modes of transition, such as revolutionary mass movements or coups by counter-elites. The 'round tables' in Eastern Europe are examples of negotiated transitions and have become a role model for consensus-building across political divisions during regime change.

However, in the long run, negotiated transitions come at a price too. If, for example, the arrangement includes reserved seats in the first election, this can provide the old elites with the resources to reorganize themselves, allowing them to obstruct, or even reverse, the democratization process. In other cases, for example in Chile and Argentina, protection from prosecution of individuals who were involved in human rights abuses during the old regime might be the only way of getting rid of the dictator. But the amnesty, even if temporary, usually violates popular feelings of justice and thus undermines the legitimacy of the new democratic order. Beneath the surface, the wounds of the past remain open and the victims will continue to demand a full investigation of the crimes that were committed under the old regime. In other cases, particular non-elected groups, most notably the army, have been granted formal or informal veto power in some areas of decision-making that are relevant to their interests. Veto players often use their blackmailing power to hijack the elected government, thereby preventing the new democratic institutions from gaining full autonomy and legitimacy. Chile and Turkey are examples of a scenario where pacts between transitional elites and the veto power of the army have obstructed the consolidation of the emerging democracy.

The transition stage[1] is regarded as having come to an end when a new constitution has been agreed upon and a founding election has been held, leading into the phase of *consolidation*. Consolidation encompasses the long process of making the new democratic institutions work, a process that can take decades before arriving at a mature and stable state of affairs. During this phase the newly established institutions begin to work and put down roots. Democratization scholars have suggested various criteria for a completed consolidation (for example, the number of free and fair elections, alternation of government, etc.), all of which have proved to be insufficient to capture the complex and ambiguous post-authoritarian realities of the 'third wave'. However, there is wide consensus that consolidation requires more than just institution-building. It also involves a democratic political culture that permeates both everyday practices of ordinary citizens and the actions of elites (Linz and Stepan 1996: 3–15; Merkel 1998). A democratic political culture is anchored in a set of beliefs and attitudes that are compatible with, and supportive of, the working of democratic institutions. These include notions of citizenship, toleration of diversity, cooperation across lines of difference and – last, but not least – a political communication culture that enables informed participation. In their seminal book *The Civic Culture*, Almond and Verba (1963) assert the close relationship between culture and institutional stability. The book, written to compare three new democracies of the 'second wave' (Germany, Italy, Mexico) with the established democracies of the US and Britain in the 1950s, has recently enjoyed a lively renaissance (see, for example, Klingemann et al. 2006; Dalton et al. 2008). The notion of an interdependency between the micro and macro levels of politics chimes with the experience of many recent new democracies that have been fairly successful in setting up institutions, but apparently lack the cultural qualities that make these institutions work in the desired manner.

While liberalization, transition and consolidation look like logical steps towards building democracy, the attempt to specify distinct phases has been criticized for various reasons. First, the process of regime change is not linear; nor does it occur in an orderly and predictable sequence of developments whereby one step is neatly built upon the previous one. In some countries, different stages occur simultaneously, for example when the authoritarian regime collapses without a preceding period of gradual liberalization. Romania and Bulgaria are cases that illustrate this pathway in Eastern Europe, in contrast to Poland, which constitutes an almost paradigmatic case for the three-stage sequence of transition. Yet even here, the cautious liberalization that led up to the founding of the independent trade union Solidarnosz in 1980 was harshly cut short by the martial law that was introduced soon after, in 1981. Eventually, the round table of negotiations between the government and Solidarnosz led to the first, albeit only semi-free, election, in June 1989. In order to account for the fact that the timing and sequencing differ across individual cases, Schneider and Schmitter (2004) refer to the three concepts as 'components' rather than phases.

A more fundamental critique comes from Carothers (2002), who rejects the developmental approach to democratization altogether because of the implicit teleological assumptions that underlie the notion of subsequent stages. He argues that many new democracies, rather than progressing towards the liberal model of institutions and practices, are stuck in the transition process, often at an early stage of consolidation. In fact, a recurrent problem that can be observed in a large number of 'third wave' democracies is the lack of liberalization even after democratic forms of government have been implemented. There are also instances of reverse transition where, after a period of rapid democratization, freedoms are restricted again – for example in Russia. Conversely, it would be wrong to assume that liberalization within the authoritarian regime always triggers change towards democracy. Some regimes have been remarkably successful in stabilizing their power basis through controlled opening, thus giving way to new types of autocracy that combine a certain degree of competition and oppositional organizations with a weak rule of law and persistent censorship of the media (Levitsky and Way 2010; Zakaria 1997).

While these are valid arguments, rejection of a notion of stages and democratic development is not without conceptual shortcomings either. It often results in an overemphasis on outcomes and the degree to which they match, or deviate from, normative expectations of liberal democracy, while ignoring the processes that have led to the present situation. Taking into account the specific journey that countries undertake in order to escape from autocracy, it can be seen that they do not necessarily arrive at the same destination – even if they are at least in the same region, broadly labelled democracy. Without assuming that there is a recognizably regular or sequential pattern, the notion of stages of democratization can be of great heuristic value if we are to understand the interaction between the numerous forces that drive, or obstruct, transitions from autocratic to democratic rule. More specifically, looking at different phases of the transition process helps us to come to a realistic evaluation of the decisions made by the actors involved, as any judgement of achievements has to consider the particular circumstances and the options available at a given point in time. The developmental view of transition also helps to avoid mono-factorial explanations about the causes of regime changes. In some stages of the process the political elites are the driving force, as actor-based theories of democratization imply. At other times, civil society and the voice of the people are of crucial importance. Even the normative framework that guides particular decisions may vary across different phases, with some actions being justified at some times and in some circumstances, but not in others.

These arguments are particularly valid with regard to the media and the transformation of public communication. Because of the media's dependency on their political, economic and social environment, and the ambiguity of communication values, the role of the media changes sometimes dramatically over the course of the transition process. At some stages, the media can be the driving force of change; at others, their role is confined to serving as instruments in the hands of other actors. Equally, during some phases the media have a significant impact on the course of the transition process primarily through the opportunities and constraints provided by particular technological features for political action – for example, the speed and visuality of television or the non-hierarchical network structure of the internet. In other phases and circumstances it is journalistic agency – i.e., the deliberate decisions of particular media organizations or reporters to speak out, investigate or advocate certain ideas – that affect the way in which citizens or elites behave. When evaluating the democratizing role of the media we might come to the conclusion that at certain times the media serve democratization best by taking on an advocacy role, but at other times objectivity and neutrality are of paramount importance to ensure the quality of public communication. In a similar vein, Rozumilowicz (2002) argues that throughout consecutive phases of the democratization process, different policy measures take priority when the media are being transformed into a free and independent institution.

The following sections utilize the notion of stages of democratization to explore the changing role of the media in processes of regime change, while taking into account that the direction and outcome of the process are uncertain. The most unanimous phase is probably what is usually labelled 'transition' – i.e., the turning point between the old and the new regime, the moment when the old order ceases to exist and a country embarks on establishing democratic procedures. In some cases this happens in a dramatic acceleration of events with mass demonstrations and statues of the old dictator being toppled; in other cases, like in Taiwan or South Korea, the transition proceeds in a more gradual fashion. An election that is recognized both domestically and internationally as fair and free is usually the marker of a country that has formally transformed into a democracy. To avoid undue assumptions as to what kind of developments precede and which follow this watershed, in the following sections the other two phases are simply labelled 'before' and 'after regime change'.

There might be liberalization with increasing toleration of freedom of speech before the demise of the authoritarian regime, but not necessarily; and consolidation of the new democratic order might not happen in cases where the persistent risk of a return of authoritarian politics and censorship still exists.

Before regime change: pushing the boundaries of control

Media are always closely linked to, and dependent on, the political system in which they operate. They reflect and even amplify its features and resonate the dominant ideology of a society. However, under certain circumstances they can also undermine the stability of the status quo, either deliberately or as an unintended consequence of their performance. Close congruence between media and political power is not confined to authoritarian regimes; similar patterns of interaction can be observed in democratic systems as well. In both democratic and non-democratic contexts, the media occupy a central space in the power structure of the political system, and provide the legitimization of the status quo. All authoritarian regimes use the media as a mouthpiece and propaganda instrument to secure public support – or at least to denounce and delegitimize any alternative views that generate from within or outside their societies. The more that media technologies and communication infrastructure – like airwaves, mobile phone networks or broadband – penetrate even the most remote parts of the world, the more dictators develop sophisticated communication strategies to stabilize their power. In fact, 'spin' – i.e., the professional use of communications to shape the public perception of politics – is not only a necessity for winning elections in modern 'media democracies'; it has also become a *sine qua non* in authoritarian systems, as they are less and less able to insulate themselves from global information flows.

It would be a mistake to assume that the relationship between the media and authoritarian regimes relies solely on suppression. Rather, for most of the time the media provide their services quite willingly. Usually there is a finely tuned system of give and take between the media and the government, which ensures that the media benefit from the system and thus have a stake in preserving it. For example, in many authoritarian countries the media enjoy generous state subsidies that protect them from the risks of market competition. In communist countries journalists held secure jobs even though the stories they wrote never saw the light of day. Elsewhere, the media are regarded as a key industry in the country's economic development, and governments have invested large sums of money in the technological infrastructure of the media to make them fit for global competition. Pre-democratic South Korea, Taiwan, Chile and Brazil are all examples of a policy that helped the media industry to grow into strong players, both on domestic and global markets.

In spite of the close interdependency between the media and authoritarian power, the former have frequently been instrumental in liberalizing authoritarian regimes. To understand how the media are involved in political and social transitions, it is useful to distinguish the direction and origin of change:

- bottom-up liberalization
- top-down liberalization
- external influences

In reality, these processes are closely interrelated and often respond to each other. For example, top-down liberalization initiated by the ruling elites may be a reaction to growing demands for liberalization from below, while demands for more freedoms grow as the government introduces reforms. Meanwhile, in a globalized world, external influences and transborder communication have become an important factor in democratic transitions. However, although they might strengthen existing internal developments towards liberalization, they are unlikely to trigger change independently from the preferences and choices of domestic actors, be it ruling elites or grass-root activists. Whatever the processes of change, it has to be stressed that the outcomes of attempts to liberalize an authoritarian system are uncertain. Liberalization can be the beginning of the end of the old regime leading to democracy; in other cases, the process settles on an equilibrium that allows some freedoms without affecting the foundations of the authoritarian power structure. But demands for liberalization can also trigger fierce counter-reactions and a relapse into authoritarianism and brute repression.

Bottom-up liberalization

Bottom-up processes of liberalization are driven by grass-root groups that are pushing for political change. Since these groups have only few chances, if any, to express their views in public, the demand for freedom of expression and press freedom is usually a centrepiece of their political agenda. Many opposition groups have their own media in order to circulate their ideas. Depending on the degree of liberalization of the political environment, the situation of dissident media under autocratic rule differs widely. In some instances, they enjoy a certain amount of toleration by political officials as long as they do not overstep a certain boundary; in other instances, they are entirely confined to clandestine outputs that are produced and distributed illegally and with high personal risk for those involved. An example of the latter is the so-called *samizdat* literature in the Soviet Union and Central and East European countries under communist rule (Goetz-Stankiewicz 1992; Johnston 1999; Skilling 1989). *Samizdat* literature was laboriously typed and retyped in individual copies and then personally passed on to trusted others. It started with the publication of underground literature, but then broadened to also cover explicitly political issues. However, the subversive potential of non-political communications should not be underestimated. For in highly politicized societies, like those under communist rule, writing purely aesthetic pieces of literature without any educational or social purpose is in itself a highly political act of resistance. Communist communication culture created an almost impenetrable thicket of 'double speech', probably more so than any other authoritarian regime type because of the huge gap between the utopian ideology, which provided the legitimacy for the regime, and the actual reality of scarcity and fear that governed the everyday lives of most of its citizens. The *samizdat* literature set out to regain honesty and authenticity in language, regardless of whether a text covered the personal or the political.

Another example of a vibrant oppositional press can be seen in South Africa (Switzer and Adhikari 2000). Hundreds of pamphlets, newsletters and newspapers, alongside music groups and choirs, gave voice to the suppressed majority of the country and finally helped to overcome the apartheid regime. These means of communications were not only weapons in the struggle against apartheid, but were also crucial in creating and maintaining a sense of community where people supported each other in times of hardship. Olukotun (2002) describes similar strong links between underground media and civil society in Nigeria during the Abacha military dictatorship in the 1990s. A wide network of supporters both within and outside the country helped these media to survive economically – for example, by 'patriotic buying' (ibid.: 318) of large numbers of copies, but also by providing help for families of journalists who were arrested because of their involvement in oppositional activities. Another important aspect of the strength of the Nigerian underground media involved their links to parts of the political elites. Frequently, dissident members of the ruling class passed on information from inside the centres of power, for example, giving advance warning of imminent raids, violations of human rights or practices of corruption and self-enrichment. These close-knit networks of clandestine media and broad sections of the population differ markedly from the situation in Romania under Ceausescu (Hall and O'Neil 1998). Here, dissident journalists took on an elitist position, often using esoteric language that could hardly be understood by anybody outside the inner circles of intellectuals. As a consequence, they remained very isolated from their environment and did not develop any significant mobilizing power.

It has to be noted that dissident media under autocratic rule can hardly be classified as being independent as liberal models of journalism would suggest. They are independent from the government and associated groups they are opposing, but they are utilized by advocacy groups as instruments in their political struggle. In most cases, the content of oppositional media is produced by activists rather than professional journalists; thus, the selection of news follows a 'political logic' rather than 'media logic'. In other words, issues and events are selected for coverage because of their significance for the particular cause of a dissident group, whereas news values and journalistic norms are less important. As Olukotun (2002: 341) notes: 'Newspapers and journals produced in struggle are political tracts rather than professionally balanced publications. . . . [I]naccuracies, slips and exaggerations were overlooked if they served the cause of the struggle.' In fact, it is fair to say that under autocratic rule, objectivity and neutrality are fairly meaningless concepts – on either side of the divide. Balancing competing truth claims about the virtues of dictatorship or the legitimacy of suppressing and mistreating particular ethnic groups would be an absurd exercise for the media of a pro-democracy movement. Nevertheless, factuality, which is one of the defining dimensions of the objectivity concept (see McQuail 1992: 196–204), can play a crucial role when dissident media uncover suppressed information – for example, about the brutality of the security forces or the corruption of the ruling elite – thereby breaking through the fog of propaganda that dominates official media coverage. However, these investigations are not pursued in a detached and neutral manner, as Western norms of journalism would require. Their aim is to delegitimize the regime and its propaganda and ultimately bring about regime change. In this respect, oppositional media, like government media, are political mouthpieces, albeit employed for entirely different purposes. They contribute to expanding the diversity of views, not by being objective, but by adding partisan perspectives that are otherwise excluded from the public discourse.

While dissident media of the 1970s and 1980s used low-key, often makeshift technology, recent oppositional movements have turned to the new digital communication technologies to create an alternative public sphere that challenges the official account of political reality. In many countries where opposition groups are unable to gain access to the mainstream media, websites and blogging have become important forums for oppositional voices. In fact, blogging has been dubbed the new *samizdat* media of the twenty-first century. In China, for example, dissident bloggers have become influential opinion leaders with considerable numbers of followers who regularly read their blogs. Some of them – for example, the democracy activists Hu Jia, who won the Sakharov Prize for Freedom of Thought in 2008, and Han Han, arguably the most popular blogger in China today – have gained almost cult status in an environment where newspapers and broadcasting are still heavily censored. With a sophisticated use of new media technologies and a new style of communication, the present generation of dissidents differs markedly from the pro-democracy movement that was finally suppressed in Tiananmen Square in June 1989, as does the society of contemporary China, which is more open to foreign influences, but also more self-confident of its own values and achievements when engaging with other cultures. Dissident blogs are usually run on foreign servers to evade government interference. They address issues that are not covered by the mainstream media, or only in a one-sided, negative way, such as environmental problems, poverty and homosexuality. By expressing discontent with the existing power structure in a provocative style of language that violates established norms of good taste, these blogs challenge the sterile phrases of official political language that dominate mainstream media. It is this style that often blurs the line between political opposition against the regime and the rebellion of a young generation against traditional norms and hierarchies. Many of the young generation of bloggers and their readers use the space on the internet to express new forms of identity and lifestyles that refute the primacy of collective goals. Their ideas are often not outspokenly political. Yet it might well be that the evolutionary power of cultural change will turn out more of a threat to China's rulers than head-on political opposition (MacKinnon 2008). Even though traditional media, such as newspapers and magazines, have responded to the growing demand of China's educated and increasingly wealthy middle class, the internet seems to be at the real centre of this cultural turn towards more individualism and plurality, as a young generation of 'internet natives' is trying to tailor cyberspace according to their own needs for individual self-expression and new forms of social interaction.

Even so, authoritarian governments have learned to cope with the new digital *samizdat*. The Chinese government has built a second wall, the 'Great Firewall', to protect the hearts and minds of its citizens from the invasion of foreign ideas. Sophisticated software to filter the content of online communication, blocking addresses and domains alongside the infiltration of discussion forums by regime loyalists – these are only some of the weapons used by authoritarian governments in the arms race with their digital opponents (Abbott 2001; Rodan 1998). Frequently, these tools of surveillance and suppression have been developed with the help of Western companies. For example, the search engine Google agreed with the Chinese government to filter out certain unwanted content, but withdrew from its contract in a spectacular move in March 2010. And back in the Middle East, Nokia Siemens provided the Iranian government with the technology to trace mobile phone users who used their phones to organize anti-government protests in the aftermath of the rigged election in June 2009 (Weinthal 2010; for a general account of the struggle for the control over the internet in the Middle East, see Howard 2010).

Equally important as the spread of oppositional ideas to wider parts of society is the role of dissident media for the opposition movement itself. Producing and distributing illicit publications requires a high level of planning, mutual trust and cooperation. Hence, oppositional media help to strengthen the coherence of dissident groups and their capability of collective action. The need to produce texts on a regular basis, whether in written form or through the airwaves, encourages internal discussions about the ideological identity of the group, their long-term political objectives and their strategies to achieve these goals. This social and political capital is of tremendous value if and when the authoritarian regime eventually falls. A well-organized opposition would then be able to step into the emerging power vacuum and drive the democratization process forward. If the opposition lacks coherence and a clear vision of the way forward for the country following the dictatorship, the power vacuum is usually taken over by counter-elites from the old regime, whose ambitions to transform the country into a functioning democracy might fall short of their determination to secure control over the centres of power and access to the resources that come with it. An example of the first scenario is Poland, where the oppositional trade union Solidarnosz organized itself around a plethora of underground publications and played a leading role in Polish politics ever since it won the first semi-free election in 1989.[2] It is indicative of the close relationship between Poland's oppositional movement and journalism that some of its leading figures moved on to become influential journalists in the new Poland – for example Adam Michnik, who is now the editor of

Poland's biggest newspaper *Gazeta Wyborcza*. Conversely, Vaclav Havel, a playwright and one of the leading figures of the *samizdat* movement in Eastern Europe, became the first democratic president of the Czech Republic.

In contrast, Bulgaria's opposition movement started organizing itself only in the late 1980s, and hardly any *samizdat* publications provided intellectual focus for the various actions. When the Union of Democratic Forces was founded in December 1989 as an umbrella for the fragmented pro-democracy groups, there was almost no shared vision of the future political course of the country, and the only glue that united the diverse groups was a strong anti-communist sentiment. As a consequence, the communist leader Todor Zhivkov was brought down by a putsch from within the leadership of the Communist Party rather than by the democratic opposition, thus allowing the Socialist Party, the successor organization of the Communist Party, to cling to power until 1997 (Dobreva et al. 2011).

In the case of South Africa, Switzer (2000) observes that the United Democratic Front (UDF) used the media to great effect not only to organize the diverse groups of the opposition movement, but also to build alliances across the divisions of race and class. As a result, the South African opposition could rely on an extensive network of a multitude of both strong and weak ties (Granovetter 1973). With growing internal unrest and international isolation, many of the mainstream white-controlled media gave up their compliance with the regime and began openly to report on and support the activities of the anti-apartheid movement. The spill-over between dissident and mainstream media was then an important factor contributing to weakened public support for the regime and to reaching out to the 'softliners' within the government, thereby paving the way for the negotiations between President de Klerk and Nelson Mandela to end apartheid rule in the country.

It remains an open question whether, and if so in what way, the new internet-based *samizdat* is as effective in building organizational power as was the self-published printed material of earlier transitions. Undoubtedly, digital media, in particular social network sites such as Twitter or Facebook, in conjunction with mobile communication technology, have demonstrated an extraordinary capacity to mobilize large numbers of people and bring them onto the streets. From the first internet-based mass protests of the anti-globalization movement at the 1999 WTO summit in Seattle to the 'Arab Spring' in 2010–11, new communication technologies have helped to activate social networks within days or even hours, resulting in spectacular public protest events that put political leaders under extreme pressure –

either to restore public order by any means or to engage in a dialogue with the protesters. However, these new media also have their drawbacks and in some ways seem to be less effective than their humble predecessors. Blogs are typically run by individuals who might attract substantial followings, but these are usually dispersed fans. Interaction between them rarely goes beyond discussions in response to the blog, and there is hardly any sense of group identity amongst them. Social network sites also have their limitations when it comes to collective action. They bring together thousands of 'friends', but if these virtual networks are not rooted in strong offline social networks, they remain loose and ephemeral. The ability instantly to bring large numbers of people out onto the streets might even give the movement a false sense of strength, as Egypt's democracy movement had to realize at the end of 2011 when the 'Arab Spring' had turned into an 'Arab Winter'. At this time the activists of Tahrir Square were outmanoeuvred by a hard-nosed military elite and the well-organized Muslim Brotherhood, which could draw on their influence in poor urban neighbourhoods and villages. What can be learnt from this case is that for online opposition movements to overcome their weaknesses, it is important to build sustainable ties beyond their online communities and to translate these networks into real-world organizational structures, which are able to take on a political role in national politics if the window of opportunity opens.

Top-down liberalization

Even though one of the prime goals of most authoritarian regimes is to preserve the status quo, the lack of change can equally pose severe threats to the regime's ability to survive. The longer an authoritarian regime exists, the more the propaganda rhetoric becomes blunt and loses its ability to stir enthusiasm amongst the population. Charismatic leaders are a great asset for maintaining the momentum of public propaganda by employing their personality (and often that of their wives) to capture the imagination of their populations – even though it is often difficult to say to what extent the public display of regime support is genuine or down to the fear that silence might be interpreted as opposition. The pitfall of manipulated information by state-censored media is that it can lead to unintended consequences when the gap between the ideal world of propaganda and the reality experienced by people in everyday life widens. Images of enthusiastic masses, busy factories and lush crops on the television screens contrast with the experience of queues in front of empty shops; images of a baby-hugging dictator contrast with the experience of marauding militia on the streets; and abuses by security forces not only undermine support, but also bear the risk of unrest and mass protests. Where political elites have not entirely lost touch with the population, they often initiate top-down liberalization to pre-empt the spread of frustration that might quickly become difficult to control once these feelings and experiences have found a channel through which to express themselves.

Since the effectiveness of propaganda is uncertain, authoritarian regimes have to seek legitimacy through economic performance – unless they resort to brute suppression. Singapore is an example of an authoritarian regime that successfully secures stability and popular support, at least acquiescence, by providing high living standards and public order (Tremewan 1994). However, in an ever more globalized world, the dynamics of the market require constant adaptation, which are bound to have repercussions on the expectations of the population and even the power constellation among competing elites. Changing economic conditions usually produce winners and losers, both of which can lead to disaffection with the regime and become a potential threat to its stability. Economic high-performers often demand more liberties to satisfy their growing self-confidence, whereas economic losers are a dangerous source of social revolts.

Faced with the risks of both stagnation and change, authoritarian leaders may have no choice but to allow for more diversity in the public expression of opinions. However, the decision to open up the system almost inevitably deepens existing divisions between softliners and hardliners amongst the ruling elites (O'Donnell and Schmitter 1986). Hardliners are unwilling to make concessions and, rather, rely on repression as a means of securing the existing power structure. Softliners recognize the need for change and might even expect gains for themselves if the hardliners lose the hegemony over the definition of the political reality. The success of top-down liberalization depends to a large degree on the ability of the reformist camp to negotiate a political compromise with the hardliners and/or to build effective alliances with civil society groups.

One prominent example of top-down liberalization consists of Gorbachev's policies of *glasnost* – or 'openness' and transparency of public debate – and *perestroika* – or 'reconstruction' of the Soviet economy from an inefficient command economy to a more decentralized and competitive economy. When Gorbachev came to power in 1985, he was acutely aware of the disastrous condition of the Soviet economy and, indeed, of Soviet society as a whole. Both principles, *glasnost* and *perestroika*, were closely interlinked, and together it was hoped they would initiate a controlled renewal of the

Soviet Union. Television was at the centre of Gorbachev's reform policy, which he believed was a prime instrument of power that could be used to change people's beliefs and behaviour (Mickiewicz 1999: 23–51). Gorbachev understood that the strict censorship exercised by the Communist Party had undermined the credibility, and hence the effectiveness, of television in particular and the media in general. He therefore invited journalists to join his *glasnost* project and explore new ways of communicating political matters to the Russian public. Instead of using the old cryptic and ritualized rhetoric, political news was presented in a more accessible and engaging language. More importantly, for the first time in Soviet history citizens were invited publicly to express criticism without running the risk of losing their job – or worse. Even powerful groups like the military and the KGB were not excluded from this public critique. Gorbachev's reforms divided the political elites from the lowest to the highest ranks, and this division was also reflected in the media, some of which supported the old Soviet values while others aligned themselves with Gorbachev's *glasnost* policy. Most journalists realized that *glasnost* opened up a unique opportunity for them to gain more independence and to play a more active role in the public debate. In fact, the *glasnost* years under Gorbachev's reign were experienced as a honeymoon period between political power and free public expression of ideas, which ended during the 1990s when the media fell increasingly at the mercy of rival political and economic players.

In the end, the new freedoms in public communication turned out to be a fragile and short-lived promise that was not sustainable enough to survive the crises that eventually brought down the Soviet Union. Most media remained closely aligned to one of the rival political groups, on which they depended for economic survival and whose interests they promoted in turn.[3] The collapse of the Soviet system, followed by the break-away of numerous regions and former allies in East-Central Europe, the Chechen War and the breakdown of the Russian economy, would have pushed even established democracies to their limits. The fundamental defect of Gorbachev's media revolution – and of liberalizations from above in general – was that he saw the media essentially as an instrument to serve his policy objectives, benevolent as they might have been. The new freedoms were granted to them for a purpose, rather than established as constitutional rights. They therefore lacked the legal guarantees as well as the independent economic revenues that would have served as a protective shield against political interference in situations where the media decided not to support the goals of the government. Most probably, Gorbachev believed that he had the legitimacy to recall and curb *glasnost* and media freedom if this had become necessary in the interest of his wider political goals.

Another prominent example of top-down liberalization is China. The violent crack-down on the pro-democracy movement on Tiananmen Square in June 1989 was preceded by a decade of reforms initiated by the then chairman of the Communist Party, Deng Xiao-ping. The decision to call out the tanks against the protesters was a strong message of the Chinese government sent out to its people and the outside world that it was determined to keep control over the reform process and to dictate the scope and timing of change without pressure from below. Contrary to the fears of many observers at that time, the Tiananmen massacre did not mark the end of the reform process in China. Since then, the Chinese economy has been merged into a state-controlled market economy and has risen to become one of the big players in the world economy.

In this truly breathtaking process, the media are playing a key role. While commercialization and decentralization of the media have helped them to increase their economic independence and to establish a closer relationship with their audience, the government has maintained editorial control. In this process of progress without change, the print media have responded to their readers' growing interest in matters of individual lifestyle by introducing a large range of specialized outlets and supplements that cover issues like sport, fashion, home and career. Yet in spite of the marketization of the media industry, a strict licensing system and state subsidies ensure that the media remain closely tied to the state (Ma 2000; Zhao 1998). More importantly, when it comes to political issues censorship remains still intact. Like Gorbachev, the Chinese government regards the media as an instrument to promote its reform policy. Even though this does not exclude critical discussion of certain issues, it is the government that determines the scope and tone of the debate. For example, the media frequently address problems of corruption in business and state bureaucracy, but this follows strictly hierarchical patterns and in no way does it touch the centre of power. Chan and Qiu (2002) point out that the combination of economic liberalization and political control has resulted in a close symbiosis between the media and the state. The Chinese government's media policy of 'sticks and carrots' offers the media enough benefits to let them accept the persisting limitations of their journalistic independence, resulting, as Chan and Qiu put it, in a 'partially liberalized authoritarian media system' (2002: 36). Hence, as long as newspapers and broadcast organizations gain more from complicity with those in power than from pushing for political independence, it is unlikely that they challenge the status quo in any fundamental way.

External influences

Even with the strictest censorship measures in place, it is no longer possible today for any country to completely isolate itself from the outside world. In a globalized world that is connected by extensive networks of advanced communication technologies, it becomes increasingly difficult to prevent unwanted ideas from crossing the borders. Opposition groups in authoritarian regimes are usually keen to establish links with the outside world for moral and material support. Support by Western governments, either expressed publicly or through diplomatic channels, as well as financial and material aid from international donors, help to strengthen the organizational structure of opposition movements and their ability to communicate their ideas. However, the influence of international organizations can also become problematic, even detrimental, when they push for the wrong kind of change at the wrong time. Since outsiders are often not sufficiently aware of the cultural sentiments and situational constraints inside a country under autocratic rule, they might misjudge the chances for successful change at a given point in time.

Links with the exiled opposition is another source of external influence and plays a vital role in sustaining opposition over longer periods of time. People who fled the country not only provide financial support, but are also important conversation partners in the process of discussing ideological issues and developing political strategies. For example, exile groups of the South African ANC were instrumental in mobilizing international criticism of the apartheid regime and provided a constant supply of printed material to be circulated in townships and amongst oppositional groups (Switzer 2000). Iran too has a long tradition of exiled opposition groups, beginning with Ayatollah Khomeini, whose system is now fiercely contested by the 'green movement'. However, as the actual situation of the Iranian diaspora shows, opposition supporters abroad are often divided among themselves and, the longer they remain outside their home country, the more they become detached from the developments and moods there (Deasy and Kaviani 2010).

Before the advent of the internet, the main channel that linked dissidents in autocratic countries with the outside world was shortwave radio, most notably Radio Free Europe, Radio Liberty (RFE/RL) and Voice of America, alongside international programmes of various national broadcasters, like the BBC World Service or Deutsche Welle. These stations saw their role as offering independent information to countries where the censored domestic media provided only a distorted view of the political situation. The assumption was that the availability of the 'truth' of uncensored information would delegitimize the propaganda of the regime and eventually mobilize popular resistance. At the same time, these broadcasters, especially those in the US, were themselves instruments of Cold War propaganda and played a central part in the overall strategy of the West to bring down the rival regimes of the communist bloc (Rawnsley 1996). Transborder shortwave radio might not have had mass appeal, since for the majority of the population the domestic news media remained the main source of information. But it was extremely important for those who were already opposed to the regime and who were looking out for alternative information (Puddington 2000). RFE/RL also frequently replicated material from domestic clandestine media, thereby expanding their reach to audiences who were not part of the inner circles of the opposition movement (Sükösd 2000: 137).

Another form of external information flow is transborder transmission of television signals from neighbouring countries where the same language is spoken on both sides of the division. A current example of this situation are the southern provinces of China, where broadcast programmes from Taiwan and Hong Kong can be easily received. Governments do everything possible to keep this information out by jamming these programmes or imposing serious penalties on those who watch the forbidden channels. A unique situation existed in the former German Democratic Republic (GDR) where virtually the entire population was able to receive West German television and made ample use of this opportunity. Watching the evening news from the other part of the country was part of the daily routine for both the political elite and ordinary citizens (Hesse 1990). After failed attempts to suppress the use of West German television, the communist leadership had to accept the fact that the population spent their evenings in the company of Western soap operas and dramas.[4] However, bringing newspapers, magazines or books into the country remained strictly prohibited, and those who smuggled in printed material did so at high personal risk.

However, besides anecdotal accounts from individual recollections, there is hardly any systematic empirical research that provides reliable evidence for the actual impact of exposure to transnational media content on mobilizing popular resistance against the regime. Stations like Radio Free Europe were mainly preaching to the converted – i.e., were primarily used by those who already held critical views on the regime. In other words, given the self-selectivity of media exposure it is difficult to disentangle the relationship between cause and effect. In their study on West German television's influence on public opinion in East Germany, Kern and Hainmueller (2009) were in a position to use survey data that had been hitherto inaccessible. This study is based on a unique situation in East Germany that provides a natural laboratory experiment. Because of their geographical locations, two distinct areas in the northeast and the southeast of the GDR were unable to receive West German television signals, whereas the rest of the country had full access to Western programmes. By comparing these two groups of audiences the authors came to a surprising conclusion: rather than undermining the legitimacy of the communist regime, exposure to West German television was actually related to increased regime support. The data suggest that people who lived in the areas that were covered by Western television showed a higher level of support for the communist regime. This effect can mainly be attributed to exposure to Western entertainment programmes. An explanation for this somewhat surprising finding could be seen in the limited leisure facilities in the GDR. Outside the big cities, cinemas, restaurants, sports facilities, etc. were in short supply. Hence, having a bigger and better choice of television entertainment must have improved the subjective quality of life experience. Access to Western television might also have eased the claustrophobic feeling that haunted many people in the GDR. While travelling outside the Eastern bloc was restricted to a privileged few, watching West German television opened the proverbial 'window to the world' that allowed the imagination to expand beyond the narrow boundaries of the day-to-day life of 'real existing socialism'. In contrast, people who could not receive Western television felt significantly more detached from the system and were more likely to disagree with its ideological premises. Being cut off from the daily pleasure of escapism must have contributed to the frustration, as it made the shortcomings and false promises of the regime more salient.

Kern and Hainmueller are cautious about drawing any generalizations from their findings, and it remains an open question whether in different political circumstances foreign media do contribute to the erosion of authoritarian regimes, as most literature – even without hard evidence – suggests. When assessing the potential of foreign media to influence public opinion in countries under authoritarian rule, we have to be mindful that people use and perceive media messages highly selectively (Bartels 1993; Bryant and Zillmann 2002). Since individuals interpret information in the political and cultural context in which they live, we can assume that foreign media influence varies according to the situation within a country at a given point in time. In a scenario where people have good reason to believe that there exists a chance of political change, they might be more inclined to pick up cues that encourage doubts about the legitimacy and viability of the regime. Thus, the existence of visible opposition groups might provide reassurance that resistance would not be a solitary act of heroism.[5] Further, since media messages are decoded and interpreted in the social context of interpersonal relationships, the willingness to adopt a more critical stance towards the regime also depends on the opinions held by close family members and friends. If, on the other hand, the regime appears stable and opposition groups are either absent or weak, then most people will prefer to make peace with the present situation and try to improve their individual situation within the parameters of the existing regime. In this scenario, people will therefore filter out any information that challenges their desire to lead a normal life. This was the situation when the surveys used by Kern and Hainmueller were conducted in late 1988/early 1989. Even though this was less than a year before the fall of the Berlin Wall, political observers and scholars of East German communism alike believed that the system was stable and would remain so for years to come. As a result, most people in the GDR preferred to use West German media to withdraw into their private lives rather than to pick up information that would challenge the status quo.

Collapse and new beginning: the drama of regime change

During the demise of the authoritarian regime – whether this is in the form of a dramatic collapse of state institutions or takes place more gradually as a result of negotiations between the government and reformers – the media begin to take on a more proactive role. It is often individual media outlets that take the lead and start exposing the mismanagement, corruption and oppressive nature of the regime. Mainstream media that used to be loyal to the government are likely to be more cautious and will remain in the wings until there is enough evidence to assume that the regime has little chance of survival. At this point there is a growing fear among the elites that they might end up on the losing side of the battle. As the cracks in the regime widen, the number of defections among the elites increase, and the media follow this tune.

During the collapse of the old regime the potential of media technologies to expand conflicts and to accelerate developments that are under way becomes an important factor that can have a significant impact on the course of events. During this period of transition the media become a key cause of the so-called 'demonstration effects'. As discussed in Chapter 3, the term was introduced by Huntington (1991) to capture the dynamics of cross-border communication during mass protests against authoritarian regimes (see also Voltmer and Rawnsley 2009).

Whitehead (2002: 36–64) suggests that the compressed interval between the disintegration of the authoritarian regime and the emergence of a new order – be it a democratic alternative or a reincarnation of authoritarian rule – can best be understood as analogous to a theatrical performance where different actors enter the public stage to act out the archetypical roles of king's murderer, betrayal, heroic victory or tragic defeat. The 'drama of democratic transitions' (ibid.: 36) holds all the ingredients of high news values – confrontation, emotion, visuality – and is therefore extensively covered by international media. Further, mass protests and violent clashes between demonstrators and armed forces chime with one of the key frames used by Western media to interpret the political world: people's power against corrupt politicians. Thus, the extensive coverage of popular uprisings against dictatorships also carries a very domestic message for audiences in democratic countries, as these events and how they are portrayed perpetuate the democratic myth and reinforce the belief of living in the 'free world'.

The worldwide coverage of political protests and upheavals, made possible by new communication technologies, immediately increases the significance of these events once they have caught the attention of the international media. As the protest movement gains momentum, less involved citizens might be encouraged to join in the assumption that the global media attention serves as a protective shield that prevents political leaders from resorting to violence, thereby decreasing the potential costs of the public expressions of anti-government views. In addition, large-scale televised protests usually bring in the political leaders of other countries, who publicly support the objectives of the protesters while increasing their diplomatic pressure on the regime to respond to the demands for democratic reforms.

The transitions from communist rule in Eastern Europe in 1989 are a powerful example of the mutual reinforcement of protest, international media attention, an expansion of the protests and final collapse of the old regime. For example, when the first demonstrations started in the East German city of Leipzig in early September only about 1,000 people dared to take part and the gatherings were quickly dissolved by the security forces. Even though the GDR government tried to suppress any news about these events, amateur images made it to West German television channels which then broadcast them back into the GDR. This set in motion a domino effect that quickly went out of the control of the already fragile state institutions. For once, knowing what was going on elsewhere in the country, different opposition groups increased their efforts to coordinate activities in different cities. Then, as people felt encouraged by Western media coverage, more were able to overcome the fear that the government would call out the tanks and bring the protest movement to a violent end. This culminated in an overwhelming mass demonstration in Berlin on 4 November, when about one million people gathered in the centre of East Berlin to chant the slogan 'We are the people'. By this time, the old regime was living on borrowed time and five days later the wall came down (Lohmann 1994).

It seems that the media were even instrumental in delivering the final blow to the wall. At a press conference on 9 November 1989, the seemingly hesitant spokesman of the central committee of the East German Communist Party, Günther Schabowski, announced in rather ambiguous wording the ruling party's plan to relax travel regulations.[6] Trying to make sense of this event, the 8 o'clock evening news on West German television came up with its own interpretation by proclaiming: 'GDR opens the border.' It was arguably this headline in the evening news that made East Germans leave their homes to cross the border, most of them for the first time in their lives. Border controls at the check points were simply overwhelmed by the masses of people who shoved westwards and they soon gave up trying to hold back the tide. No doubt, the wall would have fallen sooner rather than later in any case. But the sensational media headline, which might even have been a misinterpretation of what had been said by the spokesman, accelerated the course of events and left the Communist leadership without any chance of maintaining at least some control over the timing and direction of the dramatic changes in their country.

Another 20 years on, the use of new communication technologies, especially the internet and mobile phones, has complemented traditional strategies of influencing international news during anti-regime protests. For example, in the 2009 protests in Iran against what was believed to be fraudulent election results, mobile phones were used for the first time to coordinate actions across different groups and localities. Moreover, thousands of photos taken with cell phones provided the international news media with a continuous supply of images of events and places that otherwise would have been out of reach for regular reporters. However, the Iranian example also has another story to tell: it shows that international media attention does not always serve as the protective shield from state violence that the protesters (and many observers) hope for. If the preconditions for successful anti-regime protests are missing and if the regime is still able to grant rewards that make it more worthwhile for potentially dissident elites to remain loyal rather than join the opposition, street protests and global media pressure are unlikely to change the existing power structure. Once the protests have been stamped out, media attention will quickly withdraw from the scene, leaving the opposition to their own devices and often in a worse situation than before. Little is known of the protesters who have been arrested in the aftermath of recent protests, for example in Burma or Iran, or who have been terrorized in other ways after the streets have been cleared. Media attention is short-lived and volatile. Political leaders who are determined to cling to power know this and have learned to adapt to it. However, with the rise of the internet, patience might no longer be a guarantee for remaining in power. The open and unlimited capacity of the internet allows anybody who seeks it to find visual and written material that can be potentially dangerous for authoritarian regimes. Unlike traditional mass media, the internet does not have gatekeepers who secure information in inaccessible archives. For activists and international NGOs, the internet has therefore become an unprecedented resource for compiling and disseminating information without having to depend on the willingness of journalists to become involved.

Consolidation after regime change: a rocky journey with uncertain outcomes

As the 'third wave' slows down – and in some cases even takes a reverse direction (Diamond 1996) – democratization research turns its attention to the problems of consolidation. No longer does the main interest lie in the conditions under which authoritarian regimes collapse, but in those under which new democracies survive.

Consolidation is a complex process by which the newly established rules and institutions become routinized and accepted as the best way of governing the country (Diamond 1997). However, this complexity renders it difficult to define when consolidation starts and when it can be regarded as being completed, and indeed what it involves. Over the past two decades or so, consolidation literature has suggested an ever longer list of factors to indicate successful consolidation. Criteria stretch from simple indicators, such as the first alternation of power in peaceful and fair elections, to complex factors encompassing all areas of social and political life, which even established democracies would find difficult to live up to. However, like democracy itself (see Chapter 2), it is impossible to come up with a standardized definition of consolidation that fits all. Consolidation can take on different forms as it follows context-specific, sometimes unusual routes depending on the circumstances in which it takes place and how the new regime is interpreted by those who are involved in the transition. Institutions that might work perfectly well in one context can be detrimental in others. For example, proportional representation can broaden inclusion of divergent groups and interests, but it is also known to lead to fragmentation and instability in contexts where there are no effective mechanisms for reconciling group differences. Likewise, public service broadcasting can be a stronghold of high-quality information, but in other cases is little more than a disguise for government propaganda (for a detailed discussion of the attempt to establish public service broadcasting in Eastern Europe, see the 'Focus' section in Chapter 6).

While checklists of indicators of consolidation are of disputable value, it is useful to conceptualize consolidation as a process that involves two distinct, but interdependent, dimensions: institutional transformation and cultural change. Early democratization research has primarily focused on institutional design and market reform in the belief that making the right institutional choices would generate sufficiently strong constraints for political actors to behave like good democrats, thereby paving the way for stable and sustainable democracy (see, for example, Elster et al. 1998; Lijphart and Waisman 1996). However, as 'third wave' democracies struggle to survive, the gap between formal institutions and their cultural underpinnings is becoming a major concern. Political leaders frequently use democratic procedures to pursue undemocratic goals, and in many new democracies participation in elections is alarmingly low, while civil society remains still underdeveloped.

The following sections will discuss whether, and if so, in what way, the media matter for the consolidation of democratic institutions and the emergence of a political culture that is supportive of the stability and viability of the new political order. From a normative point of view, one would expect the media to contribute to more transparent and responsive institutions and to a better-informed and more engaged citizenry. But some observers assert a rather negative influence of the media on the stabilization of democracy. For example, Bennett (1998) maintains that the media may have been instrumental in bringing down the former authoritarian regime, but that they are a somewhat obstructive force when it comes to consolidating the new order.

Institutional consolidation

One of the main concerns about the media's role in the consolidation process is the vulnerability of immature institutions to the pervasiveness of the media in modern politics. It is often forgotten that political institutions in Europe grew their roots before the advent of the information society. Today, political decision-making takes place under the constant scrutiny of the media. In an information environment with an abundance of channels, 24-hour news, wikileaks and social network sites, there is hardly any place to hide. This unprecedented expansion of the public arena has pushed open the doors of the notorious smoke-filled backrooms, where political deals were forged away from public scrutiny. But this new openness can be a mixed blessing too, especially when it is used as a political weapon in the power struggle between competing camps. With a myriad of media hunting for breaking news, anybody who wants to circulate damaging material about a political opponent will easily find an outlet that is eager to publish 'exclusive' information. And opinions or rumours expressed in an obscure blog can quickly spread into mainstream media and dominate public opinion.

One consequence of the unpredictability of the modern media environment is that the actors operating within the newly created institutions spend more time and resources on developing effective media strategies than on establishing sound procedures to deliver the outputs and policies they are expected to produce. Those institutions that are directly dependent on public opinion are especially prone to building their structures and processes around the need to control the media agenda – directly elected presidents more than indirectly elected ones, governments more than courts, political parties more than interest groups, etc. The need for effective news management often perpetuates old practices of censorship and interference into editorial autonomy, but this is blended with an adoption of modern strategies of professional public relations and 'spin', which in turn make it difficult for the media to develop into effective democratic institutions.

Students of political communication have observed similar trends in the advanced democracies of the West. Mazzoleni and Schulz (1999) argue that modern politics has moved from 'mediated politics', where the media act as the prime transmitters of political messages, to the 'mediatization of politics', indicating a situation where political actors and institutions have aligned themselves to the operational logic of the media (see also Brants and Voltmer 2011). Blumler and Kavanagh (1999) add historical depth to this argument by identifying three 'ages' of political communication. The first 'age', starting with the two decades following the end of the Second World War when politicians had easy access to the media, came to an end with the advent of television and the need for political actors to engage in professional PR. The third, and present, age is characterized by media abundance and an acceleration of the news cycle. More importantly, journalism has adopted a more adversarial, suspicious, even hostile stance towards political office-holders. As Blumler and Kavanagh describe the situation: 'To politicians, the third-age media system must loom like a hydra-headed beast' (1999: 215). With the media moving into the centre of the political process, Meyer (2002) warns of a 'colonization' of politics by the media. This is not to say that the media are taking over, but that politics is more and more organized around the imperatives of winning the media battle.

New democracies are directly leapfrogging into the 'third age' of political communication. When autocratic rule comes to an end, freezing the relationship between political power and the media into one of master and servant, both counterparts find themselves – often rather unprepared – in a highly complex situation where policy uncertainty and limited capabilities to deliver have to be negotiated with heightened popular expectations. However, while old democracies enter this stage from a position of institutional stability, institution-building in new democracies takes place in response to, even in anticipation of, the constraints of modern media democracy. For political actors the diffuse and often hostile media environment further adds to the high level of uncertainty they have to cope with while navigating through the transition process. Surely, new democracies differ in the degree to which they adopt media-centred politics, as do established democracies. And without an independent and watchful press, it would be impossible to build accountable and responsive institutions of governance. However, if – as in many new democracies – institutions are weak, democratic norms and rules are not firmly established and public opinion is divided over the future of the country, then the mediatization of politics can be a severe impediment to the long-term consolidation of sound political processes. Indeed, some of the flaws that afflict the consolidation of many new democracies are closely related to the pervasiveness of the media in modern politics. This is not to say that the media are the cause of these problems. Rather, the dynamics of a media-saturated environment often interact with the weaknesses of a newly established democratic system in such a way that these features are further exacerbated.

In what follows, the implications of consolidating democratic institutions in a media-saturated environment will be illustrated with regard to three areas of transitional politics: the emergence of so-called delegative democracy; the establishment of political parties; and mechanisms of securing government accountability.

Delegative democracy and populism

The rise of 'delegative democracy' in a significant number of today's emerging democracies is an example of the interaction between mediatized politics and aggravated institutional consolidation. The term 'delegative democracy' was introduced by O'Donnell (1994) to describe a 'new species' of democracy that differs in important ways from representative democracy. Delegative democracy flourishes in countries with presidential systems of government. It is based on the premise that 'whoever wins election to the presidency is thereby entitled to govern as he or she sees fit' (O'Donnell 1994: 59). Most new democracies in Latin America can be categorized into the delegative type, but it has also become the dominant political form in the successor states of the Soviet Union, most notably Russia (Kubicek 1994). In delegative democracies, presidents present themselves as standing above the divisions of party politics, emphasized by their claim to embody the nation as a whole rather than particular interests or groups. In delegative democracies presidential rule is employed in a way that weakens democratic institutions, most notably parliament and the judiciary, resulting in an inefficient system of horizontal checks and balances that would keep expansive presidential power under control. Presidents frequently rule by decree to avoid the complexities and unpredictable outcomes of negotiations. Instead of relying on party organizations for winning elections, presidential candidates seek to establish direct links with the people, which, once in office, they continuously try to mobilize as a resource of power. However, the repudiation of party politics and organized articulation of group interests means that civil society remains embryonic. Instead, mass mobilization is geared towards the leader, organized as a public demonstration of unity rather than an expression of different interests or demands.

It is these populist tendencies that create a symbiotic relationship between delegative democracy and the media. One could even argue that delegative democracy would never develop without the oxygen of a media-rich environment that provides the arena for the relationship between charismatic leaders and their followers to be enacted as a public spectacle. As Waisbord (1995: 216) argues in view of Latin American countries, the fusion of personalism and a highly commercialized television industry has brought about a 'new brand of caudillos', who build their power on a successful adaptation of media logic as a political strategy. Populist leaders tick all the boxes of a good news story. Their charismatic personality and oratory power, often combined with the skilful creation of pseudo-events, is particularly irresistible for television journalists in search of dramatization and attractive visuals. What is more, the appeal to 'the man on the street' and use of anti-elite rhetoric that characterizes the communication strategy of populist leaders chime with modern-day journalism, which has become more populist and anti-establishment (Mazzoleni 2003). For example, Putin's campaign against the oligarchs has been supported by the wider public and established his image as a strong leader who is not afraid of taking on corrupt elites. Only a few voices were heard raising concerns about the procedural appropriateness of the trials and convictions that he endorsed. In Latin America meanwhile, populist appeals to the masses and attractive images have paved the way for outsiders like Alberto Fujimori in Peru or Evo Morales in Bolivia, first on to the television screen and then into political office (Boas 2005; Waisbord 2003). President Hugo Chávez of Venezuela has successfully used the media to expand his powers. In a perfectly orchestrated campaign in 2009, he secured a referendum that abolished the limitation of holding presidential office to two terms. Adopting a stance that is very typical of populist leaders, he is now turning against the very force that helped him to maintain his popularity as he increasingly streamlines the media along the official government line.

However, some scholars have rightly argued that populism – and populist media for that matter (see Brants 1998) – can play an important role in modern democracy. Abts and Rummens (2007) point at two distinct and potentially conflicting strands of democracy: the liberal element that includes rights and procedures, on the one hand, and participation that entails popular involvement, on the other. By acting 'against the alienating effects of the dry pragmatism of representative democracy' (Abts and Rummens 2007: 406), populism has the potential to mobilize groups of people who would otherwise stay away from politics. This tension between institutionalization and popular mobilization is particularly palpable in new democracies. After the excitement triggered by the breakdown of the old regime, in which widespread popular mobilization played a decisive role, the subsequent normality of politics with its horse-trading, petty power struggles and frequent policy failures must appear like an anticlimax.

And indeed, for many citizens the transition process is accompanied by extreme emotional swings between high-flying optimism and empowerment at some times, and disillusionment and alienation at others. In these turbulent times, populist leaders can provide orientation and prevent a widening rift between the new political system and the population. One outstanding example of the benevolent force of a populist leader is in South Africa. Nelson Mandela's charismatic personality, responsiveness to the emotions of the masses alongside moral integrity, helped the country to overcome a troubled past. More importantly, unlike many populist leaders and delegative presidents in other emerging democracies, Mandela used his power and charisma to promote, rather than undermine, democratic principles. It is safe to say that without Mandela's vision of a 'rainbow nation', South Africa's transition would have been more violent and probably less successful than it turned out to be.

Hence, the relationship between populism, delegative democracy and the media is ambiguous. Whether it is beneficial or detrimental to the consolidation of an emerging democracy rests on a precarious balance between the risk of democratic institutions being destroyed by the authoritarian ambitions of political leaders and the citizens' need for orientation and personalized identification.

Political parties without constituencies

The development of political parties is another case that illustrates the interdependence between institution-building and the media in new democracies. Unlike political parties that emerged from societal cleavages and dominated Western (in particular West European) democratic politics for more than a century (Lipset and Rokkan 1967), most parties in new democracies have not been able to establish durable links with substantial parts of the electorate, resulting in often dramatic shifts in electoral fortunes between successive elections. Because of the lack of sustained mass support, these emerging parties do not usually have a broad membership that would provide a pool of grass-root activists to anchor the party and its causes to the ground. Instead, emerging parties are mostly organized around a small group of elites, located at the centres of power in the capital and out of touch with their electorate. Often, these parties are relatively inactive outside election time, but are able to mobilize forces to run election campaigns that will secure them access to the resources of state institutions (Morlino 2009b). There are only a few exceptions to this general pattern, and most of them are former ruling parties of the old regime that managed to hold on to power after the transition – examples include the transformed KMT in Taiwan or ex-communist parties in Eastern Europe that relaunched themselves under new names, for example, the Hungarian Socialist Party MSZP.

The success of nascent parties that emerged after regime change is highly dependent on the media, especially television. Some of them would not even exist without the media. Lacking other viable channels of communication, like grass-root campaigners or alliances with civil society groups, the media are often virtually the only route available to political parties to mobilize electoral support. Learning how to play the media game is therefore a question of survival. With regard to the situation in Russia, Oates (2006: 152) asserts the emergence of 'media-driven parties . . . that have no real roots in the electorate, no tangible ideology beyond serving the needs of their political masters and, most ominously, no accountability to the public'. Oates's description points at the potential risks of a close interdependence between emerging institutions and the media. While the mass media and modern communication technologies help political parties to establish themselves in the post-authoritarian party system, they also prevent them from developing more sustainable structures. Having learned how to employ effective news management, parties in new democracies often do not even try to build an effective organizational structure beyond a campaign machine, which is itself usually elite-dominated and does not allow for significant member participation. Reliance on the media requires media-based parties to tailor their messages to the demands of the news media. As a consequence, parties avoid ideological agendas and complex policy issues and focus instead on symbolic politics and telegenic personalities. This strategy might help to push a party into the public spotlight and mobilize emotional popular response, but it is less conducive to establishing durable ties with electoral constituencies. Another setback of a high degree of media dependency involves the high costs of modern media campaigns, which are a hotbed for corruption and reinforce a party's entrenchment with business interests. As a result, emerging political parties often find themselves in a vicious circle of eroding public trust and the need for even more expensive media strategies.

Even though the described relationship between the institutionalization of political parties and the media can be observed in many 'third wave' democracies, there are of course large variations depending on a variety of factors. Where the media are economically weak and thus dependent on political sponsors for their economic survival, most notably in most African countries, the degree of mediatization is usually relatively low. Nevertheless, it is possible to conclude that mediatization of politics is a global trend and brings about particular institutional patterns that affect the viability of new democracies. The growing dependency of political parties on the media fosters the centralization of the party organization with a power centre around the top leader and a small operational elite, thereby preventing the nurturing of grass-root participation and the development of coherent ideologies and policy profiles.

Accountability and good governance

How successful are the media in new democracies at holding governments to account? As outlined in Chapter 3, liberal democratic theory regards the press as a major part in a system of checks and balances designed to curb the power of any single political authority. An independent press that is able to uncover inefficiencies, malpractice and the unlawful behaviour of government officials is believed to ensure the transparency of political processes of decision-making and to enforce the accountability of the elected government. In most new democracies pockets of authoritarianism inherited from the predecessor regime survive for quite a long time. An effective watchdog press can help to overcome these authoritarian practices. Another widespread problem that afflicts many new democracies is corruption. The causes are often rooted in the nepotistic structures set up by the old regime to secure acquiescence. But the transition process itself can also become the source of corruption, especially during the period immediately following regime change when a legal vacuum and regulatory uncertainty provide fertile ground for murky activities and unrestrained enrichment. Without a watchdog press that digs into these activities and brings them to the attention of a wider public, it would be difficult to protect the young democracy from those who are determined to exploit the system and its weaknesses to their own advantage. At the same time, there are also concerns that an excessively aggressive media might destabilize fragile institutions by creating a climate of suspicion and hostility that makes it difficult for the newly elected government to live up to sometimes exaggerated expectations.

Existing research provides some empirical evidence – from both large-scale analyses and individual case studies – concerning the power, but also the limitations, of watchdog journalism and its role in promoting transparency and accountability. Brunetti and Weder (2003) use econometric methodology to estimate the connection between press freedom and corruption across 125 countries. The results confirm a significant relationship between press freedom and corruption, indicating that a more independent press leads to a decrease in a country's level of corruption. This relationship remains robust even when other factors, such as professionalism of the bureaucracy, rule of law and social-economic inequality – all of which are assumed to restrict the spread of corruption – are held constant. It is interesting to note that the strength of the relationship between press freedom and corruption drops when countries with advanced economies are excluded from the calculations. One can only speculate why an independent press in developing countries is less effective in keeping corruption at bay than in developed societies. One possible explanation is that the indicators used to measure press freedom are only an imperfect proxy for the existence of a watchdog press. While investigative reporting is virtually impossible in the absence of press freedom, independence alone is no guarantee that the media actually use their freedom to uncover malpractice of political officials. The idea of an adversarial press is very much embedded in Western notions of journalism, while journalists in the developing world often regard serving their communities as their primary obligation. Further, the political institutions in developing countries might be less responsive to public allegations of corruption. Especially in 'delegative democracies' that dominate many new democracies in the developing world, presidents use their power to control whether, and if so with what consequences, allegations of malpractice and corruption are further pursued by other institutions of checks and balances, such as parliaments and an independent judiciary. Thus, although Brunetti and Weder's study (2003) provides strong evidence that an independent press is a significant factor in fighting corruption, it also suggests that a vigilant press is less likely to increase accountability in countries where public scrutiny is most needed.

Norris's (2004) study, covering 151 countries and employing similar data collections (Freedom House, UNESCO, WTO and others), comes to very similar results. Norris takes a broader approach than Brunetti and Weder by also examining good governance and development as outcomes of press freedom. These concepts include a wide range of indicators, such as political stability, rule of law, corruption, government efficiency and various human development indicators. However, Norris emphasizes that press freedom in itself is not sufficient to bring about a higher degree of accountability. Rather, an independent press has to be accessible to large parts of the population in order to unleash the desired effects. Norris's findings corroborate this hypothesis. It is only the interaction between press freedom and large audiences that enhances good governance, for the reason that media disclosures need the resonance of public opinion to gather enough pressure on powerholders to initiate change.

While global comparisons like the two studies discussed above provide reliable evidence of the general picture, we can only speculate what the underlying processes are that translate independent and critical media reporting into transparent and accountable practices of governance. Moreover, the causal direction of the relationship – i.e., the question of what influences what – remains unclear. This becomes particularly evident when considering the correlation between press freedom and the rule of law. The assumption that guides Norris's study is that a vigilant press forces political and corporate officials to stick to the rules and refrain from self-enrichment and favouritism. However, rule of law is also an essential precondition for the operations of an independent press. It provides the protected space within which journalists can investigate hidden events without risking their livelihood, their health or even their life. A reverse direction of causality can even be at work with regard to corruption, especially when corruption is systemic and also incorporates the media. In these cases the media become entrenched in an interdependent system of rent-seeking, which prevents them from digging into precisely the practices from which they themselves benefit.[7]

When assessing the role of the media in building accountable governance, it is important to keep in mind that their impact on the consolidation of democratic institutions and routines is part of a wider web of accountability mechanisms. Within these mechanisms, the media play an important role as initiators and catalysts of political change, but without further mechanisms in place their investigative efforts are unlikely to have much, if any, effect. In fact, many lives of journalists have been lost in vain because their search for the truth was met by an irresponsive and inefficient institutional environment.

To understand the media's role in the fight against corruption, it is useful to distinguish between two dimensions of accountability: a vertical and a horizontal one (O'Donnell 2003; see also Schedler et al. 1999). The vertical dimension of accountability denotes citizens' influence on government decisions. The most important mechanism of vertical accountability is the election process. But since elections do not take place very often, the continuous scrutiny of an independent press and a vigilant civil society are of crucial importance to prevent elected officials from misusing their power and from becoming detached from the needs and demands of citizens. In contrast, horizontal accountability encapsulates the system of checks and balances between state institutions. Effective horizontal controls are designed in such a way that each of these institutions restricts the power of the others in the system, especially the executive. Horizontal accountability is effective when different state agencies are able and willing to take action against other state agencies if they are involved in malpractice or violate existing laws and regulations. As O'Donnell (2003) observes, the means of horizontal accountability are weak and inefficient in most of the newly democratized countries of the 'third wave', a condition that leaves them vulnerable to continuous misuse of power and even relapse into authoritarianism.

Various instances of watchdog journalism from different emerging democracies illustrate the conditions under which disclosures of the media are likely to result in real consequences, or fail to do so in spite of considerable efforts of the media involved to push the case into the public limelight.

The fall of President Joseph Estrada of the Philippines in 2001 is an example of successful vertical mobilization against a corrupt office-holder. Ever since the fall of Ferdinand Marcos in 1986, the democratically elected governments of the Philippines have remained deeply involved in a widespread web of corruption that even includes institutions like the Supreme Court. The Philippine Center for Investigative Journalism (PCIJ: http://pcij.org), which was founded in 1989 by Filipino journalists to strengthen democratic institutions by promoting investigative reporting, became one of the most articulate and effective watchdog groups in the country. The PCIJ played a decisive role in bringing down Estrada, a former movie actor, who used the short time of his office to amass incredible wealth through numerous illegal activities, tax evasion and embezzlement of public funds. The media campaign against Estrada gained momentum when the Catholic Church picked up on the issue. Estrada's extravagant lifestyle and the open display of his various mistresses deeply violated the religious values of the church which framed the issue as a moral problem, thereby triggering a moral outcry that mobilized hundreds of thousands of people to demonstrate. Another important ally in this campaign was the business community, which turned against Estrada; it had lost confidence in his leadership abilities (Coronel 2010). Not surprisingly, Congress was reluctant to pursue an impeachment trial initiated by the opposition. However, the strong coalition of different civil society groups alongside well-researched media exposures helped to overcome a notoriously weak horizontal system of accountability.

Latin America is another region plagued by corruption and low levels of government accountability. In his study on watchdog journalism in four South American countries, Waisbord (2000b) maintains that the rise of watchdog journalism is one of the major achievements brought about by the democratic transitions across the continent over past decades. However, in spite of all the journalistic efforts for more government accountability, Waisbord observes that little progress has been made in eradicating corruption in Argentina, stopping drug-trafficking in Colombia, curbing the power of the secret service in Peru, or fighting inefficiency and corruption in Brazil's police forces (ibid.: 214). One of the reasons for the limited ability of the media to fulfil their watchdog role is the insufficient legal protection of journalists who work in Latin American countries. As a consequence, violence against journalists poses a severe threat to investigative activities (see Committee to Protect Journalists: http://cpj.org). With the exception of the ousting of President Collor de Mello in 1992, the first democratically elected president of Brazil after the end of military dictatorship, the public revelation of, in some cases, massive corruption charges did not harm those in power and did not even prevent them from being re-elected. The case of Carlos Menem, who held the presidency in Argentina for two terms, illustrates that without effective mechanisms of horizontal accountability media watchdogs are bound to be toothless. Corruption in Argentina took on mafia-like structures, permeating throughout all parts of society and infiltrating all institutions, from government agencies to the army, from the courts to the police. Soon after Menem was elected in 1989, the press started investigations into corruption and corporate bribery in which the Menem government and his extensive family were allegedly involved. Subsequent disclosures involved drug money-laundering, weapons-smuggling and the selling of rotten milk to social programmes run by the Ministry of Health and Social Action, which happened to be headed by one of Menem's close aides (Waisbord 2000b: 33–9). Even though Menem had to leave the country temporarily to evade prosecution, he managed to fence off all allegations against him. Waisbord puts the failure to hold Menem accountable down to the vulnerability of the Supreme Court to political manipulation. 'Congressional stonewalling' was another factor that prevented any further investigations. In the end, not one of the some 70 officials who were accused of corruption and drug money-laundering was convicted (ibid.: 212, 223).

Besides obstacles and weaknesses in the mechanisms of both vertical and horizontal accountability, limitations of watchdog journalism can also be put down to the way in which the media are selecting and presenting information. Most of the media's investigations focus on high-ranking individuals and their wrongdoings. If, in addition, events feature all the ingredients of a celebrity scandal, like the Estrada case, media across all genres will try to get the most out of the story and keep it in the headlines as long as possible. However, the media are much less effective when it comes to systemic problems. Once the 'king' has been brought down, the media are usually satisfied with their victory and quickly turn their attention to other topics. Yet more often than not, the underlying structures that caused the scandal in the first place still continue to exist – until the next scandal. The media's short attention span and their inability to follow an issue over longer periods of time – with the exception of a few high-quality, well-funded outlets – clearly limits their role as agents of accountability. Without new events, an issue will quickly disappear from the media agenda. For investigative journalism to be effective, it is therefore of crucial importance that the media form alliances with external actors, either civil society groups or relevant elites, to make sure that the issue remains alive until institutional agencies, like parliaments or courts, decide to include it in their agenda.

Even though it is impossible to generalize from a few case studies, the examples given corroborate the findings from global comparative studies discussed above, suggesting that the effectiveness of investigative journalism is limited in developing countries with weak democratic institutions. Evidently, in countries where corruption and official malpractice have grown roots across state institutions and the corporate sector, the exposure of single cases has little effect on the existing power structure. Long-term commitment of journalists and their media organizations to invest resources in investigative journalism are necessary to gradually challenge illegal practices and unjust procedures. It sounds like another example of the proverbial Matthew syndrome, according to which whoever has will be given more, that the media are most effective in holding political power to account where institutions are functioning reasonably well. Here media scandals function like a 'burglar alarm' that alerts citizens when things are going wrong inside their government (Zaller 2003). The problem in many new democracies is that even if the alarm goes off, the police do not show up and the neighbours turn a deaf ear.

Political culture

Institutional consolidation is only one half of the journey. The other part takes place in the hearts and minds of the citizens. Only when these two elements – political institutions and political culture – are combined is the ground laid for an enduring democracy. Without an attentive and active citizenry, accountable government is unlikely to be achieved and democracy would remain shallow.

The argument of a two-tier process of consolidation draws on Almond and Verba's (1963) concept of 'civic culture', which assumes that institutions and culture are closely interlinked. The authors maintain that the institutional set-up is not sufficient to understand why some democracies flourish and others don't. Equally important are the political orientations of individual citizens and the degree to which these orientations are congruent with the values and institutions of the democratic system. Elements of a democratic political culture include cognitive mobilization, indicated by interest in public affairs and political knowledge, the willingness to participate in political life, the sense of civic competence and the belief that citizens can have an impact on the course of politics, and finally support of democracy both as it actually exists and as a general ideal. To put it differently, if citizens are ignorant about political issues, do not make an effort to have their voices heard, despise their representatives and do not believe in democratic values, then the viability of that democracy might be seriously at risk – even if the institutions are perfectly designed.

Almond and Verba developed the concept of political culture in the 1960s with an interest in understanding the chances of democracy taking root in 'second wave' democracies that emerged after the Second World War. Not surprisingly, political culture research has seen a new renaissance over the past decade or so in response to the recent wave of democratization and the apparent problems of their consolidation (Diamond 1993; Plasser and Pribersky 1996; Reisinger 1995). Almond and Verba assumed the main problem of stable democracy to be immature and undemocratic orientations of citizens that make it difficult for institutions to function in the intended way. Results from survey research seem to confirm this concern. In many emerging democracies, democratic orientations and democratic citizenship are still fragile, turnout in elections is in decline and only a few citizens are engaged in voluntary organizations (Gunther et al. 2007). Arguably, this does not come as a surprise, given the experiences of ordinary people in transitional societies. After the excitement and drama of regime change, the hopes and expectations of citizens are running high. Even in the best possible scenario of fast political renewal and economic growth, it is inevitable that early euphoria will give way to disillusionment. Yet many new democracies do not experience a best possible scenario. Instead, for many citizens the new reality comes with economic hardship, uncertainty about the future and a rising level of violence in society. Endless political struggles, incompetent and corrupt political leaders and broken promises nurture disillusionment. As a consequence, many citizens prefer to leave politics alone and to withdraw into their private lives.

But there are also contrary trends. In fact, the reality of 'third wave' democracies seems to differ from previous waves in that there is more widespread citizen activism. More often than not, it is the citizens who push for further democratization, whereas the existing institutions prove to be incapable of transparent and efficient performance. African countries are an example of this kind of 'reversed' incongruence between citizens' democratic attitudes and insufficient institutional performance (see Bratton et al. 2005). Another example is Russia where, over the last decade or so, the political process has taken on increasingly authoritarian features. Yet after long years of acquiescence, protests erupted after the legislative election in December 2011, which was widely perceived as flawed in favour of the ruling party. Even though Putin's dominance could not be challenged so far, the demands for more democracy articulated by the new protest movement are unlikely to go away. Similar examples of citizens taking the lead to demand full democratization of their country can be observed elsewhere around the world.

Media and democratic orientations

So far, little is known about the role of the media in the development of political culture in new democracies. Are the media responsible for low levels of public trust and engagement? Or do the media, on the contrary, contribute to the democratic socialization of the new citizens by expanding their political knowledge and understanding and encouraging them to take on a more participatory role?

These questions are not confined to new democracies. With cynicism and disengagement on the rise in established democracies as well (Pharr and Putnam 2000), political communication scholars have embarked on finding out whether, and if so to what extent, the media feed the increasingly negative attitudes towards politics among citizens in advanced democracies. It is argued that the way in which the media portray politics – the general anti-political bias and the suspicion towards political officials displayed by journalists – breeds mistrust among citizens (Capella and Jamieson 1997; Patterson 1993). However, other authors have presented strong empirical evidence for a more beneficial role of the media, in particular with regard to the cognitive mobilization of citizens (Newton 1999). In fact, never before have mass publics in Western societies been as knowledgeable and interested in politics as they are today, which can, at least to some extent, be attributed to the easy availability of political information through the mass media. A survey-based analysis by Norris (2000), which comprises a large range of established European and non-European democracies, supports this trend. She assumes a 'virtuous circle' at work, arguing that exposure to the news media contributes to knowledge and encourages civic engagement, which in turn stimulates the appetite for more information.

This seems to be good news for democracy. But can these findings be generalized to new democracies? How do citizens in transitional societies respond to a media environment that is noisy, aggressive and commercialized? Are they more vulnerable than their fellow citizens in established democracies to the cacophony of voices, negative news and scandals? Schmitt-Beck and Voltmer (2007) use survey data from six 'third wave' democracies which include a set of variables to measure the respondents' exposure to political news alongside detailed measures of democratic orientations, including political interest, political knowledge, participation (measured as involvement in various campaign-related activities), evaluation of political parties, satisfaction with the performance of democracy in one's own country and general support of democracy as a preferable form of governance.[8]

The findings of Schmitt-Beck and Voltmer's study show that the media do have an effect over and above other important factors that are known from the literature to influence political orientations – in particular, age, education, gender, ideological predispositions and socio-economic position. About one quarter of the variance on political orientations can be – directly or indirectly – attributed to exposure to the news media. Very much in line with Newton's (1999) mobilization theory, media influence turns out to be largely beneficial. Citizens in new democracies might be disaffected and disengaged, but there are no indications for a media-induced malaise. On the contrary, empirical evidence suggests that the media positively facilitate democratic citizenship. However, the degree to which the media contribute to this positive result differs across media types. Not surprisingly, information-rich media have the strongest effect, with print media being more effective than television. The difference between the printed press and television also limits the overall positive picture of the media's role in transitional politics. For the media that have the most positive effect are also those that reach only a minority of citizens.

Newton's study also emphasizes that media effects vary according to different types of civic orientations. They are clearly most powerful with regard to the cognitive mobilization of citizens; that is, exposure to the news media increases political knowledge and stimulates interest in politics. To a lesser degree, the media also promote active participation. But the media have only a weak effect, or none at all, on support for democracy. Hence, it can be concluded that the main contribution of the media to democratic politics is their ability to mobilize citizens and to enhance their cognitive competences. They are less effective in changing individuals' evaluations of politics and their general values. These are formed in more complex cognitive and socially mediated processes.

Finally, the relationship between the media and democratic citizenship is moderated by the specific political situation. The findings suggest that citizens in the youngest democracies of the sample – Bulgaria and Hungary – are most affected by media influences. The strength of media effects declines the more time has elapsed since the transition. This pattern can be explained by the increased need for orientation in times of crisis or dramatic change which makes people more open to new information, whereas in stable and secure situations people avoid the costs of intensive information-seeking and rely instead on their existing knowledge and acquired heuristics.

This observation is confirmed by Loveless's (2008) study of Central and Eastern European countries in the late 1990s. Comparing countries where democratization has made good progress with those that have suffered from various setbacks, Loveless finds that in more unstable contexts people deliberately seek out information through the media. Moreover, in less consolidated democracies the media also have a stronger effect on how citizens think about politics. Mattes and Bratton (2007) confirm this general pattern of media exposure and media effects for transitional democracies in Africa. Based on Afrobarometers conducted in 12 African countries, they find that the media enhance people's understanding of the principles and rules of democracy and that this relationship is strongest in times of rapid social change. However, this generally positive news comes with a grain of salt. Nisbet's (2008) study of public opinion and the media in Mali shows that the ability to benefit from the information provided by the media differs across socio-economic strata of the population. The use of media helps especially those with higher education and urban residency to increase their political knowledge and to enhance their willingness to participate in politics. Together with other factors, such as uneven modernization and ethnic divisions, this widening 'political communication gap' further exacerbates social and economic inequality, especially in developing societies, leaving the disadvantaged even further behind. Economic inequality has far-reaching implications for political equality. If the poor and less educated are not so capable of participating in democratic politics, their concerns are less likely to be picked up by political decision-makers, who will instead spend overproportional shares of the available resources to satisfy the needs of more privileged segments of the population who are more effective in making their voice heard.

Overall, these studies suggest a positive effect of the media on the emergence of democratic citizenship and a political culture that is conducive for the consolidation of the new democratic order. Even though the gains people derive from exposure to the media is differentiated along lines of socio-economic and cultural inequalities, the media do not seem to have a detrimental effect on citizens' willingness to get engaged in politics and their support of democratic principles. Dependency on the media is particularly high during regime change and in the early stages of consolidation when alternative sources of information and opinion leadership, such as political parties, religious leaders or public authorities, are as confused and disoriented as everybody else and often disappear from the public arena altogether. Surely, the media are not much better in telling people what sense to make of the situation. But actively seeking out information contributes to strengthening people's sense of control in a situation of instability, thereby enhancing efficacy and the confidence in their own ability to cope with the ambiguities and risks of the transition. Positive media influences on citizens' attitudes towards politics might come as a surprise given the widespread concern about the low quality of journalism in many new democracies and an often shrill and aggressive tone of reporting. So far, we know very little about how individuals in post-authoritarian countries experience the new adversarial style of the media. As Schmitt-Beck and Voltmer (2007: 124) point out: 'It can well be that after decades of autocratic rule, where the media's role was confined to serving as a mouthpiece of the ruling elite, citizens welcome unfavourable news and critical accounts of politicians as an indicator of the working of democracy rather than a flaw of the new order.'

Having explored the role of the media as a democratizing force during different phases of the transition process running through liberalization, regime change and consolidation, it could be demonstrated that the media impact processes of political and social change in different ways. Before regime change, there is usually very little room for journalistic agency, as the media are playing primarily an instrumental role either to stabilize the authoritarian regime or as an organizing tool in the hands of opposition groups. This changes when the autocratic regime is about to collapse and regime change is possible. During this period the media take on a more active role by accelerating and broadening the conflict between pro-democracy forces and the old powers. With the rise of new communication technologies, transborder broadcasting, mobile phones and social media have changed the strategies of oppositional forces who have become ever more sophisticated in using these technologies to their advantage. Finally, it is disputed whether the media help to consolidate the institutional and cultural foundations of new democracies. Leapfrogging into a media-saturated environment, institution-building seems to be seriously impaired by the imperatives of mediatization. At the same time, empirical evidence suggests that the media play a positive role in strengthening citizenship in new democracies.

5

Emerging Media Systems and the Legacies of the Past

Having established in the previous two chapters how the media impact on the process of democratization, this chapter shifts the perspective from an investigation of the media as an agent of change to an analysis of the factors that affect the transformation of the media in the course of the democratization process. In reality, of course, the relationship between the media and their political, economic and social environment is a reciprocal one: the media can promote, sometimes obstruct, democratization, but are also shaped by the dynamics of the transition process and the attitudes and constraints of the political elites who are in charge of reforming the media.

For many students of transitional democracies, but also democracy activists, journalists and citizens, the outcome of the transformation of the media in 'third wave' democracies has often been rather disappointing. Even though the constitutional guarantee of the basic principles of press freedom and freedom of expression are uncontested, the rules that regulate external influences on the media and the rights and responsibilities of journalists continue to be disputed between policymakers, the media and wider parts of the society. Judged against the normative standards of democratic media, the transformation of the media often appears to have got stuck in an early stage of transition.

What could be the reasons for the delayed and, in many cases, highly conflictual transformation of the media? There are a multitude of factors that help explain the problems and difficulties involved in democratizing the media, one of which is the interpretative nature of values and norms. As has been shown in Chapter 2, the meaning of media freedom and the related norms of independence and diversity are ambiguous, and many of the conflicts surrounding the transformation of the media in post-authoritarian democracies can be attributed to the epistemic complexities of regime change.

Another factor concerns the legacies of the past. As policymakers and journalists embark on the task of rebuilding the media, they carry with them – often unwittingly – the attitudes and patterns of behaviour that are inherited from the preceding authoritarian regime. There is an element of 'old habits die hard', which would imply that 'normalization' is a matter of time and it is simply a question of waiting for all old elites to be replaced by democratic leaders. Surprisingly enough, though, attempts to restrain the independence of the media and to muzzle open debate are not confined to politicians who have been part of the old power structure and who might be suspected of being caught in an authoritarian mindset. Once in a power, former opposition activists are equally unwilling to ease control over the media. Undoubtedly, personal ambitions for power, money and fame can override the beliefs of even the firmest democrats. Yet the currents of the past run deeper than that. They are inscribed in the mechanisms of institutions and social relationships that are beyond the choices of individuals.

Hence, in order to understand the politics and economics of post-authoritarian media, we have to look at the role they have played in the preceding regime. This chapter sets out to explore the historical trajectories of media transformation in new democracies. It argues that authoritarian regimes differ in significant ways that affect both the process and the outcome of the transition process. The chapter distinguishes four specific pathways of democratic transition and their consequences for the transformation of the media and their relationship with political power.

Pathways of democratization

The notion of path dependency suggests that the characteristics of the old regime still shape the way in which the new institutions are designed and how they operate, often in very subtle ways (Greener 2005; Hollifield and Jillson 2000). This is not to propose a deterministic relationship between the old and the new regime. What the notion of path dependency implies, though, is that particular historical legacies tend to generate specific problems that need to be addressed after the demise of the old regime. Furthermore, cultural orientations and institutional structures inherited from the past often constrain the options of policymakers who are involved in reforming the media of their country, thus making some outcomes more likely than others.

Milton (2000) argues that the democratization of existing institutions that have their roots in the old regime, like the news media, is more difficult and usually yields more fuzzy results than the creation of entirely new institutions, such as the electoral system or the central bank. Milton maintains that it is almost impossible to eliminate the 'institutional traces' (ibid.: 23) inherited from the past when transforming institutions that have already served the old regime. These 'institutional traces' are not only imprinted in the procedures and rules according to which institutions run and interact with their environment; they also shape the expectations and behaviour of both their own members and of extra-institutional stakeholders. A further obstacle to the transformation of the media is – ironically – the transition itself. During the period of transition – i.e., the interregnum period between the collapse of the old regime and the creation of the new polity – all available energies are concentrated on the enormous task of designing the new institutions of government, while the existing ones and those that are regarded less vital for the survival of the new system receive just enough attention, if any, for them to adjust somehow to the new circumstances. Quite understandably, negotiating the new constitution and the rules of the foundation election preoccupies both domestic and international transitional policymakers. However, postponing the transformation of existing institutions, like the media, can have negative implications for the quality of the emerging democracy in the long run. Once patterns of behaviour have become routinized and are perceived as the 'normal' way of doing things, it can be extremely difficult to rectify them. As a consequence, media 'reform . . . is less likely than the persistence of dependence' (Milton 2000: 8).

The argument that transformed institutions bear the 'traces' of their pre-democratic existence is based on a view that regards new democracies as the product of a complex juxtaposition of the old and the new, a compromise between an ideal vision and what is possible, a conjuncture of the trajectories of the past and the decisions of post-authoritarian actors who are in charge of shaping the democratic future of their country. Even though we are used to thinking of transition as the end of the old regime and the beginning of a new order, there remains a significant degree of continuity between the two worlds. Sparks's (2008) critique of transitology draws precisely on the assumption of a revolution, a fundamental break between old and new that seems to underlie the assumptions and theorizing of much of the existing democratization research. Drawing on the experience of three post-communist cases (Poland, Russia and China), Sparks argues instead that a theory of elite continuity is much better able to explain the emerging patterns of media and politics in new democracies. Continuity can be observed not only in the power structures inscribed in the existing institutions, but also in the personnel in positions of power, thus perpetuating the logic of the old regime.

Rather than just putting this continuity down to a failure of comprehensive transition, it is important to recognize that continuity is a necessity for keeping the business of politics – and indeed society as a whole – running. Old elites possess invaluable know-how which is needed to run the country, even if this knowledge has been acquired under non-democratic circumstances. In fact, countries where post-authoritarian actors go for a radical break with the past often run into severe difficulties. For example, the decision of the American occupying power to dismantle Iraq's police and army left a power vacuum that enabled non-democratic forces to (re-)establish their spheres of influence. Yet elite continuity comes with a price. Not only does it bear the risk of clandestine obstruction by the unconverted; it can also undermine the legitimacy of the emerging democracy. Seeing the old faces in top positions again inevitably violates feelings of justice in the population, especially those who suffered under the old regime. For them, the new order might look like nothing more than 'old wine in old bottles'.

If the transformation of the media differs significantly depending on the distinct features of the old regime and the role they played in its power structure, then we need a more differentiated understanding of variations across non-democratic systems. Siebert et al.'s *Four Theories of the Press* (1956) has been the main point of reference in comparative communication studies since the book was published more than half a century ago. Siebert and his co-authors set out to provide a global framework to categorize the relationship between media and politics by distinguishing between four ideal-typical models: authoritarian, libertarian, social responsibility and Soviet communist – that is, two democratic and two non-democratic ones. These four types are arrived at by identifying the specific normative assumptions that provide the 'philosophical and political rationales or theories' (ibid.: 2) for the role of the media in a given society. With regard to the non-democratic models, Siebert et al. maintain that the authoritarian model is the oldest 'philosophy' of the press originating in the late Renaissance in Europe. In the context of the absolute monarchies of this period, the role of the press was seen as serving state power and ensuring social stability and public order. In Soviet communist theory that emerged at the beginning of the twentieth century, the media were expected to take on a more proactive, even revolutionary role, by mobilizing and educating the masses and propagating social change.

Even though *Four Theories* has been acknowledged as making a major contribution towards understanding variations between media systems, the book has also been widely criticized, mainly because of its exclusive focus on normative ideas and a lack of empirical grounding (for an overview, see Nerone 2004). Other authors have suggested additional models that recognize current developments in world politics – for example, a developmental and democratic-participant model (McQuail 1994: 121–33) or a social-democratic model (Picard 1985). However, most of these amendments are confined to capturing variations within the media systems of advanced democracies – with the exception of the development model, which cuts across democratic and non-democratic contexts.

Hallin and Mancini's study, *Comparing Media Systems* (2004), stands in the intellectual tradition of *Four Theories* (in fact, the book begins by quoting its famous predecessor), but it extends the conceptual framework by employing a multidimensional approach that takes the political, economical, social and journalistic elements of media systems into account. Like Siebert et al., the authors operate on the assumption that media systems reflect and are shaped by the political system in which they operate, but also affect the way in which politics works. They suggest three models of media and politics – polarized pluralist, democratic corporatist and liberal – to classify variations of media–politics relations in Western democracies. Hallin and Mancini's book has hugely revitalized both theoretical and empirical scholarship on the origins and forms of media system structures across different political contexts. However, since the study is confined to democratic systems of advanced Western societies, it provides even fewer insights into how media and politics interact in non-democratic contexts than does Siebert et al.'s *Four Theories*.[1]

The ongoing debate on the classification of media systems in comparative perspective can be further informed by political science transition research, which has contributed various typologies to categorize authoritarian regimes. For example, Linz and Stepan (1996: 55–66) propose four types – authoritarianism, totalitarianism, post-totalitarianism and sultanism – each characterized by various degrees of autonomy of non-state institutions and agents, such as civil society, rule of law, bureaucracy and the market, from the central power of government. They argue that areas that had only low degrees of independence require more radical reforms during the democratization process than those which had some discretionary power in organizing their own affairs. The dimension of autonomy in relation to an authoritarian state is particularly important for understanding the legacy of structural and behavioural patterns that media organizations carry with them into the new democratic era.

Brooker's typology of non-democratic regimes (2009) takes the question of who is in control as a point of departure and distinguishes between monarchical, military and one-party rule. Today, there are hardly any monarchies left in which the royal dynasty is still truly in control of power rather than just fulfilling a merely representational role. There are several cases of monarchical rule in the Arab world (e.g., Jordan, Morocco, Saudi Arabia). But even though these regimes have been challenged in the wake of the popular uprisings in the region in the early months of 2011, almost none of the present 'third wave' democracies was preceded by a controlling monarchy.[2] Hence, there are only two broad categories of authoritarian regimes from which 'third wave' democracies over the past couple of decades have originated: military and one-party rule. Given the large variation within these regime types, especially one-party rule, it is necessary to distinguish them further according to how power is legitimized and maintained in these regimes:

- military dictatorship;
- communist one-party rule;
- one-party rule in contexts of statism;
- personalized one-party rule in contexts of weak state institutions.

Without going into a detailed analysis of current political science discussion on non-democratic regime types, these four categories are well suited to capture the distinct constellations of political, economic and social forces in which the media operated under the old regime. These constellations have generated particular patterns of interaction, mutual dependencies and expectations as to the role of journalism in society that continue to shape public communication after the demise of the old regime. Each of the four regime types has dominated a particular geopolitical region, even though there are no clear boundaries, and individual cases of each regime type can be found in any area of the world (Doorenspleet 2005). However, it is safe to say that military dictatorship has been the most frequent predecessor of 'third wave' democracies in Latin America, with numerous instances in virtually all other parts of the world; communist one-party rule has dominated Eastern Europe under the hegemony of the Soviet Union, while China and North Korea remain prominent examples outside this region; one-party rule operating within strong state institutions could frequently be found in Asia, especially East Asia; and personalized one-party rule in conjunction with weak state institutions has been, and to some extent still is, the prevailing political regime type in sub-Saharan Africa.

However, caution is needed when referring to the previous regime as an explanation for the failure or success of democratizing the media after regime change. History can cast long shadows, and legacies that reach much further back than the authoritarian regime which immediately preceded the current democracy might also influence and shape the interpretations and preferences of a society today. In fact, in some of the countries that are classified as 'third wave' democracies the authoritarian regime lasted only a few years, interrupting an otherwise long tradition of democratic governance. For example, Chile experienced relatively free elections and progressive politics before Pinochet came into power after a *coup d'état* in 1973; and Czechoslovakia went through a 20-year period of democratic rule before it was occupied by Nazi Germany at the outbreak of the Second World War, followed by the communist takeover in 1948. However, for most countries of the 'third wave', democratic governance is a journey into unknown territory and history provides little direct bearing either for citizens or for policymakers as to how to put the ideal into practice.

Authoritarian regime types and media transformation

How then can the role of the media be described in each of the four authoritarian regime types? Surely, they all used the media as propaganda tools and imposed censorship and controls on what could be reported and what not. But the degree and nature of the media's entrenchment in the regime differed considerably.

Military dictatorship

Military rule has left a traumatic legacy in Latin America, but generals have also been in charge of government and ruled their countries with an iron fist in Spain, Portugal and Greece at the southern fringes of Europe and many other parts of the world, most notably South and Southeast Asia and Africa. Government under the military, or a military leader, is usually characterized by massive human rights violations, such as imprisonment without fair trial, torture and even murder of those – and sometimes their families too – who oppose the regime. In Argentina, Brazil and Chile, tens of thousands of people 'disappeared' during the rule of the generals, among them countless journalists who were brave enough to break the silence imposed on public speech. Military coups to replace a civilian government are frequently legitimized by the necessity to protect the national interest that is allegedly under threat, for example, by an incapable government, the breakdown of public order, the imminent outbreak of civil war in a situation of hostile divisions between antagonistic groups, or external enemies. However, one of the strongest arguments employed by military leaders, especially in Latin America, to justify their rule was to establish a bulwark against a purportedly looming communist takeover. Beyond these justifications of protecting the national interest against internal or external enemies, military dictatorships lack any elaborate ideological narratives to win the hearts and minds of their populations. They simply rely on a general sentiment against 'chaos' and, most importantly, on the display of physical force.

The absence of an ideology has important implications for the role of the media in military regimes. Apart for using them for occasional nationalist appeals or anti-communist propaganda, the media rarely play a central role in the power structure of military regimes. The main purpose of censorship is to suppress oppositional views from being expressed in public. The ultimate objective is quiescence and depoliticization of the population, rather than mobilization. In this respect, politics–media relationships in military regimes correspond largely with the normative assumptions of Siebert et al.'s (1956) authoritarian model.

However, some military dictatorships tolerated a limited degree of pluralism, allowing certain groups or parties to continue their activities on condition that they did not fundamentally question the legitimacy of the regime (Linz 1975). For individual media outlets and journalists, it was therefore possible to operate without excessive state interference, provided they stayed away from sensitive issues and open criticism of the existing power structure. In Latin America, the best way for the media to avoid the risk of being in the (literal) 'firing line' of military powerholders was to confine their activities to the provision of entertainment, thereby further fostering the withdrawal of citizens from public life. In fact, the dominance of entertainment programmes in Latin American television was – and still is – unsurpassed. Hollywood soap operas were imported in large quantities, providing the cultural underpinnings of the dubious political alliance between the US and military regimes in their Latin American 'backyard' (Skidmore 2001).

In line with their anti-communist ideology, Latin American military regimes protected and supported a free market economy in their countries, which also included the media industry. Apart from government-owned organs, most media were privately owned. In some instances, the media industry even started to flourish during the military years thanks to active state investment in modern communications infrastructure. TV Globo's global success story started under the military regime in Brazil. During the years under the generals, the network served as a central pillar of the regime and in return enjoyed protection from foreign competition, thus allowing the corporation to establish itself as a dominant player in the region (Amaral 2002). Likewise, the Pinochet government initiated the modernization of the media industry in Chile as part of a policy scheme to boost the national economy (Fuenzalida 2002; Tironi and Sunkel 2000).

The consequences of the economic and political constellation under military rule are still visible in Latin American countries today. Media policy under the old regime has created strong media conglomerates, some of which have successfully positioned themselves on the global market. However, the high degree of commercialization diminishes the potential for broadcasting organizations to play an active role in the democratization process of their countries. Television programming remains dominated by cheap entertainment, while political information leads a rather marginal existence. Further, political elites and media owners continue to nurture their intimate relationship to mutual advantage, thus obstructing the ability of the media to take on a more independent and critical role vis-à-vis political power.

Communist one-party rule

In many respects, communist one-party rule is exactly the opposite of military regimes. One crucial feature of communist rule is the central role of an elaborate ideology to legitimize the regime and the penetration of the state into virtually all parts of society, even the private lives of citizens. The power, and to some extent the appeal, of communist ideology derives from its utopian promise according to which people will eventually be freed from the yoke of capitalist exploitation and enjoy an equal share in the economic wealth. It was this belief and hope that mobilized the masses under communist rule, at least in earlier stages, and even gained supporters outside the countries where it was implemented. The ruling party presented itself as the spearhead of the historical development towards communism and embarked on a comprehensive and relentless programme of (re-)

educating the masses. The goal was to create the 'new socialist personality' who sees the meaning of life primarily in the well-being of the collective rather than in individual self-realization (Inkeles 1951). In this indoctrination programme, the media played a pivotal role. They were not just mouthpieces of the ruling class, but vital propaganda tools to disseminate the socialist ideology and to shape people's thinking and even their feelings.

Another key part of communist regimes was the radical reorganization of the economy. Private property was abolished, agriculture collectivized and the means of production nationalized. As a consequence, there existed no privately owned media. All outlets, whether newspapers or broadcasting stations, were owned either by the party or by allied organizations, like the official trade unions, youth groups or other organizations of mass mobilization. Even though the ideological mission of the media left little, if any, room for deviant views, the media were also beneficiaries of this system. As long as they did not overstep the accepted boundaries, they were released from the risks of market competition and the pressure to respond to volatile audience tastes. Journalists could also see themselves as part of a utopian project of historical dimensions, and many accepted their role as educators and mobilizers of the masses with great enthusiasm (Aumente et al. 1999).

The more it became evident that communist rule did not fulfil its promise of equality and abundance, the less it was possible to mobilize support through ideology and the more the system had to resort to persecution and terror. Millions of lives were destroyed over the decades of communist rule in Eastern Europe and beyond, one of the most gruesome examples being Cambodia under the rule of the Khmer Rouge. However, it has to be emphasized that the grip of the regime on its population and the media varied across countries and in response to key events. For example, after the death of Stalin in 1953 the regime distanced itself from the excessive use of terror, even though the scope for openness and public debate remained extremely restricted. In Hungary, the suppressed revolt in 1956 led to a new balance between society and the political regime that brought some leeway for the media in covering political matters. Meanwhile, the situation in the GDR, Romania and Bulgaria remained tight until the very end of the regimes in 1989 (Paletz et al. 1995).

The transformation of post-communist media had to cope with immense economic problems. Many media organizations did not survive the shock-therapy of privatization and the pressures of market competition. Few of those that made it succeeded in playing a significant role in national media markets, while, because of language barriers, access to global markets remains limited. Meanwhile, a sense of mission still shapes the self-perception of many journalists in post-communist countries, which is reflected in a style of news reporting that values opinion and commentary over factuality and 'hard' news.

One-party rule in contexts of statism

Authoritarian one-party rule as a vehicle of rapid economic modernization was a typical regime type in East Asia, most notably the so-called tiger states of South Korea, Taiwan, Thailand and Singapore. Often referred to as developmental dictatorships, these countries were characterized by a highly centralized state, frequently and for sustained periods of time with military figures occupying key positions in the power structure of the political system. Further, a well-organized and efficient state bureaucracy provided a powerful resource for the state to take on a leading role in implementing a rigorous policy of modernization and economic growth (Cotton 1997). Even though the official rhetoric proclaimed free market principles, the economy was actually extensively controlled and directed by the state, which intervened directly into market structures, prices and production policies.

The media were part of this ambitious development project. They were used to propagate the government's development policies and as an industry were part of the government's modernization project. Deliberately created oligopolies protected the media from any threatening competitors, while investment in media technology and infrastructure created an ideal environment for the industry to consolidate and expand. Official censorship was concentrated on ensuring that the media followed the official line, but there was some degree of autonomy in non-political areas. In contrast to most other authoritarian regimes, East Asian dictatorships chose not rely solely on brute suppression of public expressions of deviant ideas, but implemented a subtle and highly effective system of 'sticks and carrots' that combined coercion with a broad range of benefits. Media companies enjoyed extensive tax privileges and exclusive advertising allocation. In South Korea, these favours were even extended to individual journalists who, as a reward for conformity and cooperation, could expect extra cash flows, gifts and even lucrative posts in government and the state bureaucracy (Park et al. 2000). Over time, this system created a close-knit network of patron–client relationships between state and media that guaranteed compliance and loyalty and made direct censorship almost superfluous (Lee 2000).

Political change did not occur with a 'big bang', but came gradually and did not create dramatic disruption. In fact, a high degree of continuity is a striking feature of this transitional pathway. As Grugel (2002: 222) notes with reference to Taiwan, '[i]t is hard . . . to identify much that has changed within the state'. However, in both South Korea and Taiwan the alternation of power in recent elections has marked these countries' successful consolidation of democratic mechanisms. New parties and candidates from outside the established elite circles have successfully challenged the hegemony of the old centres of power. In spite of these achievements, most observers agree that oppositional forces and civil society remain markedly weak in these new democracies. Meanwhile, the media have entered the post-authoritarian environment in a state of economic strength. At the same time, the inherited oligopolistic structures continue to pose a severe obstacle to pluralism in the new 'marketplace of ideas', as new entrants are markedly disadvantaged and have little chances of survival in a market that is dominated by big players who can rely on sustained state support. Even though basic liberties, including freedom of the press, are now guaranteed, the realm of what is tolerated in the public debate remains fenced. The state keeps firm control over the media , while substantial parts of the industry, most notably national television and high-circulation newspapers, are still owned by the state.

One-party rule in contexts of weak state institutions

One-party rule also dominated the developing countries in sub-Saharan Africa. Unlike the state parties in East Asia, though, African one-party dictatorships were utterly inefficient in initiating development and delivering goods to their societies. On the contrary, personalized rule in the hands of 'Big Men', who monopolized the resources of the state to their own advantage, are one of the reasons for stagnation and mass poverty that seems to be the trademark of the continent. One-party rule has been frequently justified as a means of ensuring national unity after the end of colonial rule and as a barrier to ethnic divisions. While in many countries statehood and nation-building are indeed unresolved issues and the cause of brutal civil wars, the dominant parties of the authoritarian era have done little to unite the diverse populations of their countries. Instead, central power has been used by particular ethnic groups to exclude other groups from access to vital resources.

One of the enduring legacies of the past in Africa's new democracies is neo-patrimonial leadership in which political power is maintained through personal patronage and networks of kinship rather than through the employment of formal rules and institutional power structures (Bratton and van de Walle 1994). Since neo-patrimonial leadership ignores clear distinctions between the personal and the private, it has led to widespread corruption and the emergence of what Grugel (2002: 177) calls 'predatory states'.

As in most authoritarian regimes, both broadcasting and newspapers were directly controlled by, and economically dependent on, the state. However, it is fair to say that the media have played a fairly minor role in the power structure of authoritarian regimes in sub-Saharan Africa, for the simple reason that they never actually reached significant numbers of the population. Deep rural–urban divides have led to sharp inequalities in the distribution and consumption of media products, leaving large parts of the poor population excluded from the national public sphere.

The speed with which democracy has swept across the continent is only surpassed by the East European experience (Bratton 2009). The downward spiral of economic stagnation and poverty was an important factor that ignited a growing popular quest for democracy during the 1990s. Protest against economic hardship frequently turned into pro-democracy movements that attributed the miserable conditions in which the majority of the population was living to the corruption of the political elites (Bratton 2009). However, the emerging democracies in sub-Saharan Africa continue to struggle with the baggage of problems inherited from the past. Even though political systems have opened up to multi-party competition, the old ruling parties have been able to keep a firm hold on the state. Hegemonic power structures are underpinned by national media that are still dependent on state subsidies and struggle to develop their own independent voice. As a consequence, only few elections have resulted in an alternation of power. But while the political elites' support for democracy often appears to be rather lukewarm, change is on its way: civil society organizations are mushrooming alongside a new breed of private media, both committed to holding power officials to account (Hyden et al. 2003).

In conclusion, analysing processes of democratization through the lens of the past helps us to understand that history is always one of the many architects of the political institutions and political cultures of the present. The past provides meaning to what is happening now either as a point of reference for continuity or for a radical break: 'never again!' In any case, the institutional and cultural traces of the previous regime continue to live on in the way in which the role of the media is perceived in the new political order. The path dependency of political change precludes a simple import of the institutions and norms from Western models. Rather, the emerging forms and practices have to be judged in their own right and transformed from within the framework of their particular trajectory.

Part III

Transforming the Media

The chapters of the third part of this book explore four key arenas of media transformation – political, economic, social and professional – and the factors that promote or inhibit the development of an independent and pluralist press. Drawing on Hallin and Mancini's (2004) comparative framework of media systems, the analysis conceptualizes the media as multidimensional systems that maintain relationships with virtually all processes and institutions of the society in which they operate. Hallin and Mancini distinguish between four 'dimensions' that constitute modern media systems. First, the media are closely interrelated with the *state* and the institutions of power, causing a highly ambivalent relationship that oscillates between dependency and antagonism. At the same time, the media are – with few exceptions – profit-seeking enterprises that are competing in rapidly expanding information and entertainment *markets*. Furthermore, the concept of *parallelism* denotes the various ties and allegiances the media form with particular interests in society, be they ideological, religious, class-based or ethnic. Finally, the fourth dimension of journalistic *professionalism* describes the media's own norms and rules that constitute a distinct professional identity and serve as standards for the quality of journalistic production.

What makes the transformation of the media so challenging is that each of these dimensions – political, economic, socio-cultural and professional – is governed by different principles and objectives. As a consequence, media organizations incorporate a variety of often contradictory norms, operational modes and regulatory policies that exist in parallel and are sometimes almost impossible to reconcile – a task that is rarely achieved even in established democracies, which do not have to struggle with the legacies of an authoritarian past and the turmoil associated with transition. The four dimensions of media systems identified by Hallin and Mancini constitute distinct, but interconnected, arenas of transformation that often include different participants each pursuing their particular preferences and objectives. Because of the interdependence of the arenas of media transformation and the diversity of stakeholders involved in the process (ranging from politicians of different camps, to owners and advertisers, to international donors and NGOs, to audiences and organized groups, and to journalists) policy inconsistencies and unintended side-effects of policy decisions are unavoidable. For example, commercialization of the media can be an effective measure to ensure greater independence from the state, but may also undermine the quality of information provided by the media. Similarly, strong ties with social, cultural and political interests (parallelism) ensure stable audience loyalties, but might go against recognized standards of journalistic professionalism.

Numerous media assistance programmes have been set up to support policymakers in their endeavours to transform the media of their countries. There is no shortage of checklists to guide policymakers through the process (see, for example, Kalathil 2011; Kumar 2006). However, these guides, usually written from a Western perspective, often fail to capture the complex constellation of conflicting interests, historical legacies and situational constraints that are involved in media transformations. As outlined in Chapter 5, the legacies of the preceding regime together with enduring cultural patterns and the immediate turmoil of the transition itself constitute unique constellations of opportunities and constraints, making it difficult to import policy models from elsewhere. There is no one size that fits all. Solutions that work out in some contexts might be detrimental in others, and achievements in one of the four dimensions might impede the progress in others.

Together, the four chapters of Part III provide a comprehensive overview of the challenges and achievements of media transformations in new democracies. Chapter 6 starts off with the media's relationship with the state, arguably the most crucial aspect of democratizing the media. The chapter covers the main issues of media legislation, such as freedom of information, libel and broadcast regulation. Problems of a (too) strong and a (too) weak state are discussed, as are the obstacles placed by each condition on the independence and viability of the media. The 'focus' section of this chapter examines the attempt to establish public service broadcasting in

Eastern Europe. The limited success of this project illustrates the particular challenge of reconfiguring the relationship between political power and the media, but also raises questions about the exportability of complex institutions that have their roots in particular historical constellations in the West. Chapter 7 analyses the uneasy relationship between democracy and the market. Even though the commercialization of the media is widely regarded as a way to protect the media from undue state interference, the chapter also shows how market forces work as an obstacle to the media's ability to provide the information that is needed for a robust public debate. The 'issue' of political ownership highlights the often intimate relationship between political power and media ownership, especially in Russia and Latin America. Chapter 8 explores various forms of political parallelism. It is argued that partisanship can play an important role in building political communities and even in holding governments to account. But it can also work as a divisive force that inhibits cooperation and unity. The situation of post-conflict societies, which is the subject of the 'focus' section of Chapter 8, highlights the risks of 'uncivil' parallelism and raises crucial questions about the legitimacy of restrictions on public speech. Finally, Chapter 9 turns to the professional norms and values of modern journalism. Journalists in transitional democracies often find themselves torn between the professional ideals that have developed in the West and alternative models that respond to the specific demands and constraints of their own culture. The struggle experienced by journalists in transitional democracies to find a new place in the changed political environment is further complicated by a global crisis of journalism. One of the main challenges is the internet, which is increasingly replacing traditional media as a source of information and a forum for expressing opinions where citizens can debate current issues without journalistic gatekeepers, thereby eroding the economic and normative foundations of journalism as we know it. The subject of corruption in journalism, discussed in the 'focus' section that concludes this chapter, highlights the economic, social and cultural conditions that lead journalists to sell their services to interested parties. As experiences from Asian and African countries, but also Russia, show, truth-seeking and the need to survive are often difficult to reconcile.

6

Media and the State

Arguably, the key arena of democratizing the media is concerned with the reconfiguration of the relationship between the media and the state. However, the role of the state[1] – and subsequently the relationship between the state and the media – in new democracies is highly ambiguous, in some cases and at some times taking on the role of a benign force that protects rules and rights, and at other times being a malignant force that violates these very rules and destroys the human and natural resources of a country. As a consequence, the relationship between the state and the media oscillates between complicity and hostility, attraction and repulsion, collaboration and confrontation. Tainted by the legacies of the past, post-authoritarian states are marred by a history of suppression, disregard of the rule of law and a culture of 'doublespeak' that has undermined any sense of truth and honesty in public life for a long time to come. Under a dictatorship, state institutions, such as the police, army and secret services, were frequently involved in violence against citizens, while bureaucracies built networks of favouritism and privileges that excluded large numbers of citizens from a fair share of a society's wealth. Quite understandably, then, public trust in politicians and political institutions is alarmingly low in most new democracies and any attempt at strengthening the role of the state is met with great suspicion (Catterberg and Moreno 2006; Mishler and Rose 2001; Klingemann 1999).

However, it is important to keep in mind that democracy is only possible within a functioning state, and successful democratization requires effective state institutions because it is the state that, by initiating institutional and legal reforms, acts as the primary agent of change. Likewise, democratization of the media would be impossible without democratization of the state (Price et al. 2002). The dilemma of democratic transitions is that they are led by, and are dependent on, state institutions that are still infused with authoritarian structures and practices and populated by people who, to varying degrees, have been involved in the old regime. Given the ambivalent role of the state, democratization seems to be an almost impossible task, very much resembling one of the tales of Baron Münchhausen, a German nobleman of the eighteenth century, who told his amazed audience that when he fell into a swamp he managed to pull himself out by his own hair.

This chapter starts with a closer look at the post-authoritarian state and political leadership. Two main problems are identified: the weak state that lacks the capacity to introduce and enforce reforms, and a state that dominates the various non-state sectors of society to an extent that makes it impossible for civil society and the media to take on an independent role. The chapter then moves on to discuss the legislative and regulatory provisions that constitute an enabling environment for an independent media to thrive. Finally, the issue of implementing public service broadcasting in Central Eastern Europe illustrates the problems of building media institutions that are subjected to a high level of regulation and at the same time are sufficiently safeguarded against being hijacked by the government.

Between two evils: dominant state and weak state

Given the legacy of authoritarian rule, the main emphasis of democratic transitions has been on reducing the all-powerful position of the state by implementing systems of accountability to ensure that the newly elected officials, once in power, remain responsive to the needs and demands of the citizenry. This view of transitional politics corresponds with the liberal tradition in political philosophy that regards the state as the main enemy of individual freedom. However, transition scholars have become increasingly aware of the threats that arise from state incapacity (Fukuyama 2004; Grugel 2002: 68–91). Frequently, it is not so much an all-powerful state that obstructs the path towards democratic consolidation, but rather a weak and inefficient state. In many emerging democracies of the global South the state is unable to deliver even the most basic goods and services to the population. Poverty and inequality remain high in spite of the promise of newly elected democratic governments to improve the living conditions of citizens; inadequate infrastructure prevents large parts of the population from participating in and benefiting from global information flows, while crime and violence committed by gangs and militia groups pose a constant risk to the daily lives of countless citizens. In Chapter 5 different pathways to democracy were discussed, as were the ways in which they are shaped by the preceding autocratic regime. In particular, the fourth pathway of transition from one-party rule in contexts of weak state institutions constitutes a context where the transformation of the media is hampered not only by the dominance of state influence, but equally by its absence.

Paradoxically, a seemingly strong state is in fact often a weak state. Unable to enforce its own legislation across all sections of society, weak states tend to resort to disproportionate displays of force and to the suppression of public expressions of opposition in order to mask their own fragility. Post-Soviet Russia demonstrates this double-faced nature of the strong, but weak state very well. Despite both Yeltsin's and Putin's strong-man style of leadership, the Russian state is alarmingly incapable of enforcing its own rules, indicated, amongst other things, by its inability to control large-scale tax evasion, corruption and the activities of illegal militias. Many African and some Latin American states experience a similar inability to act forcefully. Undermined by civil wars, economic inequality and the threat of military coups, state institutions in these countries are characterized by limited authority that is accompanied by authoritarian practices. State debility has now become the main threat to civil liberties, including an independent press. Democratization of the state therefore involves both strengthening and curbing state power. For a functioning democracy encompasses both a strong state that is capable of implementing and enforcing legislation and the allocation of resources, and a 'self-restraining state' (Schedler et al. 1999) that is willing to devolve power and to tolerate and encourage public spaces where divergent views and dissent can be expressed.

The transformation of the media from an instrument of state power into an independent institution of public debate reflects these dilemmas of the transformation of the state in many respects. Arguably, insufficient regulatory certainty and persistent state interference in media affairs are often the result of both an unrestrained, illiberal state and a weak and incapable state. One of the immediate challenges to democratization of the media is how to create an enabling regulatory framework that ensures the media's professional and economic viability. Without effective state action and the willingness of the government in power to act in the wider public interest, the media would fall into the hands of whoever has the means to hijack them for their own interests. Experience shows that lack of regulation almost always means less independence. However, this is precisely what has happened in many new democracies. Media legislation is delayed for many years following the demise of the old regime and remains disputed between opposing political camps even after a media law has finally been passed. There can be many reasons for the absence of effective media legislation. In some cases, the passing of new media legislation is put on hold because of the inability of different parliamentary factions to reach a compromise, thus causing a regulatory vacuum that allows uncontrolled media concentration and political interference to spread. In other cases, the obstruction of media legislation can be a deliberate indirect way for the government to maintain its influence on the media by using the regulatory ambiguity to strengthen those media enterprises that report about the government in a favourable way, while punishing the critical ones.

What makes media regulation in emerging democracies so difficult is the fact that the same politicians who are in charge of securing the independence of the media are those who would lose most by doing so. Democratic politics bears new and often unpredictable risks that make politicians even more dependent on access to the media than they were during the autocratic regime when power positions were maintained by coercion and skilful intra-elite manoeuvring. In contrast, success in a democratic environment depends on the ability to negotiate across different stakeholder groups, to deliver election promises and, last but not least, to win the support of the citizens. However, public support can shift rapidly in response to unforeseen events and developments that are largely outside the control of national governments, like changing trends in the global economy or international crises. Furthermore, media exposures of corruption or the involvement of particular politicians in the crimes of the past can bring political careers to an abrupt end at any time. It therefore comes as no surprise that after an election has been won incoming governments try to take advantage of their regulatory power by manipulating media legislation in a way that allows the ruling elites to expand their control over the media. A consistent pattern in new democracies is therefore that conflicts over the control of the media, especially broadcasting, flare up every time a new government comes into power.

Is there any prospect of overcoming the vicious circle of dependency on the media and the suppression of media freedom? One possibility is political learning. Political parties that find themselves in opposition after losing power realize that the same media laws that they introduced to their own advantage now serve the interests of their opponents. Thus, as rational actors they might come to the conclusion that in the long run it does not pay to tinker with media laws. However, for most political actors the situation looks – rightly or wrongly – different. Instead, they follow the rationality of the 'prisoner's dilemma' – i.e., a situation in which it is difficult for rational, selfish agents to take a more cooperative and moderate course because they cannot be sure that the opponent, rather than sticking to the rules, will not in fact take maximum advantage of the available power resources (*Stanford Encyclopedia of Philosophy* 2007). In many new democracies multi-party competition is experienced as a jungle where everybody has to survive now and think of long-term consequences later. Both elites and voters often view politics as a zero-sum game where there are only winners who 'take all' or losers who 'lose all', but no territories of negotiation and compromise in between (Anderson et al. 2005; Kirschke 2000). In a political culture that regards the political opponent as an enemy who cannot be trusted, and that interprets a compromise as defeat rather than achievement, it is almost impossible to agree on rules that in the end would benefit both sides. As a consequence, the short-term objective of maintaining power takes priority over the long-term perspective of adapting to periodic alternations in government.

If one of the reasons for continuous interference into the media is the dependency of political actors on the media to secure electoral success, then the professionalization of government communication skills can help to break the vicious circle. Democratic political communication involves the art of persuasion, which involves providing arguments that not only convince partisan supporters, but also appeal to broader audiences and even oppositional groups (Canel and Sanders 2012). International NGOs that are engaged in media assistance programmes, like the World Bank, have recognized the fact that supporting the independence of the media must include strengthening the communication capacity of national and local governments (World Bank 2009). Equally important, though largely ignored so far, is the communication capacity of parliaments and parliamentarians for the viability of democracy. Parliaments play an important role in the democratic system of checks and balances. Especially in presidential systems – as most new democracies are – parliaments are supposed to counterbalance and curb the power of the executive. As representative bodies, parliaments are also a key institution in fostering citizens' trust in the effectiveness of democratic politics and building an informed society. The more that parliaments are able to communicate their activities and those of parliamentarians, both through traditional and new media, the more they will be able to perform these roles (Coleman, Taylor and van de Donk 1999;

see also the activities of the Commonwealth Parliamentary Association, www.cpahq.org).

Governments, parliaments and other political agencies that adopt more professional communication strategies are less likely to resort to the old games of manipulation and threat as a means of influencing the media agenda, thus broadening the space for the development of media independence. Developing communication capacity includes professional election campaigning, but also extends to 'normal politics' and the effective organization of citizen feedback and participation in the policy process (Lees-Marshment et al. 2010). Research on political communication cultures in Eastern Europe suggests that the younger generation of politicians is more inclined to adopt professional communication skills than their older colleagues who have been socialized under the old regime. As a result, their relationship with the media seems more relaxed and 'business-like', whereas the older generation tends to cling to strategies of interference and threat, resulting in the recurrent 'media wars' in the region (Pfetsch and Voltmer 2012).

State incapacity affects the independence of the media in an extreme form when the state fails to enforce the rule of law across its territory and all sectors of society. In many new democracies, especially in developing countries, the weakness of state institutions has led to large areas of 'statelessness' (Waisbord 2007) where extra-state actors – warlords, mafia-like groups, drug barons, local bosses, etc. – control the scene and dictate what can be reported and what not. It is often overlooked that these actors can pose a bigger threat to independent and investigative journalism than the state. In fact, they are probably responsible for more instances of violent attacks against journalists, and even murder, than state agencies are. As Waisbord (2007: 120) points out:

> Illegal networks profit from remaining invisible to public scrutiny. By making them visible, reporters endanger their lives . . . Thus, it comes as no surprise that a large number of journalists who are often the targets of violence are not those who uncover illegal affairs mainly or only involving government officials or corporations but, rather, illegal traders who prefer to operate below the publics' 'radar'.

Organizations like Reporters Without Borders (Reporters sans frontières: RSF) or the Committee to Protect Journalists (CPJ) confirm the dangers of state incapacity for an independent press. According to CPJ, Colombia, Mexico, the Philippines, Pakistan and Russia not only head the list of the most dangerous countries for critical journalists, they are also the countries where violent crimes against journalists largely remain unpunished because the judicial system is either unwilling or unable to put the perpetrators on trial. The consequences of this 'statelessness' is a devastating degree of self-censorship that undermines not only the media's democratic capacities, but also any form of open debate or participation by citizens in public life. One example of this development is Mexico, where the judicial system has proved to be incapable of eradicating organized crime. Large regions of the country are, in effect, under the command of drug cartels that show zero tolerance to any critical coverage. A special report commissioned by the CPJ shows that since December 2006 (when President Felipe Calderon came into power, whose call on the military to fight organized crime allegedly led to the problem spiralling out of control) more than 30 journalists and media workers have been murdered or have gone missing (Lauria and O'Connor 2010). The principle is 'plomo o plata' (lead or money), meaning 'either we pay you or we kill you' (ibid.: 1). After traditional media have been effectively muzzled, the internet becomes the last domain where issues of organized crime are exposed, though most netizens prefer to remain anonymous. In fact, bloggers have taken on the role of watchdogs who are investigating the criminal activities of the cartels. As a consequence, organized crime has now turned against bloggers. A series of gruesome murders in autumn 2011 signalled the determination of the cartels not to tolerate any unwanted publicity (Reporters Without Borders 2011). However, hardly any of the murderers have ever been prosecuted. The impunity rate for crimes against journalists in Mexico is higher than 90 per cent. It is because of the uncontrolled violence against journalists, committed mainly by non-state actors, that Freedom House has downgraded Mexico's media from 'partly free' to 'not free'. Mexico might be formally a democracy and has recently overcome its decade-long one-party rule, but the inability of the state to guarantee the safety of critical journalists remains a serious obstacle for the viability of the country's democracy.

Cornerstones of an 'enabling environment' for media independence

Power is essentially the ability to control information. As Schattschneider famously pointed out: 'The definition of the alternatives is the supreme instrument of power' (cited in Dearing and Rogers 1996: 1). Control over the flow of information not only involves the selection of topics and how they are presented and interpreted in public, it also involves determining what information is to be kept out of public reach. As research has shown, the information that is available to individuals greatly affects the outcome of their decisions. This can be the voting decisions of citizens, policy decisions of governments or even the decision whether or not to go to war. In other words, individuals and organizations would often decide in a different way if, at the time of the decision, different pieces of information had been available or different aspects of the problem had been highlighted (for an overview, see Dearing and Rogers 1996). It is for this reason that the battle over the independence of the press is, in effect, a battle over the hegemony of the definition of reality and the boundaries between what is said in public and what remains secret. As Michener (2011: 146) maintains, 'the question of secrecy versus disclosure is becoming one of the most important political issues of our time'. Thus, some of the most important pieces of media legislation are laws that affect the power balance between the state and the media and the ability of each side to determine what can and what cannot be communicated in public.

Freedom of information laws

Freedom of information laws restrict the power of the state and strengthen the side of the media in the struggle over public information. This legislation endows journalists, but also the wider public, with the right to access information held by public agencies. Access rights are essential for the media to provide meaningful information to citizens and to perform their role as watchdogs of state power. Without the ability to search proactively for information and to double-check claims, the media would be reduced to a mere platform for conveying the announcements of political actors who feed the media with their readings of current issues. Freedom of information laws are believed to serve a plethora of benefits, ranging from overcoming the authoritarian culture of secrecy in emerging democracies, to promoting transparent and effective governance, to encouraging citizens' participation. International organizations like the UN and the World Bank have therefore pushed for freedom of information laws – with considerable success. Today, about half the countries around the world have implemented freedom of information legislation, even though there is significant variation across regions. Africa is clearly lagging behind, with fewer than 10 per cent of countries having enforceable right of information laws (Darch and Underwood 2009). Surprisingly, Zimbabwe, one of the most oppressive countries on the continent, is one of the few to have a freedom of information law in place. The background of this piece of legislation illuminates how an idea that is designed to strengthen the position of the media can be manipulated actually to strengthen the position of the state. The Zimbabwean government used the freedom of information bill, which was passed in 2002, to restrict access to data that were previously available. Since the bill includes a substantial list of exemptions, it effectively allows the government to lawfully deny the disclosure of information (Michener 2011).

The Zimbabwean case, albeit an extreme one, points at the conditions under which freedom of information legislation is paid anything other than lip service. One crucial factor involves the content and wording of the bill itself. However, even though there is a range of issues that legitimately need to be excluded from the public realm, like, for example, national security issues, these exemptions have to be kept to a minimum. Even though exempting national security issues from freedom of information rights is widely accepted, the clause is frequently used to deny access to information even when the connection with national security is dubious. According to Noorlander (2011), offences against national security regulations have become the most commonly used justification for the imprisonment of journalists. In other cases, ambiguity in specifying the areas that are excluded from public access are used by state agencies to manipulate access to information. References to something as woolly as the 'national interest' are an invitation for officials in charge of keeping state records to deny requests for access. It is precisely this that might be the Achilles heel of the Nigerian freedom of information act – and many similar cases – that was passed in early 2011 after 12 years of struggle between media activists and a government determined not to give up control over its information monopoly. One of the exemptions stipulated in this bill concerns trade and financial information that would violate the privacy of individuals involved (see Obe 2007). However, in a country rife with corruption this clause might prove to be a serious barrier for the media when investigating, for example, dubious practices of business arrangements and the selection of contractors, especially in the booming oil industry.

In democracies emerging from a traumatic past of human rights violations or civil war, official records often contain highly sensitive information about the perpetrators of these crimes. These files are a potential time bomb and can be a big obstacle for negotiating access to information rights, especially when the information is a threat to groups and individuals who are still holding positions of power in the new democratic system. Indeed, 'pacted transitions' (Karl and Schmitter 1991) that are the result of negotiations between members of the old elite and reformers are often only achieved on condition of amnesty guarantees and exemptions from legal prosecution for key figures of the old regime. In young democracies that succeed military dictatorship, this 'birth flaw' is almost unavoidable because the military controls the means of physical force, which can be used as a blackmailing ploy whenever certain policies are perceived to violate the political or economic interests of the army. Latin America is an example of this dilemma, where in many countries the military secured protective guarantees as a condition of regime change, thus effectively preventing attempts to investigate the details of the torture and 'disappearance' of thousands of people that took place under their regime. For example, in Brazil the concerns of the military establishment can be regarded as one of the main reasons why President Lula was less than eager to promote an effective freedom of information law (Michener 2011). Lula introduced a freedom of information bill at the beginning of his second term, and the law finally came into effect in May 2012 under his successor, President Dilma Rousseff. Given the high level of corruption in the country and the continuing restrictions of the media (Freedom House classifies Brazil's media as 'partly free'), the bill has been hailed by human rights and watchdog groups across the country as a long-awaited tool to fight an embedded culture of secrecy that permeates through all levels of bureaucracy as well as the political class. The introduction of the freedom of information act coincides with the inauguration of a truth commission to investigate human rights abuses during the military rule of 1964–85. Even though an existing amnesty prevents any legal consequences from the findings of this commission, more than 25 years after the end of the dictatorship people in Brazil can still hope to find out what happened to those who 'disappeared' (Barbassa 2012; McLoughlin 2011).

Another important factor for the effectiveness of freedom of information legislation – and this holds for any other legislation to promote and protect the independence of the media as well – is its grass-root support. Formal regulation might create an 'enabling environment' (Krug and Price 2002), but it only comes to life through the active support of civil society and the media themselves. As Neuman and Calland (2007) put it, access to information rights is the 'co-responsibility' of a broad range of stakeholders, not just state agencies and the media. Experience has shown that in cases where pressure from international organizations or donors was the main reason for governments to implement freedom of information law, the legislation remained largely ineffective and was often systematically undermined by non-compliance of the agencies responsible for answering requests for access. The case of Bulgaria illustrates the importance of broad societal involvement for the successful implementation of freedom of information legislation. Bulgaria was one of the first countries in post-communist Eastern Europe to pass a freedom of information bill in spite of mounting corruption allegations against politicians who therefore tried everything in their power to prevent such a law. However, a forceful coalition of human rights activists and economists, together with journalists who frequently covered the issue in current affairs programmes, kept the topic on the agenda. After the bill came into effect in 2000, an explosion of requests from both private individuals and the media made sure that adequate systems were put in place to warrant effective implementation (Michener 2011).

Finally, state capacity is again a factor that determines the effectiveness of freedom of information laws and their implementation. Where no adequate information management systems are in place and bureaucracies do not have the skills of systematic record-keeping and archiving, even the best access to information law remains pointless. In addition, custodians of public records who are still caught in a mindset of secrecy are unlikely to ensure the effective enactment of the law. In fact, 'mute refusals' – i.e., unanswered requests for access – are the most common response to journalists or private individuals seeking access to public files (Neuman and Calland 2007). Gills and Hughes (2005) observe that, in the Mexican case, even though the country's access to information is the most advanced in the hemisphere, lack of resources for the newly established agencies prevents effective implementation. An even bigger obstacle is a surviving authoritarian bureaucratic culture that supports closure and secrecy rather than openness and access. A similar gap between the wording of a bill and its implementation is also evident in South Africa, whose implementation of the right of access to information into the constitution is regarded as a role model on the continent. However, as Darch and Underwood (2005) show, lack of administrative capacity and cases of deliberative non-compliance have hampered the effectiveness of the law. Even more importantly, low public demand caused by language problems and inequality has prevented the law from developing any significant impact on the transparency and accountability of governmental procedures.

Libel laws

While freedom of information legislation has the potential to strengthen the democratic role of the media, libel laws are a powerful weapon in the hands of governments used to stifle open and critical debate. Nevertheless, libel and defamation laws fulfil an important role in public communication, as they protect individuals against harm to their reputation caused by unverified accusations in the media. Libel laws force journalists to act responsibly when reporting about individuals by making sure, as far as they can, that the coverage is based on sound facts. However, libel laws are amongst the most commonly abused regulations employed to restrict critical journalism. As Noorlander (2011: 5) points out: 'It is relatively easy to bring a claim but very hard to defend one.' An important way of lessening the potentially detrimental effects of libel laws is therefore to put the burden of proving the truth of a disputed publication on the complainant rather than the journalist. Moreover, where libel laws are part of the criminal rather than the civil code of the legislation, journalists accused of libel or defamation frequently face hefty prison sentences. Undoubtedly, for most journalists this is too high a risk to take, and as a consequence many of them will prefer to stay away from critical coverage that has the potential to trigger lawsuits against them. Decriminalizing libel and defamation is therefore one of the main concerns of national and international NGOs campaigning for media freedom (see, for example, Committee to Protect Journalists, www.cpj.org).[2] However, even where libel laws are part of the civil code, excessive damage charges can be equally ruinous to life and career. Noorlander (2011: 6) lists examples of libel awards as high as $36 million claimed by a supermarket chain in Thailand, Tesco Lotus, against three journalists, or $11 million against the Russian newspaper *Kommersant* claimed by Alfa Bank.

Yet the most notorious cause of state interference into journalistic freedom comes from a very specific type of libel: seditious libel, or insult laws that criminalize criticism and negative coverage of state institutions and political leaders. As a result, instances of exposure of corruption, accusations of government inefficiency, failed policies and misadministration have been prosecuted under the remits of seditious libel laws. In contrast to libel, accusations of seditious libel or insult hold regardless of whether the claims made by the media are true or false. Hence, it is the criticism that is prosecuted, not the distribution of false information. Obviously, this is not an 'enabling environment' of media independence, but one that makes it impossible for the media to perform their role of holding officials to account. Walden (2002: 206) states that seditious libel laws 'constitute one of the most pervasive, repressive, and dangerous forms of media regulation'. Instances of gaoling journalists for critical coverage regularly trigger global protest, but they are only the tip of the iceberg. Underneath lies the expansive mountain of silence built up by fear and self-censorship.

Insult laws are still in place in most African countries. At a meeting of the World Association of Newspapers (WAN) in 2007 the delegates issued the 'Table Mountain Declaration' that condemns insult laws as a violation of press freedom and calls for African governments to abolish this libel legislation in their countries (WAN 2007). It was noted that in the first five months of 2007 insult laws had led to the imprisonment of 103 journalists in 26 African countries. When WAN met again three years later in 2010, progress had been slow. At this point Ghana was the only country that had fully scrapped insult laws; a handful of other countries had abolished at least parts of their legislation. Hence, in most African new democracies, journalists have still to fear criminal charges when they criticize government officials (WAN 2010).

Meanwhile, progress has been made in Latin America, where the honour of public officials has traditionally been protected from *desacato* (contempt or insult) by extensive libel laws. Recently, countries such as Argentina, Chile, Mexico and Uruguay have abolished their insult laws, while in Brazil media laws originating from the era of military rule are still employed to deal with complaints against the press, thus leaving the media potentially vulnerable when uncovering corruption and other misconduct of political figures (Wendell 2009).

Thailand is frequently criticized for its extensive protection of the royal family from even moderate criticism. The country's constitution describes the King as an object of 'worship' who must not be exposed to any kind of criticism; and the criminal code stipulates that '[w]hoever defames, insults or threatens the Sovereign, his Queen or her Consort, Heir-apparent . . . shall be punished with imprisonment' (Walden 2002: 223). The immunity of Thailand's monarchy against public questioning has not only resulted in the imprisonment of a large number of Thai journalists, but has also been used to gaol foreign correspondents (see Fuller 2011). It is indicative of the backsliding of Thailand's young democracy that the military is taking on an increasingly leading role in persecuting journalists and ordinary citizens for insults against the monarchy. This show of active loyalty is not without reasons, as it was the King who gave his formal approval to the 2006 military coup.

The battle over the degree to which public figures can be exposed to public scrutiny was also the cause of a bitter 'media war' between the government and the media in South Africa. Under the Mbeki presidency the media had already been accused of being excessively critical (Tomaselli and Teer-Tomaselli 2008). Mbeki's successor,

President Zuma, saw himself subjected to increased critical media coverage that scrutinized not only his private life, but also the involvement of the government in mounting corruption in connection with the allocation of lucrative state contracts. It comes as no surprise that Zuma accused the media of anti-government bias and a lack of respect for the dignity of public figures. In March 2010 the South African government issued a proposal for a protection of information bill that aims to counterbalance the liberal provisions of the existing freedom of information regulation by expanding the range of classified material that falls under broadly defined 'national interests'. If put into effect, this law would make whistle-blowing and investigative reporting falling into the category of 'national interest' issues a criminal offence with prison sentences of up to 25 years. The bill was passed amidst allegations of mounting corruption in the high echelons of the ANC, which are said to also include controversial arms deals (Nkosi 2011). In July 2012 a review of the United Nations Human Rights Commission (UNHRC) expressed unprecedented international condemnation of the bill as a threat to press freedom and civil rights in South Africa (Smith 2012).

Parallel to this highly controversial proposal, President Zuma suggested a media appeals tribunal to act as a complaints agency for those who find themselves exposed to defamatory or incorrect media coverage. Zuma claims that the existing mechanisms of press self-regulation have proved to be ineffective. Instead, the media tribunal should be answerable to parliament, and thus would no longer be an independent agency (Smith 2010). Although a president who is unable to tolerate public criticism together with an uncontested majority of the ruling ANC pose a threat to civil liberties and an independent press in South Africa, the country is lucky enough to have a vivid and vigilant civil society that is determined to defend the young democracy and its newly gained freedoms.

It is widely acknowledged among students of media law that public figures have to tolerate a higher degree of exposure to public criticism than ordinary citizens. Being elected to public office comes with the expectation of being praised for successful policies, but also of being held accountable for policy failures and breaches of ethical codes that are attached to holding political office. However, the distinction between undue offence and mudslinging, on the one hand, and legitimate investigation and control, on the other, is often a grey zone and will be judged differently at different times and in different circumstances. To understand the intensity of the conflicts between governments and the media, which are characteristic of most new democracies of the 'third wave', it is worthwhile remembering that these countries are leapfrogging within a very short period of time from the stifled culture of dictatorship and oppression into an environment of a global journalistic culture that applauds adversarialism as the key norm of independent news coverage. Yet in the established democracies of the West, the culture of tolerating, and even promoting, a critique of public authorities took a long time to develop. For example, during the first two decades of the young post-1945 German democracy, politicians enjoyed almost untouchable authority. The relationship between journalists and their political counterparts was governed by a degree of deference that would be unthinkable today, and the private lives of politicians were generally regarded as outside the reach of public interest. One can put this attitude down to the country's legacy of authoritarianism; however, similar patterns were also prevalent in Britain during the same historical period (Blumler and Kavanagh 1999). The cultural change of the 1960s then transformed popular attitudes towards authority forever – and with it journalistic professionalism – giving way to more adversarial and cynical attitudes towards politicians. Obviously, the recent transitions to democracy take place at breathtaking speed, and it takes time to develop, and adapt to, a new culture of openness. What is important in this process is that campaigns for the abolition of silencing legislation are accompanied by an open and inclusive public debate on the standards and norms a society expects in order to govern the communicative practices of both politicians and journalists. The outcome of that process might not always mirror the practices of public communication in Western democracies, which – as some observers argue – are in fact 'out of order' (Patterson 1993) and detrimental for a healthy democracy. Successful transformation of public communication would be indicated by a state of affairs in which principles of freedom are supported by elites and citizens alike. Acceptance of freedom of speech needs time to develop. At the same time, as discussed in Chapter 2, practices of press freedom have to consider the rights of both the speaker and the listener. Thus, any judgement of how far the media can go should take into account how a particular piece of news affects the audience and the communication culture of a country as a whole.

Regulating media structures

While freedom of information regulations and libel laws aim directly at media content – in either an enabling or a restricting fashion – the structural regulation of media organizations does not censor what is being published, but it can nevertheless have a significant indirect effect on content. Much more than the press, broadcasting is subjected to a high degree of regulation, which provides governments with a variety of avenues within which to interfere in the operation and even the programming and output of broadcasters. This is why it is mainly the transformation of broadcasting that causes bitter and endless 'media wars' in transitional democracies. In virtually all authoritarian regimes, broadcasting – at least the main broadcaster – has been under the direct control of the government. Transforming these state channels into independent media outlets is an enormous challenge that is hampered not only by the unwillingness of governments to withdraw from what is believed to be a vital resource of power, but also by economic and technical constraints.

There are two main reasons why broadcasting allegedly requires more and denser regulation than the press. First, the scarcity of the available airwaves makes access to this resource a crucial issue and rules are necessary for the allocation of frequencies to potential broadcasters. Licences are therefore granted for fixed periods of time and periodically renewed subject to a positive outcome of a formal review process. With the expansion of the spectrum following satellite and cable technology and the digital convergence of different media platforms, the scarcity argument has come under severe attack (McQuail and Siune 1998). Since the beginning of the technological revolution in broadcasting in the 1980s, advocates of deregulation have been campaigning for an abolition of the distinction between the printed press and broadcasting that shaped media regulation for most of the twentieth century. While regulators have maintained some degree of separation between the two sectors of the media system, broadcasting policy since the 1980s has been dominated by deregulation and commercialization. Even in countries with strong public service traditions, most notably in Western Europe, this paradigm shift in media regulation has been accompanied by a fundamental shift in the understanding of the role of broadcasting in society away from the notion of a public good to a notion of information as a commodity.

The second reason for the more extensive regulation of broadcasting is the belief that television, in particular, with its visual appeal, has an extraordinary power over public opinion. Even though empirical research does not provide unanimous evidence for this assumption (see Bryant and Zillmann 1991; Street 2011: 101–27), broadcasting is regarded as a medium that is crucial for mobilizing mass support and winning elections. Because of its mass appeal and reach, television often serves as the main national medium, a platform on which the cultural and social diversity of a country is represented, but also as a channel through which political leaders can address the nation as a whole. It is this second argument that prevents policymakers from giving up the exceptional regulatory status of broadcasting.

Public service broadcasting is widely regarded as a regulatory model that serves the objectives of national and cultural integration best. It stands for an ideal that emphasizes the general public interest rather than the interests of the government of the day or any particular group in society. However, the label 'public service broadcasting' is often not much more than a convenient smokescreen used by the government to exploit the main national broadcaster for promoting its own interests. Thus, in many new democracies the distinction between public service broadcasting, which serves general political purposes but keeps at arm's length from the government of the day, and state television, which is dependent on and serves the interest of the government, is blurred and provides the battleground for endless power struggles between the ruling elites and broadcasters. Even though in most new democracies policymakers set out to transform the state broadcaster of the authoritarian past into a broadcaster that serves the public interest, the main national channel(s) remain vulnerable to interference not only in the structure and management of the broadcaster, but also in its programming and political coverage. A brief look at the main regulatory devices demonstrates the many options governments can employ to manipulate broadcasting to their own advantage.

It starts with licensing. The allocation of licences determines who is entitled to use the available frequencies and under what conditions. Vague regulations, arbitrary procedures and a culture of secrecy provide the governing elites with plenty of opportunities to use their discretion to favour political allies, friends and family members as well as to punish opponents and keep out critical and independent voices. A report by the Open Society Justice Initiative (2008: 72) on media freedom in Latin America observes that 'capricious allocations' of licences have led to the concentration of ownership in the hands of a few powerful television companies, most of which have close ties with the political elites of the country. An example of licensing being used as a political tool is Venezuela, where, in 2007, President Chavez refused to renew the licence of the country's second largest television channel Radio Caracas Television (RCTV). The decision was obviously aimed at silencing a broadcaster who had been an outspoken supporter of the opposition. RCTV was able to continue broadcasting via cable and satellite, but was finally taken off air three years later (Forero 2010).

It is not only dissenting voices that are often systematically disadvantaged by licensing regulation and the way in which they are applied, but also minorities and non-profit organizations. This is particularly the case when the allocation of frequencies is dependent on investment requirements, which most civil society groups are unable to meet. Uruguay's licensing policy, like that of many other Latin American countries, has been characterized by political and big business favouritism. But in 2007 the country issued a progressive new law that emphasizes community media as a recognized third sector in the media industry alongside privately and state-owned media. One third of the available licences are reserved for community broadcasters, thereby providing a strong counterbalance to political and economic hegemony (Open Society Justice Initiative 2008: 72–5).

Another element of broadcast regulation that governments and other powerful state actors frequently employ to influence the editorial policy of broadcasters is the appointment of personnel. Whether it is the supervisory body that oversees the audiovisual sector and decides on the allocation of licences, or the management board of broadcasters, it is extremely difficult to insulate these bodies from political interference. Usually it is the president, the government or the responsible government department, or the parliamentary majority that appoint at least some of these broadcasting bodies either as a whole, or their chairpersons. As a result, the broadcasting supervisory bodies are often highly politicized. Governments use their capacity to appoint to place people loyal to them in key positions to ensure favourable coverage. Political interference is even exacerbated when the government has the power not only to appoint top broadcasting personnel, but also to fire the persons in charge. As a consequence, incoming governments are quick to replace figures who were appointed by the previous government with their own candidates. Under these circumstances there is hardly any incentive for broadcasting regulators or managers to adopt a more professional, independent, non-partisan approach to their role.

The third element of media regulation that determines the degree of government control over broadcast organizations is funding. There are three main sources of revenue for broadcasting: state subsidies, a licence fee and advertising, each of which constitutes particular dependencies that affect the broadcaster's performance as a democratic – and democratizing – actor. As Tracey (2002: 31) explains, there is a clear correlation between the source of funding and the content produced by a media outlet: 'Programmes funded by advertising necessarily have their character influenced in some shape or form by the demand to maximize the garnering of consumers. Programmes directly funded by the government, and with no intervening structural head shield, inevitably tend to utter the tones of their master's voice.' Evidently, state subsidies are the least desirable form of funding because it is unlikely that media that are dependent on state support are able to monitor and criticize political power effectively. In contrast, advertising revenues are regarded as a way of keeping an arm's length distance between the media and the state. However, economic interests can be as obstructive as political interests in distorting news coverage, even though their influence on media outputs is often more subtle and less easy to detect than political bias. The licence fee, which only applies to public service broadcasters, is believed to square the circle by shielding broadcasters from the perils of both political and economic influences. In reality, this is often difficult to achieve. The experience of established public service broadcasting in the West over the past two decades has shown that in an increasingly competitive media market it is impossible to insulate the broadcasters from commercialization; neither is public service broadcasting safe from government interference, in particular when the amount of the licence fee is determined by the government or the parliamentary majority. To dilute the disadvantages of both models, most public service broadcasting systems rely on a combination of advertising and licence fee income.

For policymakers in many transitional democracies, considerations about the right balance of advertising and licence fee must sound like a luxury debate. In developing countries, advertising revenues are often not a viable source of income to cover the operational costs of broadcasting. Being dependent on mass consumer markets, advertising is usually confined to the urban middle classes and hence is too small and too susceptible to the ups and downs of the economy to provide a sustainable stream of revenue. The licence fee is equally impractical because household incomes are generally too small to cope with an additional tax. Consequently, more often than not the state remains as the only, or main, possible source of funding for nationwide broadcasting. In these circumstances, the transformation of state–media relationships has to cope with two simultaneous challenges: the structures and practices of domination inherited from the authoritarian past, and the constraints arising from broadcasting's persisting economic dependency on the state.

The controversy about Hungary's new media law that was passed and amended in 2011 can serve as a vivid illustration of the whole range of regulatory issues surrounding journalistic independence and structural control. It also highlights the persisting vulnerability of public service broadcasting to state interference, which will be discussed in more detail in the 'Focus' section below.

When Victor Orban, the leader of the right-wing party Fidesz, won the parliamentary election in May 2010, he set out to create nothing less than a 'revolution'. An unprecedented two-thirds majority allowed him to embark on far-reaching policy projects, including changes to the constitution, without having to negotiate with other political parties. Key to Orban's agenda has been a major overhaul of the existing media law. The legislation came into force in January 2011 and triggered widespread protests both within Hungary and across Europe.[3] The new media law might have passed largely unnoticed outside Hungary's borders if Hungary had not been in charge of the European presidency for the first time since the country joined the European Union. Interventions by the European Commission and several European governments led to a couple of amendments of the media law, which was then passed in March 2011, that soften some of the most controversial elements. But many Hungarian government officials – and probably citizens as well – regarded these interventions by the EU as undue interference into the country's sovereignty, driven by European stereotypes of Hungary being still an immature young democracy even 20 years after the fall of communism (Marcus 2011). While the amendments satisfied the EU, others remain worried. For example, the Organization for Security and Cooperation in Europe (OSCE) maintains that the revised law still violates norms of press freedom (Nyman-Metcalf 2011). It is indicative of Orban's illiberal views that he returned to a restrictive course as soon as Hungary's EU presidency came to an end.

One of the most problematic innovations of Hungary's new media law is the establishment of a 'super-regulator', a new regulatory authority (National Media and Communication Authority, NMHH) that oversees both the printed press and broadcasting. With its far-reaching competencies, the NMHH can issue excessive fines for what is regarded as imbalanced reporting. Yet the regulator itself is anything but balanced. All its members are government appointees with a mandate of nine years – i.e., more than twice as long as a normal legislative term. Moreover, the law restricts journalistic independence by forcing them to reveal their sources if the coverage is related to something broadly defined as 'national security'. Meanwhile, the government started to scale down the number of employees at the public service broadcaster MTV by a planned target of around 3,000 staff. Even though cutting down an oversized organization might be a necessary step to make it more efficient, the cuts appear to have been used by the Orban government as an opportunity to get rid of critical and independent journalists. For example, the anchor of the radio news magazine '180 minutes', Attila Mong, was one of the first to be suspended from his post. He had held a minute of silence on his programme in December 2010 to protest against the new media law (Verseck 2011).[4] It seems that there is some truth in the stereotype and 20 years is not a long enough time in which to democratize Hungary's media; but it is enough time to dedemocratize them.

FOCUS: TRANSFORMATION OF STATE BROADCASTING TO PUBLIC SERVICE BROADCASTING IN EASTERN EUROPE

When the countries in Central Eastern Europe emerged from the collapse of state socialism, they inherited huge bureaucratic broadcasting organizations that were hopelessly overstaffed, inefficient and governed by an attitude of subservience to their political masters. One option for dealing with these 'dinosaurs' would have been to privatize them like most of the other formerly state-owned industries in the region. However, both local policymakers and international policy advisers agreed on the necessity of transforming state broadcasting into public service broadcasting for two main reasons. First, a privatized ex-state broadcaster would have created a massive monopoly that would have distorted the emerging audiovisual market right from the start, leaving little chance for newcomers to successfully compete with an established and powerful player. Second, and more importantly, it was felt that the young democracies were in need of a national broadcaster that serves the public interest by taking on a leading role in educating and informing the citizens. A similar situation existed about half a century earlier after the defeat of fascism, when the allied forces that emerged as the victors of the Second World War insisted on establishing public service broadcasting in Germany and Japan. In both countries, these public service broadcasters have developed into strong institutions providing high-quality programming. And even though it is difficult to provide hard empirical evidence, it is safe to say that NHK in Japan and ARD and ZDF in Germany have played an important role in promoting and consolidating a viable democratic culture in their respective countries.

Public service broadcasting is seen as a democratic, and democratizing, force in public life. It provides a forum for public debate by providing space to address the important issues a society is facing and by giving voice to a broad range of views and opinions. In order to act as a facilitator of public debate, public service broadcasting has to remain impartial when covering conflicting interests and positions. The forum function extends beyond providing a platform for the powerful to also include those who are normally excluded from mainstream broadcasting, like minorities, disadvantaged groups and working-class people. Through diversity and inclusiveness, public service broadcasting hopes to create a shared sense of national unity that reassures cultural identity and prevents fragmentation in a globalized world. As Richard Hoggart, a leading figure in British cultural life, puts it, public service broadcasting 'allows a nation to speak to itself' (cited in Tracey 2002: 29). Two key principles are the pillars that carry the mission of public service broadcasting: independence from any vested interests – be they political, commercial or otherwise – and adherence to the highest-quality standards that encompass all genres from drama to news to entertainment (Blumler 1992; Raboy 1998; Tracey 2002).

At least this is the ideal. In reality, many public service broadcasters have grappled to live up to these expectations. Caught between elitism and paternalism on the one hand and populism and commercialization on the other, they struggle to position themselves in an increasingly competitive market. The pervasiveness of popular culture makes it difficult for public service broadcasters to stick to their mission to provide relevant and high-quality programmes. Further, public service values are increasingly challenged by both market forces and political pressures (Blumler 1992). For example, Italy's public service broadcaster RAI is firmly in the hands of the dominant political parties, Spain's TVE is barely distinguishable from any commercial broadcaster, and even the BBC, the undisputed role model of what public service broadcasting stands for, has been accused of being too close to the centres of established power as well as giving in to demands for trivial entertainment, at least in some of its offerings. Nevertheless, the principles of independence and quality remain the yardsticks against which public service broadcasting is judged and which legitimate its privileged position in the media system of a country. A more severe threat to the institution of public service broadcasting comes from the dominance of neoliberalism and the belief that the market is a better regulator than any public body whatever the policy matter is – from healthcare to education, from public transport to public information (Couldry 2010; Hesmondhalgh 2005).

Compared to many other transitional democracies that embarked on introducing public service broadcasting, the countries in Central Eastern Europe seemed to be particularly well positioned to successfully transform state into public service broadcasting. Public service broadcasting is often perceived as a Western, specifically Western European, concept which might be difficult to export to political and cultural contexts outside the Western tradition. For East European countries, adopting public service broadcasting was one of the defining steps in their 'return to Europe' after having been cut off from their natural historical and cultural ties by the Iron Curtain. Conversely, the European Union and the Council of Europe made it a condition for the accession states in Eastern Europe to bring their media legislation into line with European standards, as outlined in the directive 'Television Without Borders', and to adopt the European model of public service broadcasting. This policy was in open contrast to American preferences for a fully commercialized broadcasting system believed to be a bulwark against undue state influence. During the 1990s when post-communist policymakers drew up their media laws, countless Western experts arrived in the capitals of Eastern Europe to advise on media policy and legislation. In addition, there was a great deal of financial aid flowing from Western governments and organizations, for example the Open Society Institute, Konrad-Adenauer Stiftung, Bertelsmann Foundations and many others, to the East to help building democratic media structures (Harcourt 2003). So, with a genuine desire to become 'European', combined with considerable external incentives and pressures, public service broadcasting in post-communist countries was bound to succeed.

However, the present state of public service broadcasting in Eastern Europe paints a different picture. From the start, media policy in Eastern Europe was highly contested and continues to be so up to now. In fact, the notorious 'media wars' that unfolded across the region were mainly concerned with the regulation of, and ultimately control over, public service broadcasting. There were two main frontlines in these wars. On the one hand, governments clashed with public service broadcasters over the degree of political influence; on the other, there were struggles between the government in power and the main opposition parties, both of which were trying to secure and expand their control over the main broadcaster. As a result, broadcasting legislation was often delayed for several years, and even after a law was finally passed it quickly became subject to further amendments.

Taking stock after almost 20 years of transformational media policy, the results presented in reports published by the Open Society Institute (2005, 2008) in conjunction with the EU Monitoring and Advocacy Program are disheartening, in some cases even devastating. After a period of progress, the 2008 Report gives testimony to a new trend of 'repoliticization' of public service media with intensified political pressure and diminishing editorial independence (Open Society Institute 2008: 20–1).

At the centre of the ongoing conflicts over public service broadcasting in the region are attempts by governments to compromise the independence of the broadcast organization by manipulating the regulatory and administrative bodies. The issue of who controls these bodies has been contested right from the start of media transformation in Eastern Europe. Hungary's notorious 'media war' was sparked immediately after the first democratic election in 1990, when the incoming national conservative government under Prime Minister Jozsef Antall fired the director generals of public radio and television and replaced them with pro-government candidates. When President Arpad Goencz refused to countersign the dismissals, the conflict developed into a constitutional crisis about the competences of different branches of government. In the end, the conflict was only solved when both directors resigned – probably not entirely voluntarily. But the issue of control remained unresolved, thus making it impossible to pass a new media law which would have clarified the relationship between the government and the public broadcaster. The law was finally passed by parliament in 1995 after the Socialist Party (MSZP) had won an absolute majority in the previous year (Hankiss 1994; Splichal 2001).

Meanwhile, in Poland President Walesa dismissed the chairman and two members of the National Broadcasting Council (KRRiT) in 1994 because the regulator had granted a commercial television licence to an applicant that did not have the approval of the president; and two years later Walesa dismissed the entire management board of the Polish public service broadcaster TVP. Similar instances occurred even after the broadcasting act had been amended to the effect that members of the Council could not be recalled during their term (Jakubowicz 2002). Since its first fully free election in 1991, Polish politics has been characterized by extreme shifts in power. Up to the election in October 2011, when the ruling coalition secured a majority for a second term, no governing party had been re-elected, and in most cases had suffered devastating losses. In response to the highly volatile political landscape, each party has been keen to secure a majority on the broadcasting supervisory body (KRRiT), if possible until after the end of the current term in power. Placing one's supporters on the KRRiT was used not only for rewarding loyalty, but also, and more importantly, for keeping control over programming and content even after an electoral defeat. The situation even deteriorated when the Law and Justice Party (PiS) under Jaroslaw Kaczynski won the general election in 2005, with his twin brother Lech Kaczynski winning the presidential election the same year. One of the first actions of the newly elected president only one week after his inauguration was to amend the broadcasting act in order to reduce the number of members on the KRRiT – a move which allowed him to dismiss unfavourable members. During PiS's term in power between 2005 and 2008, there was a new director general of TVP virtually every year (Open Society Institute 2008: 289–92). Committed to replace the Third Republic of post-1989 by a 'Fourth Republic' that would be based on a strong state and a moral revolution, the Kaczynski brothers were driven by hostility against the media, which they accused of moral relativism and of being part of a communist conspiracy. It therefore came as no surprise that during the PiS government indirect interference turned into direct censorship, as a TVP journalist states: 'Formerly, TVP's directors asked you as a favour to find a way of supporting a certain party or politician. Today they just give you orders to follow, no matter what' (ibid.: 292).

As a consequence of continued politicization, the quality of the information produced by public service broadcasters across Central Eastern Europe has suffered severely. Since regulators and managers are primarily selected for their political credentials, they often lack the professional skills and expertise that are necessary to make informed and balanced decisions. Frequent instances of members of the executive dismissing directors and editors who take a critical, or simply balanced, stance on government policies inevitably discourage journalists from developing habits of independent thinking and incisive observation, both of which are the hallmarks of high-quality journalism. Moreover, political bullying has led to a brain-drain from public service broadcasting to commercial channels. Against these odds, however, in most East European countries public service broadcasting provides significantly more political information in news, current affairs programmes and documentaries than their commercial counterparts, which have largely resorted to entertainment and sensationalist soft news (Open Society Institute 2008). Thus, it is fair to say that even in its strangulated form public service broadcasting plays an important role in providing a space for public debate and political information.

Do people care, or is the battle over public service broadcasting just a kind of shadow-boxing between power-hungry politicians and idealists? The low ratings of public channels that are often below those of their commercial competitors seem to indicate that they did not succeed in gaining the popularity and trust enjoyed by their Western counterparts in the strongholds of public service broadcasting (Britain, Germany and the Scandinavian countries).[5] However, this does not mean that citizens are indifferent to the independence and quality of their media. Time and again there have been public demonstrations in various East European countries to protest against the hijacking of independent media and public television by political power. The 'media war' in Hungary under Prime Minister Antall's government brought thousands of citizens onto the streets in support of the beleaguered broadcaster (Hankiss 1994). When in December 2000 the Czech government under Vaclav Klaus placed their man at the top of Czech TV and announced a change in the broadcasting law, employees of the channel went on strike and television screens remained black for several days. Large crowds demonstrated for the independence of broadcasting on Wenceslas Square where in 1989 the 'Velvet Revolution' began (BBC News online 2011). In 2005 a public campaign was launched in Slovenia against changes in the broadcasting law that would have subordinated public service broadcasting to the government. In Poland several demonstrations were organized between 2005 and 2007 to protest against the government's motion to force journalists to declare possible collaboration with the Communist regime. When the Russian government closed down the only remaining independent (commercial) television channel NTV, tens of thousands of people gathered on the streets to express their support for the broadcaster (Jakubowicz and Sükösd 2008: 12). And in early 2011 several demonstrations mobilized tens of thousands of people in central Budapest to protest against the above-mentioned new Hungarian media law proposed by the Orban government (Index of Censorship 2011). And these are just some of the examples of protests around issues of media independence.

Looking back at 20 years of transition policy, it is fair to say that the transformation of state television into public service broadcasting in post-communist Eastern Europe remains in flux, and some would even argue that it has failed altogether (Mungiu-Pippidi 2003). However, even though some of the broadcasting laws are undoubtedly deficient, changing legislation to implement better safeguards against political interference, important as they might be, is unlikely to create truly independent public service broadcasting that is capable of delivering high-quality and balanced information. To solve the problem more is needed than simply changing the words written on paper; the cultural values and patterns of behaviour of both politicians and journalists also need to change in order to pave the way for a full transformation of former state broadcasting. The legacies of communism have left countries in Eastern Europe not only with an overbearing state and the arrogance of political elites who feel entitled to impose their view of the world on society, but also with a journalistic culture that sees its mission as (re)educating the purportedly ignorant and irrational masses. In a subtle way the mission of public service broadcasting of playing a leading role in educating and informing the audience might chime with the political role of the media under communism, making it difficult for managers and journalists in public service organizations to distance themselves from the centres of power. By the same token, the emergence of governments in Eastern Europe who embark on a 'revolution' – usually a conservative one – that would radically change society and the role of the media therein echoes in an unsettling way the radical rhetoric of communist politics. According to Jakubowicz (2004), it is the 'ideas in our heads' that define the rules of the game, not just the formal arrangements of legislation and organizational structures. As he points out, 'it was only when "imported" legal and institutional frameworks failed to function as intended that the importance of their cultural underpinnings became apparent' (ibid.: 55). Thus, in order to make public service broadcasting work, cultural changes are necessary on all sides of the process: politicians, journalists and citizens.

One of the many cultural factors for the intensity and persistence of the 'media wars' over the transformation of the relationship between state and public service broadcasters can be seen in the inability of political elites to negotiate a compromise across party divisions on issues that are of overarching importance for the viability of the emerging democracy. As Agh (2001) observes, the political culture in Hungary – and many other post-communist democracies in Eastern Europe – has taken on a majoritarian rather than a consensual understanding of democratic politics, where the 'winner takes all' by imposing domination over other centres and resources of power, be it material benefits or access to the media. With regard to journalists, it is important for them to break out of the circle of interdependency, and this means distancing themselves from the seduction emanating from the feeling of being part of the power elite. For example, in hindsight the strike by Czech media workers in 2000 appears like a turning point in the relationship between the state and the media. By refusing to accept the imposed director and by leaving the screen black, journalists were able to overcome ingrained attitudes of deference and a fear of losing their jobs. Supported by mass protests, their resistance established an invisible line between political power and the broadcaster – even though attempts by government to interfere did not stop, at least conflict remained at a manageable level. Finally, the widespread mobilization of protest in support of media independence shows that civil society in Eastern Europe is not dead, but is vigilant and alive. Any strategy of strengthening public service broadcasting – and civic-minded media in general – therefore has to incorporate civil society.

Nevertheless, at a historical moment, when public service broadcasting is under threat worldwide from digital convergence, the imperatives of deregulated markets and fragmented audiences, it might be impossible to recreate an institution that perfectly suited the needs of society at a particular point in time (i.e., in the middle of the twentieth century), but has to reinvent itself to preserve the values of independence, quality information, impartiality and integration in the age of the internet and globalization. In this respect, both new and established public service broadcasters are sitting in the same fragile boat.

7

Media Markets

Liberal democratic theory conceptualizes democracy, the market and the media as mutually reinforcing forces. In this view, democracy provides the legal framework and freedom for entrepreneurship to unfold its innovative potential, leading to growing national wealth; conversely, the rise of a liberal market economy is believed to increase the quest for individual self-determination and to restrict the role of the state in society; and finally, the media are seen as vital for providing the informational environment that is needed for rational popular participation as well as rational market activity. In the West, democracy and capitalism developed in tandem, each creating conditions that allowed the other side to progress, even though by no means in a peaceful and harmonious way, as millions of people paid with their health and their lives in the 'Satanic mills' (William Blake) of untamed capitalism. The unleashed forces of the industrial revolution that unfolded in Europe and North America during the eighteenth and nineteenth centuries brought about an increasingly wealthy and self-confident class of entrepreneurs, inventors and explorers who demanded freedoms and rights from the state that would allow them to pursue their interests without the restrictions of the traditional order of social subordination and customs. But it was also in the interest of the state to create favourable conditions for the exploding markets, as economic development enabled it to finance its growing ambitions in the global competition for domination. This interdependency between the interests of the state and the market gave birth to the twin conditions of democracy and capitalism. The media were part of this dynamic development from early on. The printing press allowed ideas to spread across space at an unprecedented speed; and with the invention of the telegraph even space no longer mattered. The instant availability of information provided entirely new opportunities for businesses to coordinate within and across national boundaries (Thompson 1995). Equally important were the social implications of the emerging mass media. It has been argued that the rise of a mass-circulation press significantly contributed to nation-building and nationalism. By creating 'imagined communities' (Anderson 1983), the media helped to strengthen the centralization of power as well as social cohesion between the diverse segments of the population that were dispersed across the territory of the nation-state. Yet mass communication and nationalism were also the driving forces that orchestrated the mobilization of the masses which resulted in the totalitarianisms of the twentieth century. For both communism and fascism, the mass media were a pivotal instrument of power that was brilliantly employed by political leaders to control the hearts and minds of the population.

However, even though capitalism and democracy create conditions that are favourable to each other, their close relationship also produces contradictions that threaten the stability of democratic rule. The close interdependency between state and market that helped to kick-off the industrial revolution was designed in such a way that kept the masses out of the equation. Universal suffrage, be it for the non-proprietorial classes, women or ethnic minorities, had to be fought for in long and bloody battles. The demands of ordinary people for equal rights and participation have always been – and still are – a potential threat to the vested interests of political and economic elites. Indeed, the tension between the ideal of democracy and how it is put into practice, between inclusion and exclusion and between power and powerlessness remains a constant fault line in contemporary democracies (Bernhagen 2009b). Robert Dahl was one of the first to understand the structural inequality that is built into the institutional arrangements of contemporary pluralist democracies – or 'polyarchies' as he calls them (Dahl 1971). As he points out, the competition between divergent interests is not a level playing field. Economic elites are much more effective in influencing policy decisions – through extensive networking, lobbying and, if necessary, bribery, etc. – than interests without stakes in the economy, leading to a structural under-representation of the majority of the citizenry in the policy process. Today, the balance between democracy and the market seems to have shifted at the expense of the former, as the concentration of power created by multinational conglomerates and global financial markets has effectively undermined the autonomy of democratically elected governments and, consequently, their legitimacy and accountability.

It is even questionable whether markets have an intrinsic preference for democratic rule. What markets need are secure property rights and contractual reliability, whereas mass participation, whether in elections or by means of unconventional mobilization, remains a source of uncertainty and instability. Usually, democracies are better able to guarantee the rule of law, but they are also susceptible to unpredictable mood shifts in public opinion and voters' demands for a fair share in the economic wealth of the society. For this reason, business has frequently supported dictatorships and has sided with *coups d'état* against democratically elected governments as long as the emerging authoritarian regimes promised to deliver the kind of stability and security needed for capital to grow. Without doubt, the military dictatorships in Latin America and the statist one-party regimes in East Asia turned out to be to the advantage of the corporate interests of these regions.

Whether or not the old regime fostered a capitalist economy, 'third wave' democratization always involves market-oriented economic reforms, albeit to varying degrees. Post-communist transitions constitute the most dramatic change because they involve a fundamental restructuring of the economic system from a state-controlled to a market-driven economy. Other pathways did not involve economic regime change, although democratization generally required a reduction in the role of the state in the economy, abolition of protectionism and the building of sustainable financial institutions.[1]

Economic transitions in the wake of the recent wave of democratization have taken place during the rise of neoliberalism to an almost undisputed global doctrine. The results, though, are not wealth and happiness for all. While for some (individuals, groups, countries) the liberalization of markets has brought about significant gains of wealth, for others it simply led to disaster and a downward spiral of poverty. Some decades into the 'third wave' it has become obvious that market reforms do not necessarily foster democratization. True, economic growth has been an important factor for democratic consolidation; but empirical evidence suggests that the ability of newly established democracies to reduce income inequalities is equally, if not more, important (Przeworski 1991; Przeworski et al. 1996). Some new democracies, like Brazil, have made significant progress in reducing their inequality ratings. But in most new democracies the gap between winners and losers, those at the top of the income distribution and the growing number at the bottom, is widening, providing a breeding ground for disillusionment and social conflicts. Sadly, South Africa today is at risk of taking exactly this route. Two decades after the

ANC came into power the country is still, according to a report by the World Bank (2012), one of the most unequal societies in the world, even though race is no longer the main determinant of poverty. It is not only the gap between rich and poor that is widening in South Africa's society, but also the gap between the promises of democratic rule and unfulfilled hopes.

This chapter investigates the ambivalent relationship between the media and the market and the implications this has for a healthy democracy. As the first section outlines, the inbuilt dynamics of media economies often work against the normative objectives of diversity and a plurality of voices. Furthermore, as profit-seeking actors, media companies aim to maximize audiences that are attractive to advertisers, which systematically limits the media's ability to produce content that encourages informed citizenship. Finally, the 'focus' section of this chapter on political ownership challenges the view that commercial media are the best guarantor for political independence. Instead, the situation in many new democracies – and not only new ones, it has to be said – shows that the joint interests of political and economic elites frequently hijack the media to pursue their own interests by controlling the range of issues that can be covered by the media.

The political economy of the media

The tension between democracy and the market permeates the organization and performance of the media in a fundamental way and sets them apart from any other business. Due to their dual nature as economic enterprises and political institutions, the contradiction between the selfish motivation of making a profit and the civic motivation of serving the public interest characterizes mass communication from the production of messages down to their consumption by audiences. In liberal democracies, free media usually means a free market system of commercial media, sometimes supplemented by publicly funded media segments. Market-based media are regarded as a way of organizing public communication that guarantees both independence from the state and other political interests and a diversity of voices competing for recognition in, to quote John Stuart Mill's metaphor, a 'marketplace of ideas' (1972/1859). This is understood as a commercial marketplace where 'ideas' are exchanged for profit and where consumer demand – rather than the prescription of a more or less benevolent authority – determines which ideas stand the test of competition.[2] As mentioned in the previous chapter on the relationship between the state and the media, for most of the post-war period policymakers in established democracies – with the US being one of the main exceptions – have deemed it necessary to invest in public service broadcasting as a sphere of public communication fenced off from market forces. In spite of a general commitment to free market principles, during the decades following the end of the Second World War a certain degree of scepticism remained as to whether competition and profit-seeking would, left to their own devices, bring about the quality and diversity of information necessary for a viable democracy. However, during the 1980s the coincidence of advances in communication technologies with the resulting proliferation of channels and the rise of neoliberal ideology led to a fundamental paradigm shift in media policy. With the media no longer regarded as a cultural good but as an industry, far-reaching deregulation became the prime media policy objective. In Europe, the European Union took on a leading role in the redefinition of the media as a consumer-oriented industry rather than an institution in the public interest. As a consequence, public service broadcasting as a non-commercial organizational form of mass communication has come under severe pressure. With the argument that the licence fee and the protective regulatory environment of public service broadcasting distort the free play of market forces, public service broadcasters are now struggling not only against an increasingly competitive commercial media sector, but also against an indifferent, if not hostile, political environment (Harcourt 2004; Ward 2001).

But how efficient is a market-driven media system at fulfilling its democratic purpose? In their analysis of the role of the media in established and emerging democracies, Mughan and Gunther (2000: 7) note a 'growing disillusionment over the extent to which the media present to the electorate an unbiased flow of a plurality of viewpoints, or even an adequate volume of the kinds of information that democratic theory implies should be available to voters'. Based on these observations, they come to the conclusion that 'the traditional stereotype of the uniformly positive contribution to democracy by free, unregulated communications' has to be challenged and scrutinized (ibid.). Similarly, Hackett and Carroll (2006: 2) identify a 'democratic deficit' of corporate media, which cannot be put down to a temporary policy fault that could be easily rectified. Rather, the deficiencies of the media as a social and democratic institution are the result of an inherent flaw of market forces as a regulatory mechanism for ensuring media outputs in the public interest. Several factors are responsible for the mismatch between commercial media and the requirements of democratic public communication.

First, media industries operate in two different markets, whose interests are not necessarily compatible: audiences and advertisers (Picard 1989). The discrepancy between these two markets becomes even more evident when we understand audiences as citizens who are seeking information that enables them to participate in the democratic process in a meaningful way. Only a relatively small proportion of the income of media companies is generated by sales, whereas the lion's share of returns depends on selling the attention of audiences to advertisers. Thus, the media are primarily answerable to their advertising clients and shareholders and there is no effective mechanism that makes the media accountable to those who are consuming their products. The consequences of the media's dependence on advertising are systematic inequalities in access and representation. Since the value of readers and viewers depends on their potential capacity to consume the advertised goods, population groups with little purchasing power will find less information that suits their needs and will be less likely to be covered in a positive way than the affluent segments of the population who can afford all those cars, cosmetics, clothes, foods, insurances, etc. that fill much, often most, of the space and time of media content. Media content analyses have consistently shown that the news, but also entertainment and screen fiction, are dominated by white, urban, middle-class men (Zhao and Hackett 2005). Thus, what Dahl found with regard to the misrepresentation of interests in pluralist democracy is paralleled by a similar imbalance in the public sphere: women, the elderly, working-class people, ethnic minorities, the rural population rarely make it into the news, and, if they do, the image that is projected is more likely to reinforce prejudices and stereotypes.

Second, media markets tend to be highly concentrated. Both national and global markets are dominated by ever fewer conglomerates that are highly integrated both across media markets, such as print and audiovisual formats, and across the entire distribution chain, including content production and distribution. Media production generally, and in particular the production of political information, is characterized by the logic of economy of scale where the initial production costs (i.e., creation of a news story, documentary or in-depth report) are relatively high, whereas the costs for the subsequent production and distribution of large numbers of copies for audience consumption are low. In other words, whether a particular programme or a particular newspaper is consumed by 5,000 or 500,000 people does not affect the resources that have to be invested in producing the initial master copy. As a consequence, the trend towards huge media conglomerates and oligopolistic market structures is virtually unavoidable, as large media companies with high circulation rates are better able to maximize returns from their products (Doyle 2002). The internet is no exception to the trend towards oligopolistic concentration. Despite its claim of being an open space that provides access to everybody, the internet has effectively fallen prey to a handful of giants – Microsoft, Google, Facebook, AOL/Times Warner – which divide the global market amongst themselves. Concentration dramatically reduces diversity because it allows media companies to reproduce the same – or only minimally modified – content through multiple media channels. Contrary to its pronounced intentions, the policy of deregulation that has been adopted by governments around the world since the 1980s has in fact not resulted in more choice and pluralism, but rather in a higher degree of ownership concentration and uniformity of media content (McChesney 1999).

Good journalism is still a hand-crafted product, despite the technological developments and resources available from the internet that have made news production more efficient. Investigative journalism, in particular, which is so crucial for a healthy democracy, often does not conform to the requirements of routine content production. In order to keep costs down, many news media rely increasingly on what international news agencies can provide, especially for the coverage of foreign affairs, without engaging in their own independent research or investing in in-house foreign correspondents. The picture is not much better for domestic politics, as for many news media the official material issued by government press offices has become the main source of news production. As a result, political information is becoming more standardized not only within, but also across countries, thereby reducing diversity and marginalizing the locale, where most people are actually experiencing politics. Meanwhile, broadcast journalism is increasingly giving way to formats that can be produced at low cost, such as talk shows and so-called reality shows. Only a few high-quality outlets can afford in-depth reporting, whereas middle-market media and the regional press provide a rather thin and hardly critical account of current affairs.

The third reason for the inefficiency of markets to create a democratic public sphere is that distance from the state or any other powerful political agents by no means implies that the information provided by commercial media is free of political bias. Dependent on advertising revenues, commercial media aim to create a communication environment that is attractive to potential customers. Hence, media content, even when noisy and sensationalist, implicitly supports the status quo by favouring mainstream ideas and opinions that do not fundamentally challenge the existing state of affairs. Groups that resist accepting the doctrine of growth, deregulation and unavoidability of social inequality are often marginalized or even criminalized. Dissident groups that directly challenge the interests of the media industry are even met with outright hostility or are ignored altogether.

Moreover, owners have their own agenda of interests, which they promote through their media outlets. Two types of ownership – profit-seeking and policy-seeking – lead to different kinds of biases, even though both orientations frequently coincide. Profit-seeking owners are mainly concerned with the economic success of their enterprise. They keep their media out of the political struggles of the day, even though they interfere in politics, either by lobbying and/or through editorial policy, if certain policy proposals contradict their business interests. For example, Rupert Murdoch's support for the Conservative Party during the Thatcher government in Britain and his switch of allegiance to the Labour Party in 1997 was arguably driven less by political conviction than by the observation that the public mood in the country was changing and that it would be a bad thing for his popular media outlets to find themselves on the losing side. Media outlets of profit-seeking owners can take on any political stance or pursue a neutral editorial line, but would take sides if and when their business interests were affected by particular policy proposals, for example anti-trust or privacy legislation. In contrast, policy-seeking owners use their media to promote a particular political idea or party, occasionally even when this is against their economic interests. For example, the late Axel Springer, a German press baron and owner of the biggest tabloid paper in the country, was always an outspoken supporter of conservative politics and the Christian Democratic Party. Throughout the Cold War he pursued an aggressive anti-communist editorial policy, insisting on always putting 'GDR' in inverted commas, thus indicating his refusal to recognize the East German state, but also portraying student activists, environmentalists and other social movements as 'Moscow's fifth column'. The Springer press consistently stuck to this political line regardless of which party was in power – though it should be mentioned that this did not affect the success of his media empire in any obvious way.

However, against the odds of the inherent limitations of media markets to produce outputs in the public interest, the media provide citizens with a surprisingly high amount of information that encourages public debate and participation and forces governments to legitimate their actions. Some of these products might be the result of a strategic economic decision to exploit niche markets of politically interested audiences who are part of small circles of political 'anoraks' who look out for more than the daily diet of headline news. Yet, more often, quality information is the result of the professional commitment of editors and reporters to serve citizens and communities and to contribute their share to a robust and viable democratic life. In fact, the tension between economic objectives and journalistic priorities, between maximizing returns and the commitment to professional standards and ethics, characterizes the production process in most of the media industry. As Doyle (2002: 5) points out, the 'principal–agent problem' is particularly prevalent in the media industry, where the 'agent' – i.e., the editor, reporter or producer – and the 'principal' – i.e., the owner, advertiser or shareholder – differ in terms of their goals and values. Even though many owners understand that the credibility of their outlets can pay off in the long run, journalistic quality remains a secondary objective, a means to economic success that would be sacrificed if other media formats were to promise higher returns. Because of the 'principal–agent problem' in the media industry, a strict division between the management of a media firm and its editorial decision-making process strengthens journalistic independence and broadens the space where investigative journalism and commitment to non-economic values like democracy, social responsibility and truth are possible.

Democratization and media markets

Given the deficiencies of corporate media to provide a democratic public sphere even in established democracies, it comes as no surprise that the relationship between market reforms and the democratization of the media has been an uneasy one in most new democracies. International donors and organizations that support democracy have promoted the privatization of the media as the main route to media independence. And indeed, given the legacy of state interference into the operation of the media under autocratic rule, there seem to be hardly any alternatives to marketization as a means of media democratization. As was demonstrated in the discussion of the problems surrounding the creation of viable public service broadcasting in Central Eastern Europe (see the 'Focus' section in Chapter 6), post-authoritarian states are unlikely to refrain from manipulating media that are in one way or another dependent on revenues managed by state agencies.

In most new democracies, the liberalization of the media market in the immediate aftermath of the breakdown of the old regime opened the way for a plethora of new media outlets to enter the 'marketplace of ideas'. Countless enthusiastic editors and journalists seized the opportunity to make their voices heard, thus serving a hungry audience that was eager to absorb the new abundance of information. However, very soon almost all these new media outlets found themselves in severe economic difficulties, and only a few eventually survived. The hyper-politicization of the period of regime change soon gave way to disillusionment and depoliticization, as the demands of everyday life took over again. In many post-communist countries newspaper markets virtually collapsed after a short period of post-euphoria flourishing. For example, between 1996 and 2000 readership in Poland declined by 73 per cent (Carrington and Nelson 2002: 233; see also Johnson 1998). Not only did newspapers lose the generous state subsidies that kept them afloat under communist rule, the radical economic reforms of most post-communist governments also destroyed existing audience markets, as the economic hardships that followed market reforms forced people to cut down on any possible expenses to make ends meet. As incomes declined and unemployment rose, newspapers became a luxury good that many people could no longer afford. As a consequence, oligopolistic structures, well known from Western countries, now dominate most post-communist media markets in Eastern Europe.

But there are also instances where the liberalization of media markets has led to more pluralism and brought new life to the public sphere. When African governments opened the airwaves for commercial broadcasters, it was small independent FM radio stations, in particular, that flourished everywhere across the continent (Nyamnjoh 2004). Radio is particularly popular in Africa among producers and audiences alike because it is relatively cheap and extremely flexible in its usage. Radio seems to suit the oral tradition of African cultures extremely well and neatly merges with what has been called 'radio trottoir', referring to gossip and storytelling that circulate on the streets (Hyden and Leslie 2002: 20–5). Radio has the capacity to reach those parts of the population who are illiterate and live in less developed rural areas. Even though most of the new independent stations are concentrated in and around towns and cities, radio plays an important role in providing the rural population with information that helps to strengthen participation and citizenship. As Myers (1998) describes in the case of Mali, independent radio stations see themselves as part of the democratic project and have played an active role in promoting civil society at the grass roots. Radio stations have also been actively involved in holding officials to account and monitoring the democratic process.[3] In several other instances, for example Senegal and Ghana, independent radio stations were at the forefront of reporting about irregularities during elections, thereby preventing widespread fraud that would have invalidated the electoral process (Blankson 2007).

Yet as the experience in many new democracies has shown, the main challenge facing the transformation of media markets is how to translate temporary growth into long-term sustainability by securing a continuous flow of advertising revenue. Since advertising only develops in wealthy economies, a thriving national economy and media development go hand in hand. As Carrington and Nelson (2002: 230) note, a wealthy economy sets in motion a virtuous circle providing 'more sources for advertising revenue, along with the basis for less political paranoia, [and] more opportunities for media companies to expand into new markets and/or formats'.

In the post-communist countries of Eastern Europe the development of media markets was closely linked to the transformation of the whole economic system from a command to a market economy. Locked in a 'dual transition' of economic and political transformation, the marketization of post-communist media probably involved the most radical change of all democratization pathways. In an environment where major parts of the national industries in the region collapsed when exposed to international competition, consumer markets remained weak and underdeveloped for quite a long time, thus leaving the media without reliable revenues. At the same time, the countries of Central Eastern Europe benefited from their proximity to Western Europe, further supported by the political will of the European Union to get the economies in the prospective member states on their feet as fast as possible. Encouraged by the – to some extent exaggerated – expectations of a speedy recovery of the economies of Central Eastern Europe, Western media companies invested in the transformation of existing media outlets or launched new ones, sometimes even before the wider economic conditions had consolidated. West European media corporations quickly divided the market among themselves, with the Swedish Bonnier Group concentrating on Poland and the Baltic States, the Swiss-based Ringier AG on the Czech Republic and Slovakia, and the German Bertelsmann AG on Hungary, Poland and Romania (Carrington and Nelson 2002: 234). In many cases, the engagement of foreign ownership led to extraordinarily high levels of concentration and thus to a marked decline in diversity. For example, in 1996 the German WAZ (Westdeutsche Allgemeine Zeitung) bought up almost 80 per cent of the total print circulation in Bulgaria, including the country's two best-selling tabloids (ibid.). In Hungary, Poland and the Czech Republic foreign ownership was already consolidated by the early 1990s, with between

50 and 70 per cent of the national print market controlled by foreign corporations; regional markets were also in some instances monopolized by foreign investors (Gulyas 1999). Lack of regulation caused by the long time it took legislators to pass new media laws, often combined with insufficient implementation of existing ownership restrictions, allowed foreign investors to accrue huge chunks of the Eastern European media market. Foreign ownership has positively helped Eastern European media markets to consolidate at a time when the economies of these countries were still struggling. For example, Western companies invested in modernizing the infrastructure of their media organizations and introduced efficient management structures. However, the presence of foreign ownership left little space for home-grown media entrepreneurs to enter the market. Today, foreign ownership is increasingly felt as cultural domination in the countries of the region, which – for better or worse – are beginning to develop their national identities by distancing themselves from the West. It is also worth mentioning that in the controversy about the new Hungarian media law (see Chapter 6) Western media companies that were engaged in the Hungarian media market remained noticeably silent when media freedom (but not media ownership) came under attack (Verseck 2011).

In spite of the drawbacks of extensive foreign ownership, the investments of international media companies in Central Eastern Europe have undoubtedly helped local media organizations to develop into strong economic enterprises, which would otherwise have had little chance of surviving the turmoil of the first years of economic restructuring after the breakdown of the communist command economy. Other new democracies where future returns look less promising hardly attract any substantial foreign investment and hence are left to their own devices. Foreign capital usually stays away from countries in the developing world where advertising markets are extremely limited. As a consequence, the media in these countries do not have much choice but to remain dependent on state subsidies. For example, in Africa only governments have the resources to operate daily newspapers, whereas oppositional papers only appear irregularly and with very limited volume (Nyamnjoh 2004).

Even if the media obtain revenues from advertising, these are often covert state subsidies, for example when the state acts as the main advertiser either for state-owned industries or its own activities. The allocation of these advertising contracts is frequently used to reward government-friendly media and penalize those who are more critical or even engage in investigations of corruption. An Open Society Institute study (2008: 31–66) on soft censorship in Latin

America found that abuse of advertising for political purposes is a widespread practice in almost all countries of the region and has a detrimental effect on the independence of the media. But there are also instances where the retaliatory allocation of public advertising has become public, which hopefully will help in the future to implement more transparent regulations to prevent unfair practices. For example, in Costa Rica the disclosure that high-ranking officials used government advertising to buy favourable coverage of the government's foreign trade policy in 2007 triggered a scandal and forced the vice-president of the country to resign. In the same year, the Supreme Court of Argentina ruled that withholding advertising contracts from a critical newspaper violates principles of free speech and ordered government agencies to refrain from discriminatory practices in the future (Open Society Institute 2008).

FOCUS: MEDIA, MONEY AND POWER

Markets are processes that are rooted in, and operate through, social relationships. Since economic activities are social activities, economic success depends not only on the quality of a product, but also on the quality of the social relationships in which a business is located. In his seminal study on economic differences between northern and southern Italy, Putnam (1993) was able to identify the crucial role of social capital as a prerequisite of economic performance. Mutual trust and the ability to cooperate are the lubricants that allow economic exchange to run smoothly. In the same way that social capital boosts economic success, so economic capital in turn enhances social influence and reputation. The interplay between economic power and political influence is also an important factor for understanding the political significance of media ownership.

Media ownership exceeds the cumulative value of economic and social capital by adding cultural power to the arsenal – a resource no other industry can offer. In modern societies the media are the prime agents of defining and interpreting social reality, making them a powerful means of influencing and manipulating public opinion, which has the potential to maximize all kinds of capital – economic, social, political. As McNair (2000: 88) puts it: 'Media power translates economic power into political and cultural power, which are key elements in the maintenance of economic power.' Since political and media power reinforce each other, it would be in the interest of neither political actors nor media owners to stay apart. Hence, the assumption that the state and the media act as antagonistic forces, which underlies the normative reasoning of liberal media theory, rarely meets reality.

In most established democracies the interdependent, sometimes even symbiotic relationship between politics and the media manifests itself as a professionalized exchange relationship where the supply of information is traded against access to the public agenda. In many new democracies this interdependency goes even further, as media ownership is excessively politicized. Especially in East Asia and Latin America, the media industry is deeply entrenched in the power structure of the country. The legacies of Asian one-party rule in the context of developmental statism and the military dictatorships in Latin America cultivated a system of clientelism and interconnected elite networks that have been almost seamlessly carried over into post-authoritarian democratic politics (Hallin and Papathanassopoulos 2002). In both regions only a few media outlets are directly owned by the state. Instead, state and media industry are interlocked in what has been labelled 'crony capitalism', where economic success depends on close relationships with government officials (Hughes and Lawson 2004; Kang 2002). In this system, the accumulation of economic and social capital is concentrated within an exclusive circle of participants who form close informal relationships with each other in order to minimize the risks of their activities and maximize the gains. The consequence of crony capitalism in the media industry is that the cultural capital of public communication primarily serves the interests of the closed circles of interlocking elites at the expense of the wider public and, ultimately, democracy.

Contrary to liberal media theory, the market does not constitute a separating shield between the media and the sphere of politics, neither does private ownership guarantee political independence of the media. Rather, they often reinforce each other, thus forming a 'media-political complex' (Curran and Park 2000a: 14) of combined political, economic and cultural capital. On the surface of it, the emerging media systems in most new democracies seem to correspond fairly well with the principles of liberal media theory, but the way in which they function is rooted in the social relationships that tie political and economic elites together. In 'media-political complexes' the relationship between politicians and media owners is rarely a balanced one. In most cases political elites take control of the media to serve their own interests, but sometimes media owners launch high-pressure campaigns which can lead to a situation whereby they, in effect, capture the state.

Media capture involves a situation in which the pay-off for financial transfers to the media is expected to be a gain in power, regardless of the resulting commercial profits or losses. For politicians, the main objective for investing in the media industry is to secure favourable coverage, in particular during election time when power is at stake. In Latin America, government officials or members of their families are frequently involved in the ownership of media companies, and high-ranking politicians and even presidents hold seats on the management boards of commercial broadcasting stations (Waisbord 2000a). In other cases media companies enjoy a variety of privileges in exchange for compliance. These privileges can involve advantages in the granting of broadcasting licences, selective relaxation of existing laws in processes of mergers and acquisitions, special tax breaks, the cancellation of debts, or simply bribes to owners or editors.[4] Strategies employed to capture the media rarely need to resort to harsh censorship. Instead, by relying on self-serving cooperation they are even more effective than direct control because they trigger less resistance on the part of the media.

Crony capitalism in the media industry, which evolves from interlocking groups of political and media elites, has created media giants that distort not only the plurality of voices in the public sphere but also the media's ability to hold public officials to account. Research has shown that a captured media fosters corruption because it provides a protected space of favourable coverage for political elites. Knowing that 'their' media will turn a blind eye to their activities encourages them to engage in dubious practices. Another consequence of media capture is the reduction of political turnover, because biased media are less likely to identify policy failures and the incompetence of incumbent politicians, who as a consequence are able to stay in power for longer (Besley and Prat 2006). In addition, media capture limits democratic citizenship and effective participation. Using comparative data across both democratic and non-democratic regimes, Petrova (2008) demonstrates that in countries where the rich spend money to influence media coverage there are higher levels of social inequality. The reason is that media that are dependent on wealthy sponsors portray redistributive policy options in a distorted way, thus withholding information that is necessary for less privileged voters to vote according to their own interests.

Hughes and Lawson (2004) provide a detailed account of the pattern of commercial and political influences on Mexican television during the 2000 presidential election when, for the first time, the ruling PRI (Institutional Revolutionary Party) lost this office to the opposition. In spite of the political opening-up experienced by the country during the 1990s, broadcast media were still caught up by arrangements made between broadcasters in collusion with politicians, with both sides trying to exploit the power of television over public opinion to their own advantage. As Hughes and Lawson show, the shifting power balance between media owners and political elites produces something like a plurality of biases. While public television remained clearly in favour of the incumbent party, private broadcasting, especially in the regions, adapted to the specific commercial incentives emerging from the political circumstances in the location where they were operating. Overall, '[c]overage appears to have been based on government subsidies of dubious legality and on the prospects of future commercial benefits' (ibid.: 99), overriding professional journalistic norms of accuracy, fairness and independence. As the authors emphasize, the Mexican situation echoes similar arrangements in other Latin American countries and demonstrates that neither privatization nor the absence of direct censorship necessarily produces an open and pluralist media system. In the same way that the media benefited from supporting, and being part of, the old regime under the generals, the big media players continue to remain close to the centres of power (Fox and Waisbord 2002). But there are also positive signs. With new spaces opening up after political and economic liberalization, an increasing number of media outlets are diverging from the culture of propaganda and giving voice to dissenting and critical views. For example, prior to Mexico's landmark election in 2000 a large number of print media started to engage in investigative coverage on the ruling PRI, which arguably contributed to its eventual defeat (Rockwell 2002).

In contrast to media capture, capture of the state indicates a situation where the power balance is tilted towards organized groups – most often businesses, including the media. In other cases, the military, religion or ethnic groups play a similar role. In contrast to lobbying, which operates within the existing legal framework, state capture involves pressure groups in shaping and bending the rules of the game to their own advantage by using payments to officials, fabricated material to damage the opponent, and even blackmail to influence political decisions. The costs of holding the state to ransom are enormous. Not only do they affect economic growth; they also undermine the efficiency and transparency of political institutions and the success of the transition process as a whole. Such a situation is a recurrent problem for weak states, many of which are transitional democracies in various hybrid manifestations – a problem that has been discussed in more detail in Chapter 6. As Hellman et al. (2003: 752) state, the problem has often been overlooked in transition research: 'In only a decade [of transition], the fear of the leviathan state has given way to an increasing focus on oligarchs with the power to "capture the state" and shape the policy making, regulatory and legal environments to their own advantage, generating concentrated rents at the expense of the rest of the economy.'

During the 1990s, Russia – emerging from one of the most brutal dictatorships of the twentieth century – represented a worrying example of a state beleaguered by a handful of powerful industrialists and bankers, often with dubious links to organized crime. The chaotic privatization within an almost lawless environment that followed Yeltsin's rise to power allowed a small group of 'oligarchs' to amass unbelievable wealth within only a few years. In their rise to power and wealth, media ownership played a crucial strategic role (McNair 2000; Mickiewicz 1999; Zassoursky 2004). As part of conglomerates that combined businesses as diverse as oil, gas, financial services, car manufacturing and others, media assets rarely contributed to the profits of these commercial empires. In fact, in most cases they made losses. The main function of the media was to manipulate the information environment of political and business decision-making. Koltsova (2006: 14) calls this 'advertising-propaganda motivation' of media ownership. Through biased, often straightforwardly fabricated media coverage, media owners tried to influence government decisions and generate support for a business-friendly environment among the population. Especially in the battle over the privatization of state property, the media were important weapons used to outmanoeuvre competitors. Koltsova (ibid.: 228) argues that for most of the time it wasn't the Russian government that put the media under pressure, but the other way around: power groups pressurized the government through their media.

The presidential election in 1996 highlights the degree to which the Russian state was captured by industrial interests and their media. With his popularity below 10 per cent, Yeltsin was entirely dependent on media support if he was to be re-elected. For the power groups around the leading oligarchs, Yeltsin had various advantages over the other candidates who were running in this race, which in their eyes made him worthy of support: he was regarded as weak and easily influenced, he was willing to secure a business-friendly environment, and he was the only candidate who had a chance to win against the communist contender Zhirinovsky. Having won the election, Yeltsin then had to distribute returns for the support he had received. However, with the rise of Putin the balance between the state and extra-state actors, including the media, changed again. Putin was determined to strengthen state authority and to break the power of the oligarchs, forcing some of them to leave the country (Berezovsky, Gusinsky) and imprisoning others on charges of tax evasion (Khodorkovsky). Putin also brought the media, in particular television, back under state control, with the effect that 'the assertive (if frequently corrupt) coverage that characterized the Yel'tsin years has given way to docile and flattering treatment of the Kremlin on the air and in the press' (Gehlbach 2010: 78). However, Gehlbach contradicts Freedom House's judgement of a return of 'Soviet-style media management', arguing that Putin's control of the media remains rather patchy, mainly focusing on the evening news and the top echelons of the media industry, whereas allowances are made for what is possible in other formats of information and the large range of entertainment genres (ibid.; see also White 2008). A return to the totalitarianism and pervasive media control of Soviet times has become unlikely.

8

Political Parallelism

The notion of 'press-party parallelism' was introduced by Colin Seymour-Ure (1974) to describe the pattern and degree to which the press system mirrors the party system of a given country. On the macro level, parallelism raises the question whether across the media system as a whole all parties are represented according to their actual strength. Evidently, distortions in favour of a particular party would diminish the chances of the underrepresented parties to win elections because their supporters are less likely to encounter information that reinforces their leaning, while potential swing voters are more exposed to information that favours the party that is overrepresented. On the micro level, press-party parallelism indicates the alignment of individual media outlets with a particular party.

Since media can form alliances with all sorts of political groups – not just political parties – Hallin and Mancini (2004: 26–33) prefer to use the term 'political parallelism'. This chapter's discussion of political parallelism returns to an issue that has been discussed in Chapter 2: the distinction between external and internal diversity. Evidently, political parallelism is closely related to the concept of external diversity, which denotes a situation where individual media promote a particular viewpoint while ignoring or even dismissing opposing views. In theory, the aggregation of micro-level biases can establish comprehensive diversity on the macro level, provided all relevant voices are represented in dedicated media outlets. But in practice it is unlikely that the biases of individual media outlets add up to a correct representation of the power relationships within the party system. In contrast, internally diverse media represent all – or at least a broad range of – the different viewpoints in their coverage. Internal diversity is closely linked to journalistic norms of objectivity, balance and detachment and is therefore often regarded as the better way of presenting political information. Without denying the virtues of internal diversity, this chapter argues that political parallelism plays an important role in democratic politics. But the mobilizing power of partisanship can easily turn into destructive forces that spread intolerance and even hatred between different groups of citizens. After discussing the pros and cons of political parallelism, the 'focus' section of this chapter turns to a particular group of transitional democracies, namely those that emerge from violent civil conflicts. Building democracy in post-conflict societies poses particular problems and dilemmas to issues of press freedom and political parallelism that defy easy and clear-cut solutions.

Parallelism, partisanship and political engagement

In nineteenth-century Europe it was fairly normal for newspapers to be closely aligned with, in most cases owned by, a particular political party or other kind of association. From its beginning, the printing press has been regarded as a channel of advocacy, be it for religious, political or philosophical causes. Seymour-Ure points at the mutual dependency of the printed press and the emerging political parties at that time: 'The growth of competing political parties in 19th century Europe was widely paralleled by the rise of newspapers supporting them' (1974: 157). The party press played an important role in mobilizing mass support that allowed parties to reach beyond the small circles of their leadership. More importantly, the press created 'imagined communities' (Anderson 1983) of interconnected individuals who were able to share ideas and learn about the experiences of people who lived in similar circumstances elsewhere. For example, the rise of the labour movement would be unthinkable without its vibrant party press that linked people who could never have afforded to leave the confined space where they worked and lived. But Seymour-Ure's statement can also be turned around: the rise of a plurality of newspapers in nineteenth-century Europe was widely paralleled by the growth of political parties supporting them. The reason for this was that before the rise of mass consumption and the accompanying advertising markets, there were no funding sources for the press other than the sponsorship of organizations or individuals who had the means to run their own newspaper.

It was only during the twentieth century that newspapers gradually freed themselves from their party sponsors. Today, the party press has virtually disappeared and newspapers have given up their institutional ties. However, in many European countries newspapers have retained the ideological identity that originates in their historical beginnings. Scholars of media history believe that neutrality and objectivity as a journalistic norm only emerged in response to changing economic conditions (Schudson 1978). The rise of the so-called yellow press – i.e., cheap, easy-to-read newspapers with mass circulation – made it imperative for media owners to produce content that would be attractive to mass audiences regardless of their particular political worldviews. The newly established news agencies also contributed to a less politicized style of journalism, as news became a commodity that was sold to a large number of different customers (Boyd-Barrett and Rantanen 1998). These developments affected the American press much earlier and more strongly than their European counterparts. Today, impartiality and balance have become widely recognized, albeit rarely practised, journalistic norms.

If media partisanship was an important precondition for the emergence of political parties that were built on loyal mass support for electoral success, then surely its decline cannot be without consequences. This is the argument put forward by political scientist Martin Wattenberg (1998) when he argues that the neutral reporting style of modern media is, at least in parts, responsible for the decline of American political parties. As voters no longer find clear partisan cues in the political information provided by the media, party identification is eroding. Instead, the personalized style of news coverage has given way to the rise of candidate-centred politics, focusing on individual politicians often without clear connections to their party affiliation. Of course, cause and effect are difficult to disentangle here. It can well be that with declining party attachment citizens avoid overt partisanship and prefer political information that is presented in a more neutral and detached manner. However, dealignment and the decline of partisanship is neither a universal nor a linear trend. For example, in the US the success of Fox News, an outspoken right-wing television channel, indicates the demand for media that provide interpretations of current events that resonate and reinforce the beliefs of their audience. Similarly, online journalism and blogs, often run by journalists, attract large followings not by taking a distanced view on the world, but by opinionated commentary, by taking sides, by being subjective.

Most of the media systems that have emerged in transitional democracies are highly politicized, with individual media clearly attaching themselves to particular groups or causes. There is virtually no new media system where internal diversity is the dominant pattern of representing the plurality of voices in the public sphere. Thus, despite all the efforts of media assistance programmes that promote norms of balanced and neutral reporting, the news media in emerging democracies are dominated by partisanship. One of the reasons for the prevalence of political parallelism is the persisting dependence of the media on state agencies and dominant parties for financial support. Where this is the case, parallelism of individual media outlets inevitably translates into a distorted pattern of media representation on the macro level, as dissident and marginal voices that cannot afford to run their own media outlets are pushed to find a platform to communicate their views to the wider public. Another reason for widespread partisanship is, quite simply, freedom. After long years of suppression, the end of censorship often triggers an explosion of voices eager to express themselves in public. Even though the resulting public debate frequently sounds more like a shrill cacophony than a harmonious choir of different voices, political parallelism in new democracies is an indicator for the emergence of a pluralist marketplace of ideas, imperfect as it might be.

Political parallelism and external diversity are often regarded as inferior to neutral reporting and internal diversity because they provide only a limited, often one-sided view on political affairs. However, it is worth remembering that most of the leading newspapers in Europe can, without much difficulty, be positioned in the political spectrum of their countries. Many of them have won prizes for outstanding journalism despite the fact that they stand for particular political ideologies and often do not even clearly distinguish between news and comment, as the Anglo-Saxon model of professional journalism implies. Examples of newspapers that combine high-quality journalism and partisanship – partisanship with a small 'p' because the editorial leaning of these papers does not involve any organizational ties with, or consistent support for, a particular political party – are the *Guardian* and *The Times* in Britain standing for left-liberal and centre-right positions respectively, the left-liberal *Le Monde* in France, the German *Frankfurter Allgemeine Zeitung* endorsing centre-right positions, and the left-leaning *La Repubblica* in Italy. Newspapers in post-communist Eastern Europe that have earned international acclaim for their quality are equally outspoken participants in the political debate, like, for example, the left-liberal *Gazeta Wyborcza* in Poland. This is not to deny the many instances of partisan media that employ aggressive, even malicious rhetoric to denigrate whomsoever they regard as their political enemies; but the examples illustrate that parallelism does not exclude high standards of journalistic reporting. Hence, neither does political parallelism and partisanship exclude quality, nor does neutrality and detachment guarantee high-quality political coverage.

External diversity can play an important role in the political and social life of a country. Similar to the history of political parties in Western Europe, parallelism helps political and cultural communities to develop their collective identities. In doing so, advocacy media support and encourage the development of a vibrant civil society, which has been weakened, often eliminated altogether, by autocratic rule. Partisan media can also play a leading role in watchdog journalism, as Waisbord (2006) notes for Latin America. Even though the driving motive is often to damage the political opponent (while keeping quiet about the wrongdoings of one's own side), investigative activities of partisan media are crucial to keeping political authorities accountable. Finally, partisan media contribute to an informed citizenry. This might sound paradoxical given the selective coverage they offer. The reason is that for individual citizens biased information has been shown to be more useful for political learning and participation than neutral information. Facts seldom speak for themselves, as proponents of objective journalism often – quite naively – assume. To make sense of facts and events, they have to be interpreted, linked to existing knowledge and embedded in the social context of those who are consuming this information. Most people are primarily meaning-seeking, rather than simply information-seeking beings. Learning about what has happened is immediately followed by the question why this happened and with what consequences. And information about a political figure is judged on the grounds of which side he or she is standing for. Biased information provides these cues, thereby serving as a key mediator for citizens' involvement in politics (for the US context, see Dalton et al. 1998; Mutz 2006).

Analysing the reasons for people's trust in the media in Latin America, Waisbord (2006) argues that for individual media users professional journalistic norms, like objectivity and balance, are much less important than is generally assumed. He distinguishes between 'journalism of information' and 'journalism of opinion', each of which makes different credibility claims. 'While one says "trust me, I'm an expert", the other says "trust me, I'm one of us"' (ibid.: 84). Many people judge the trustworthiness of information on the basis of the trustworthiness of the source of this information. If we know that a source of information shares similar values to the ones we hold, belongs to the same community or supports the same party, we conclude that the information itself must be reliable. The close relationship between 'journalism of opinion' and trust in the media could be an explanation for the 'hostile media syndrome', according to which people perceive neutral media as hostile to the political party they support. In other words, two people who support different parties would regard the same media outlet as imbalanced and hostile even if the information is presented in an even-handed, neutral manner. This observation implies that if a source of information cannot be identified as 'one of us', it is met with suspicion. Not surprisingly, the 'hostile media syndrome' is more widespread in the US, where news reporting generally follows the professional norms of balance and neutrality, than in Europe, with its rich tradition of partisan media (Gunther and Schmitt 2004).

Parallelism and the dark side of partisanship

While parallelism and partisanship are a vital part of democratic life, they can easily become a destructive force. Both have the potential to deepen intolerance towards those who do not share the beliefs of the in-group. If partisanship and advocacy are not moderated by respect for the opponent, if one's own position is taken as absolute, and if facts are ignored or even manipulated in order to serve one's own cause, then parallelism can create a toxic public sphere that jeopardizes social and political integration. Strong parallelism of the media deepens polarization between opposing groups, which makes it difficult for political leaders to negotiate across lines of division, thereby challenging the legitimacy of political compromises, without which pluralism and democracy would be unsustainable.

The dark side of partisanship often parallels the 'dark side of civil society' (Theiss-More and Hibbing 2005). Scholars of democratization often emphasize the importance of civil society for a successful rebuilding of political life from authoritarianism to democracy (see, for example, Grugel 2002). And indeed, without groups fighting for human rights, development, the environment, a local school and many other noble goals, democracy would remain a 'cold' set of rules and procedures. However, a great many activist groups are fighting for particularistic gains at the expense of public goods or are mobilizing against other groups in order to achieve domination or exclusive access to scarce resources. Obviously, collective action is not a virtue in itself. What matters are the aims of this engagement and the effects it might have on others.

Putnam (2000) distinguishes between bridging and bonding social capital, with the former referring to engagement that is inclusive and reaches out to other groups and sections of society, and the latter denoting collective action that is isolated and in the worst case directed against others. Partisan media, with their limited scope of arguments and restricted target audience, are 'bonding' media that tend to impede interaction with other groups by perpetuating us/them sentiments. A crucial precondition for external diversity to work to the benefit of a democratic public sphere is therefore the existence of one or more media that function as a forum by providing 'bridging' communication across the boundaries of group interests and worldviews. These forum media are spaces where different groups can speak and – more importantly – listen to each other. Traditionally, public service broadcasting is designed to serve this function, but the role of bridging communication can also be taken on by private media. Forum media do not emerge naturally. They require political will to be put into existence. To make them work, it is important that they are protected from being hijacked by the state or any other power group in society. This is not an easy task and might need external assistance. It requires more than simply privatization of the media because, as experience in many new democracies has shown, the marketization of the media usually results in a fragmented system of external diversity. Instead, creating a forum media involves implementing rules and incentives that encourage civic-minded journalism and ensures access for all groups and voices to the forum.

What kind of parallelism is emerging in the new democracies of the 'third wave' and what implications does this have for the possibility of moderation and intergroup communication? The parallelism that dominates politics in the established democracies of Western Europe and North America is anchored in the ideologies of political parties which developed in response to the particular conflicts associated with the political and economic modernization that unfolded during the eighteenth and nineteenth centuries (Lipset and Rokkan 1967). Even though some of these conflicts can be observed elsewhere in the world (for example, those between labour and capital or between the central political power and separatist movements at the periphery), historical pathways to democracy have often taken very different courses in non-Western societies. Thus, collective action and media advocacy often differ significantly in the emerging democracies of the twenty-first century.

In Western democracies politics is traditionally dominated by the left–right division (or the distinction between liberal and conservative in the US). Encapsulating complex sets of ideologies, beliefs and policy priorities, 'left' and 'right' have become powerful categories that help citizens to navigate through the complexities of political life. 'Left' usually stands for a progressive worldview, social equality, redistribution of national wealth and a stronger role of the state to bring about these changes, whereas 'right' indicates social conservatism, hierarchy and the preservation of the established order. In Eastern Europe, as a result of shared historical roots with Western Europe and the polarization of the Cold War, the dualism of 'left' and 'right' has maintained some of its significance for organizing the meaning of political conflicts (Markowski 1997). However, the legacy of the communist past has shifted the meaning of these categories to the effect that 'left' is seen as standing for the old order and 'right' for change and progress. At the same time, many of the political parties that emerged after the end of communism made little or no attempt to develop a coherent ideological profile. Instead, they employ other issues to serve as pointers for political distinctions – for example, nationalism (Russia), minorities (Bulgaria, Hungary, Romania) or the communist past (Poland). These issues are often more symbolic than related to any substantial policies, but they have stirred the emotions of large parts of the electorate in these countries and have polarized public debate. In most post-communist countries, parallelism on the macro level of the media system as a whole is grossly imbalanced because of the structural advantage the formerly communist government organs had at the beginning of the marketization of the media. Communist mouthpiece media entered the new marketplace with strong organizational know-how and established audiences, and used their head start in the early years of the transition to reinvent themselves as modern and professional outlets. As a consequence, most of the leading national newspapers in post-communist countries are the former official organs of the old regime.

In Latin America the left–right distinction also remains the central dimension to structure electoral choices (Seligson 2007) and the pattern of media parallelism. Across the continent there has been no 'strong cultural-political push to depoliticize the press, to downplay partisan allegiances, and to follow the canon of objective reporting' (Waisbord 2000a: 52). In contrast to Eastern Europe, Latin American countries have been marked by extreme social inequalities, which often run along ethnic lines, leaving the indigenous population at the very bottom of the income distribution. The left–right dimension therefore retains its strong class appeal, distinguishing between the haves and the have-nots, the privileged middle classes who occupy virtually all power positions and the poor masses. After the withdrawal of the generals from the political stage, the main media companies maintained their close relationships with the power elites. However, a new breed of populist leaders, some of whom come from poor and/or indigenous backgrounds – like, for example, the former President of Brazil, Lula da Silva – have been successful in forging new alliances with the media, thus shifting the power balance in the media systems of their countries.

A very different pattern manifests itself in sub-Saharan Africa. According to Bratton and van de Walle (1994), ethno-patrimonialism is the dominant feature of African politics. In societies where, because of underdevelopment, class divisions have not yet fully unfolded, ethnicity and region remain the main points of reference for collective identities. Ironically, the transition from one-party to multi-party rule has often contributed to an exacerbation of ethnic conflicts, as free elections allow the various groups to compete for resources and influence. In his study on Cameroon, Nyamnjoh (2005) observes that virtually all parties of the country organize along ethnic lines despite a law that requires them to establish multiethnic organizations. The media parallel these divisions and have allowed themselves to become the mouthpiece of the particularistic interests of tribal ambitions. Against the background of colonialism, autocracy and civil wars, the creation of a positive cultural identity is undoubtedly important for the self-esteem and development of these societies. However, by and large the media have failed to moderate partisanship and to position local identities within a wider national context. According to Nyamnjoh (2005), Cameroonian media often fuel ethnic hostilities and cultivate conspiracy theories about the purportedly sinister intentions of 'them'. For example, members of another tribe have been labelled as 'parasites' or 'traitors', and a headline reads: 'The natives feel threatened. Is there a plot against Douala?' (ibid.: 244, 252). In conjunction with the increase of interest groups that campaign for ethnic interests, the media's 'culture of one-dimensionality' (ibid.: 66) can create a hostile public sphere that polarizes citizens and, in the worst case, might even lead to interethnic violence. As Berman (1998) states, in many African countries 'uncivil nationalism' has prevented development of a public sphere founded on transethnic cooperation and social trust.

In the aftermath of the 2007 election, this became a brutal reality for the people in Kenya when ethnic violence left more than 1,000 people dead, while hundreds of thousands had to flee the country to save their lives. In this conflict, phone-in programmes on vernacular radio channels played a crucial role in fanning the interethnic violence. Before the outbreak of violence, these stations had served as a forum for citizens' involvement, but lack of training left journalists helpless when their programmes were hijacked as a platform for hate speech (Ismail and Deane 2008). However, the same mobile technology that fuelled hatred was also used to mobilize civic behaviour. Initially set up by a group of Kenyan bloggers, the website Ushahidi (www.ushahidi.com) gathered information about violent incidents sent in by mobile phone users. This information was then mapped on Google Earth to provide an immediate account of what was going on (Goldstein and Rotich 2008; Sigal 2009: 23). Ushahidi is a clever way of combining open software, citizen journalism and grass-root participation. The technique of crowd sourcing quickly spread to other crisis areas, for example, for mapping anti-immigration violence in South Africa. It was also used to alleviate the aftermath of the earthquakes in Haiti and Chile in 2010; and most recently it has helped protesters in the Middle East to organize anti-regime demonstrations. Like so many other communication technologies, crowd sourcing can be a catalyst for destructive behaviour and mob violence as well as for effective peacekeeping strategies (Heinzelman et al. 2011).

In Asia, political and social parallelism takes yet another form. In some countries the media have close ties with particular political parties (Taiwan, Thailand) or with linguistic and ethnic groups (Malaysia) (see Hong 1999; McCargo 2003; Rawnsley 2006). Yet, frequently, loyalties are diffuse and hardly follow the pattern that can be observed in the other geopolitical regions discussed above. Especially in the so-called 'tiger states', the close interdependency between state bureaucracy and businesses, including media companies, has resulted in a cosy rather than an antagonistic relationship between politics and the media, which is shaped by patron–client relationships rather than ideological affinities (Park et al. 2000). As McCargo (2003: 10) observes: 'In the absence of a stable party system organized along ideological lines, the idea of a newspaper that consistently supports a particular political party is not a valid one across the region.' In a political environment that is highly factionalized, the media prefer not to commit themselves to one particular side of the political battle. Instead, they maintain ties to multiple political actors – politicians from both government and opposition parties, civil servants, military, interest groups, etc. – that they hope can be exploited for commercial benefits. By supporting various stakeholders, the resulting partisanship is often inconsistent and ambiguous (McCargo 2012). Thus, it can be argued that the information that citizens receive from the media is not objective, nor does it provide coherent cues that can serve as guidelines when they make decisions on political issues.

FOCUS: REBUILDING PUBLIC COMMUNICATION IN POST-CONFLICT SOCIETIES

Many of the present attempts to build a democracy and a free press are taking place in countries that are emerging from civil wars fought between ideological, ethnic or religious groups. The end of military action rarely means that peace has been restored beyond its most basic meaning of absence of armed violence. Post-conflict democracies have to overcome deep divisions, while citizens are still haunted by disturbing memories of the most appalling crimes committed by fellow citizens on each other. Civil wars destroy trust at all levels: trust in the state that was unable to protect its own citizens, trust in the fairness and capability of institutions, trust in social relationships, and trust in the media which have almost always been instruments of the hate propaganda of the conflict parties. Thus, achieving sustainable peace requires more than negotiations between the opposing groups and a settlement on the future distribution of power and resources; it also involves creating conditions that make it possible for the antagonistic groups to talk to each other again and to live together in one nation.

Post-conflict societies are facing multiple challenges simultaneously: state-building, nation-building and, ideally, gradual transition to democracy. Since state institutions are extremely fragile, there is the looming risk that hostilities will break out again at any time if one of the antagonistic parties glimpses the chance of gaining more from continued military action than from collaboration. Compared to state- and institution-building, nation-building is a more diffuse and long-term process. Those who have been victimized during the conflict need to regain a sense of empowered citizenship and confidence in the rights and responsibilities this entails – if it ever existed. Most urgently, nation-building requires a new understanding of collective identities to ensure that sub-national identities, such as kinship, ethnicity or region, do not override loyalty to the nation as a whole. Ethnicity and nation, as any other collective identities, are social creations that are constructed, deconstructed and reconstructed through communication and social interaction. Hence, media and communications play a crucial, albeit highly ambiguous, role in this process. Ambiguous, because most of the media have been participants in the conflict; crucial, because democratization and nation-building require the media to be a public forum in which debates about citizenship, identities, government policies and government accountability can take place. It is for this reason that many democracy assistance programmes, which have previously regarded the media as a by-product of the democratization process that did not require any particular attention, now systematically include schemes to develop media capacity (see De Zeeuw and Kumar 2006; Kumar 2006; Price and Thompson 2002).

However, the route that is usually taken to move a country forward on its path towards democracy – competitive elections and liberalization of the media – has not always yielded the expected positive results. The unsettling truth is that in many instances elections and uncensored media have exacerbated the already fragile situation in post-conflict societies. Collier (2009) suggests that rather than pacifying society, elections frequently deepen antagonisms, even to the point of the recurrence of physical violence, because electoral competition inevitably increases the visibility of differences and divisions. Lacking a coherent policy platform, most candidates and parties employ symbolic politics, such as ethnic or religious identities, to mobilize voters, thus revitalizing and perpetuating hostilities between groups. In a similar vein, Zakaria (1997) expresses scepticism about the democratizing effects of elections (at least when held early in the transition process), as they endow illiberal elites with the electoral legitimacy that they then use to continue their authoritarian practices.

Likewise, opening up the media does not necessarily help nation- and state-building either. The assumption that liberalizing the media naturally brings about robust public debate and pluralism has proved to be mistaken, as the space that is opened up by free access to media ownership and the abolition of censorship can quickly be occupied by those who aim to manipulate public opinion. Even if individual journalists are keen to adopt a more professional approach to their work, the power of media owners and political pressures often prevent such ambitions. Where political parties campaign on a sectarian agenda, the media usually follow suit, resulting in deeply polarized pluralism. One of the many examples is post-Saddam Iraq. Helped by massive media development investments, Iraq's media landscape flourished after the dictator was ousted. However, the media soon became politicized and were drawn into the power struggle that was unleashed after the first election. As a report of the Center for International Media Assistance notes: 'The future of the country's media does not look promising on several fronts. Many of Iraq's media outlets have become mouthpieces for ethno-political factions with the potential to inflame sectarian divisions that have led the country to the brink of civil war' (Ricchiardi 2011). Quite surprisingly, in spite of this dire prognosis, the report applauds the increased consumer choice of the new media landscape and condemns measures of the government to bar coverage that is deemed to incite sectarian violence (ibid.: 6). It seems that the ideology of free market media is stronger than the search for solutions that are adequate in a particular situation. Having the choice between different varieties of hate speech seems to be rather pointless and of little value for citizens' empowerment and informed participation.

Bosnia-Herzegovina provides another example that demonstrates the dangerous combination of premature elections and unrestrained media (Thompson and De Luce 2002). Since the Dayton Peace Agreement of 1995 did not make any provisions for the future constitution of the media in the country, the first general election that took place in the following year went ahead with the main broadcaster still under the control of the government, while the rest of the media was divided along national and ethnic lines. As a result, the opposition did not have anything near to fair access to the airwaves, and the election was won by ethno-nationalist parties. The late Richard Holbrooke, then special envoy to the Balkans of the US State Department, describes the election as being conducted 'in an atmosphere poisoned by a media controlled by the same people who had started the war. Advocates of reconciliation in all three communities were . . . overwhelmed by media that carried nothing but racist propaganda' (cited in Thompson and De Luce 2002: 207). To counterbalance the ethnically divided state broadcaster, the international community, led by the Office of the High Representative (OHR), launched a commercial television network dedicated to balanced, transethnic reporting. However, in the end the initiators had to admit that Open Broadcast Network (OBN), in spite of considerable funding flowing in from international donors, had failed to live up to the expectation of serving as an alternative model of broadcasting. The audience share remained far below that of its state competitors, leaving it a fairly insignificant element in the otherwise divided media landscape of the country. Kumar (2006: 93–108) takes stock of the enterprise and identifies several factors that led to OBN's underperformance. The main flaw was probably the 'top-down' approach of the network, which was managed by an international bureaucracy without enough involvement from Bosnian journalists and managers. Consequently, the broadcaster was perceived by the audience as a foreign enterprise that only appealed to a small number of educated urban viewers, but was not accepted as 'one of us' by the wider audience. Further, the approach of launching a commercial channel in addition to the existing state broadcaster proved not to be financially viable in a small and underdeveloped television market. Some observers argue that it would have been more important to reform the three ethnically segmented channels of state broadcasting rather than investing in an additional one. Change would have been slow and against the interests of a political class accustomed to instrumentalizing public broadcasting for its own purposes. But working with the existing channels would have allowed local media workers to be involved and would have encouraged the rebuilding of public communication from within.

Allen and Stremlau (2005) take a very different approach to post-conflict media development. Based on the experience of various post-conflict societies, especially in East Africa, they suggest that in order to stabilize the fragile situation and reduce the risk of intergroup violence, some degree of censorship might be necessary. If a laissez-faire approach to media transformation leads to a proliferation of inflammatory speech, then the need to achieve reconciliation between antagonistic groups and to stabilize fragile state institutions can legitimize a certain degree of media control. Putzel and Van der Zwan (2006) are quite sanguine in criticizing what they call the 'unsophisticated liberalization of the media' by international agencies, which in their view are not sufficiently aware of the complexity of the situation on the ground. Instead, Western media development organizations have to acknowledge that hate speech and other abuses of media freedom have the potential to undermine state-building and the development of a much-needed national consensus. The authors conclude: '[I]n the case of fragile states, it may . . . be misguided and potentially dangerous to assume that encouraging the creation of free and independent media will automatically strengthen civil society, or help establish a democratic system that will hold governments accountable' (ibid.: 1).

Several African countries have taken the route of controlled media liberalization. One of the most contested examples is Rwanda where in 1994 an estimated 800,000 Tutsis were killed in a concerted attack by the majority Hutus. This genocide, which was the culmination of a centuries-old rivalry between the two groups, left the country traumatized and shattered. How could the two communities ever live together as a nation, and what could be the role of the media after they had been instrumental in stirring hatred between the groups for years, even explicitly orchestrating the killings? The government under President Kagame decided on a form of 'benevolent censorship' by passing a law that banned what was called 'genocide ideology' from public discourse. According to this ruling, any references to ethnic identity are prohibited in order to prevent the perpetuation of ethnic stereotypes and hatred between Hutus and Tutsis. The ban on 'genocide ideology' also means that journalists (and any official figures) have to adhere to the officially accepted account of the 1994 events. Almost two decades after the genocide many observers still regard the situation in Rwanda as being volatile, with hatred looming under the surface, which arguably justifies the restrictions that have been imposed on public speech (Kinzer 2010). However, it becomes increasingly apparent that restrictions on free speech in the name of interethnic peace serve as a smokescreen for endemic censorship. While it is questionable whether the cloak of silence that lies over the society helps to overcome the traumas of the past, it certainly helps to stabilize the power positions of those who are in charge of the transition. The government's policy of controlled public communication has stifled public discourse, and even spread fear, as opponents of President Kagame are quickly accused of promoting a 'genocide ideology'. Several newspapers have been closed down for the same reasons. During the run-up to the 2010 presidential election (which Kagame won with 93 per cent of the votes) restrictions on public communication were used to prevent any contestant from challenging the dominance of the incumbent. Two of Kagame's challengers were arrested on charges of 'genocide ideology', and the imprisonment of two journalists, Agnes Uwimana Nkusi and Saidath Mukakibibi, for 17 and 7 years respectively, for 'threatening state security, genocide ideology, devisionism and defamation' (PEN International 2011), might be extreme cases, but they are indicative of the authoritarian course the country is taking under the cloak of preserving peace.

The Rwandan case highlights some of the problems involved in a sequencing approach to democratizing the media, which puts stability and nation-building before other values, such as press freedom and an open expression of opinions in the public sphere (He 2001; Linz and Stepan 1996: 16–37; for a critical discussion of sequencing, see Carothers 2007). For once, the question as to who decides on the definition of what is excluded from public speech (for example 'hate speech') and how this decision is made are crucial for the legitimacy of any restrictions. If governments are characterized by ethnic, religious or regional group bias, their legitimacy to make this decision can be easily challenged. In the worst case, the government or individual members of the government have themselves been involved in past human rights violations and thus do not have the moral authority to act as an arbiter of contested interpretations of collective identities. Further, if difficult truths are swept under the carpet, they are still there and everybody in the room knows it. At some point a society that is struggling with a violent past has to address these issues, otherwise there is the risk that continuing silence will generate new hostilities, conspiracy theories and mistrust among citizens. The solution, however, is not unrestrained expression of opinions regardless of their consequences. As has been argued in Chapter 2, press freedom cannot be absolute even in the most robust democracies. Rather, the principle of free speech encompasses both the freedom and dignity of the speaker and the listener. What post-conflict societies therefore need is an open debate about possible limitations of what can be said in the public domain and how this can be justified. Even if a shared understanding across all participants cannot be achieved as an outcome, such a debate might at least lead to the mutual recognition of divergent views.

Post-apartheid South Africa has gone through various public debates about its troubled past and the consequences that the experience of racial prejudice and social exclusion might have for freedom of the press today. In 1999 the South African Human Rights Commission (SAHRC) set up an inquiry into racism in the media. Even though the conclusions of the SAHRC laid down in its final report were widely disputed, the hearings triggered a broad public debate about the way in which the press portrays race in its daily coverage. In particular, the notion of 'subliminal racism' tested the boundaries between press freedom and undue censorship (Tomaselli 2000). Two years earlier, the media already found themselves in the spotlight of public scrutiny when they became part of the so-called institutional hearings of the Truth and Reconciliation Commission (TRC). The national broadcaster SABC, itself at the centre of these hearings because of its role as an entrenched part of the apartheid regime, provided the airtime for the proceedings to be broadcast, thus allowing the whole nation to be involved in this debate (Krabill 2001). As for the TRC hearings in general, it was made clear right from the start that the aim of the exercise was not only to find out the truth about the past, but also to overcome feelings of revenge and to achieve reconciliation. The belief in 'the truth' also strengthened the acceptance of a free press, flawed as it might be in particular instances. Notwithstanding its shortcomings, the TRC was a heroic attempt by the people of South Africa to create a sense of nationhood through openness rather than silence. At least three crucial factors contributed to the TRC's success: clear rules were set up, including, among other things, that the stories of both victims and perpetrators be heard; contrary to initial plans to conduct the proceedings behind closed doors, they were broadcast nationwide; and the moral authority of Archbishop Desmond Tutu, who acted as the chairman of the Commission, ensured moderation and fairness.

To understand the dynamics and consequences of public communication in divided and post-conflict societies, it is important to think beyond mass mediated communication and to also consider social communication processes that take place between individuals, usually in face-to-face encounters. Research into media effects has consistently shown the power of interpersonal communication. There are only very rare occasions where media messages have a direct effect on their audiences. Most of the time, they are closely linked and channelled through social communication where people engage in (re)interpreting and evaluating what they have learned from the media (Lazarsfeld et al. 1968; Huckfeldt and Sprague 1987). It is through everyday conversations with family members, neighbours or workmates that media messages are transformed into socially constructed and collectively shared meaning, which can eventually change individuals' attitudes and behaviour. The strength of political talk has a significant downside, though. It usually takes place between people who share the same values and belong to the same group – class, ethnicity, religion, etc. People prefer to mingle with like-minded others and look out for information that reaffirms their beliefs and identities. Social interaction in heterogeneous groups and information from media with a different editorial orientation challenge these certainties and are met with a great deal of cognitive resistance. The tendency to rely on trusted – i.e., 'one-of-us' – sources of information and to live in homogenous social contexts is bound to fall victim to the 'law of group polarization' (Sunstein 2002), resulting in a segmented society where different groups live in parallel without ever bridging the divisions.

It is therefore all too clear that to pacify post-conflict societies, it is not enough to ensure that media messages do not perpetuate prejudices and intergroup hatred. Equally, if not more, important is that opportunities are created for ordinary citizens to listen and talk to 'the other side' (Mutz 2006). Theories of deliberative democracy have developed concepts and practices that might usefully be employed to transform not only the media, but a society's communications environment as a whole. Practitioners of deliberative democracy have developed designs for a large range of communication contexts, from intra-governmental decision-making to local conflict resolution to online forums. What these initiatives show is that talk is not a good thing by itself. It has to be set up and moderated in such a way that cross-cutting interaction and changing one's mind are encouraged. Sigal (2009) suggests the design of an online communication structure for divided and conflict-prone societies that encourages dialogue and nonviolent political solutions rather than fostering segmentation and bias (for deliberative web design, see also Wright and Street 2007). John Dryzek, a leading scholar of deliberative democracy, explores the applicability of deliberative principles in contexts where identity politics dominates the public discourse. The challenge is 'how deliberative democracy can process what are arguably the toughest kinds of political issues, the mutually contradictory assertions of identity that define a divided society' (2005: 219). Dryzek is sceptical about both agonistic pluralism, which promotes the open clash of differences, and consociational arrangements, which remove divisive issues from the public sphere and confine deliberation to behind-the-scenes negotiations between political leaders. Instead, he suggests a more pragmatic type of intergroup deliberation that focuses on specific needs and problem-solving tasks, such as security, education or water supply, rather than on general values and identities that are difficult to accommodate without risking the breakdown of the dialogue.

So far, the potential of deliberative democracy for reconciliation in post-conflict societies is still largely unexplored. James Fishkin, who developed the technique of deliberative polls, has organized these conversations mainly in stable democracies with a view to improving knowledge and considered judgement on contested issues. A deliberative poll conducted in Northern Ireland suggests that, as in less conflict-laden contexts, intergroup discussions result in more moderate opinions and a reduction of polarization between opposing positions (see Fishkin 1991; for an overview of deliberative polling projects, see http://cdd.stanford.edu/polls/). Communicative approaches to peace-building, nation-building and reconciliation in post-conflict societies are an important way of broadening the intellectual and operative repertoire beyond formal institutions, including the media, because they have the potential to create a sphere of public communication that actively involves individual citizens and encourages them to exchange and reflect on their views and experiences with others (see O'Flynn 2006; Yordan 2009).

9

Journalistic Professionalism

Chapter 8 explored the transformation of the media during democratic transitions as a reconfiguration of relationships between the media and their political, economic and societal environments. In the course of these discussions, a great deal of what constitutes post-authoritarian journalism has already been covered by investigating the various influences on journalism in transitional democracies and how these contextual changes affect the performance of the media and the quality of the information they convey to their audiences.

This chapter turns to the changes that are taking place within the media, looking at how journalism as a social field (Bourdieu 1998) with its own internal relations and hierarchies is transformed by, and adapts to, the new environment of democratic politics and media freedom. Who are the winners and losers within the journalistic field, and how does the social position of journalists affect the quality of the work they are doing? How do journalists understand their new role in society and how do they re-establish a sense of professional identity after the old norms and practices have lost their legitimacy? How do individual journalists navigate through the troubled and confusing conditions of post-authoritarian hybridity where Western notions of professional journalism might be desirable, but frequently turn out not to exist in the actual conditions under which journalists go about their work?

The first part of this chapter provides a general discussion of journalistic professionalism and the norms and standards that constitute the kind of outputs that are generally recognized as quality journalism. However, while the transnational discourse of professional journalism seems to imply universally shared norms of 'good' journalism, journalistic practices differ significantly across cultures. In fact, professional journalism encompasses multiple models that often coexist and compete even within a particular culture or country. Like notions of democracy and press freedom, journalistic norms are interpreted and socially constructed through the actions and cognitive filters of those who are engaged in journalistic work. As this chapter argues, the transformation of journalism after the demise of authoritarianism combines different streams of meanings and practices that originate from the role journalists had under the previous regime, the constraints of the post-authoritarian environment, cultural norms and the perception of Western role models. Thus, alongside hybrid forms of democracy a broad range of journalism has emerged that reflects the huge diversity of the political, economic and social realities in the new democracies of the 'third wave'. The 'issue' section of this chapter addresses a largely ignored, but endemic problem in journalism: the exchange of money for favourable coverage. Highlighting the problem of corruption of some journalists does not diminish the great work done by many others who take great risks in their endeavour to provide a faithful account of events. But the emphasis on outstanding journalistic performance often diverts attention away from the precarious situation in which most journalists do their work, especially in the countries of the developing world.

Journalism as a profession

Journalism is generally seen as a profession, even though some of the defining elements that characterize the traditional professions, such as medicine or the law, are usually missing. For example, to work as a journalist does not necessarily require a particular formal training or passing standardized tests or examinations. Indeed, graduation from one of the university programmes in communication science, journalism or media studies that have been established over the past couple of decades rarely opens the door for a career as a journalist. Even though there is now a trend towards 'academization' of journalism, most journalists learn their profession on the job by observing experienced peers and being supervised by their seniors. Nevertheless, in spite of the openness and ambiguity of the field, journalistic professionalism manifests itself through three main characteristics.

First, journalists subscribe to a set of norms that guide their activities and set the standards for what is regarded as 'good' journalism.

Seib (2002: xi) describes journalism as a 'moral enterprise', thus emphasizing the centrality of norms and ethics for the definition of the profession and its role in modern society. Journalistic norms include rules regarding practices of collecting information – for example, procedures of verifying information, the protection of sources or respect for the dignity of those who are the subject of news reporting. Other norms, like balance, neutrality and fairness, aim at safeguarding the integrity and credibility of journalism and distinguish journalistic outputs from many other narratives that describe and interpret the social world. However, the importance attached to these norms and the degree to which they are applied in the day-to-day business of news production differ significantly across cultures. Journalistic norms are constantly under challenge both from within the profession and by external forces. As societies change, so do the normative presumptions of what makes 'good' journalism. Societal value change, shifting ideological hegemonies, commercial constraints and new audience demands all exercise pressure on how journalists understand and practise their occupation.

Journalistic norms have their roots in journalists' own perceptions of their role in society (Donsbach 2008). Even though there is wide agreement about the core functions of journalism – providing information about actual events, investigation into issues of public concern – professional norms differ depending on the priorities of individual journalists or media organizations. For example, journalists who see themselves primarily as neutral chroniclers of current events will prioritize different quality standards for their work from those who see themselves as opinion leaders and educators of the masses. Journalistic role perceptions and related norms develop in interaction with the dominant values of the society and the expectations of the audiences who are consuming journalistic products. In other words, journalism as a profession is both embedded in local cultures and linked to an interconnected global community of professionals who share a particular work ethic and identity, but also differ in significant ways (De Beer and Merrill 2004; Weaver 1998). Ultimately, neither ethical standards nor professional production rules provide stable guidance for journalistic activities. Changing audience expectations and the opportunities brought about by new technologies often undermine these routines, thereby calling for a revision of the standards of what is and what is not acceptable journalistic practice.

The second characteristic of professional journalism is autonomy, which safeguards journalists from interference by actors from outside the profession. Without a certain level of autonomy it would be impossible for journalists to make their decisions according to their own norms and ethical standards. Political instrumentalization, marketization and close ties and loyalties with particularistic group interests, which have been discussed in Chapter 8, frequently undermine the professional autonomy of journalists and limit their ability to maintain a sense of professional identity. Journalistic autonomy is threatened not only by outside forces, but also from within media organizations. Journalists do not necessarily pursue the same interests as the owners of the media company that employs them. In fact, profit-seeking motives often contradict, even undermine, journalistic quality standards and ethics. The separation between ownership and editorial decision-making is therefore essential for the autonomy of journalism. Yet as competition increases and audience shares dwindle, journalists often see no alternative but to surrender to the imperatives of the market.

A third indicator for the professionalization of the journalistic field is the differentiation of journalistic activities and the subsequent division of labour between different roles (Deuze 2007). These differentiations often evolve around different genres, like straight news and commentary, or specialisms, like domestic and international politics. A high degree of specialization further strengthens the autonomy of individual journalists within an organization because it endows them with exclusive knowledge and skills that cannot be easily overridden by non-professional considerations of news decisions. However, divisions of labour also create hierarchies and unequal allocation of professional prestige both within the field and within individual news organizations. These inequalities can lead to different degrees of autonomy within the profession, as lower-status groups tend to be more vulnerable to interference and the pressures from above than elite journalists.

The global divergence of journalism

Like other professions, journalists have developed a distinct professional identity that encapsulates a sense of who they are and what the purpose of their activity is. Deuze (2005) talks of 'occupational ideologies' that provide journalists with professional definitions of their role in society and basic principles of 'good' journalism. Past research, mainly conducted in Anglo-Saxon and West European countries, has identified different role perceptions, or ideologies, of journalism, such as the gatekeeper and the advocate (Janowitz 1975); the interpreter, disseminator and adversary (Weaver and Wilhoit 1986); or the bloodhound and the missionary (Koecher 1986). Donsbach and Patterson (2004) argue that all these models can be put down to two basic dimensions. One positions journalistic work between a passive and an active pole, denoting various degrees of autonomy from actors outside journalism. The other dimension refers to the degree to which journalists take sides in the political debate of the day, thus running between neutrality and advocacy.

Comparative studies, especially those that include non-Western countries, show wide variations of how journalists in different cultural contexts understand their professional role. Even though there is some agreement, differences seem to prevail. Comparing the professional orientations of journalists across 21 countries, Weaver (1998) concludes that beyond the perceived duty to provide information 'there is much disagreement over how important it is to provide entertainment, to report accurately and objectively, to provide analysis of complex issues and problems, and to be a watchdog of government' (ibid.: 478). These observations lead Deuze (2005) to the conclusion that there is no one model of journalism, but many. Thus, journalism only exists in the plural: journalisms. Different notions of journalism even exist side by side within one national context and compete with each other (Hanitzsch 2011).

The juxtaposition of alternative journalistic ideologies is particularly prevalent in emerging democracies where the path dependency of cultural and institutional development blends professional orientations that live on from the past with those that are adopted during the transition process. Professional journalism does not start with democratic regime change. Journalists in emerging democracies build on their experience under the old regime and may even draw professional pride from what they have achieved during that time. Even though under autocratic rule their autonomy was widely restricted, journalists did develop distinct professional identities with particular values and ethical standards. The demise of the old regime and, with it, old models of journalism does not necessarily bring about a higher degree of professionalism. On the contrary, the ambiguities of transition and the fall-out from radical market reforms often lead to a manifest decay of journalistic standards and a loss of professional identity.

Media development organizations have made it their mission to implement norms of objectivity, neutrality and fact-based reporting in the newly emerging democracies of the 'third wave'. The response of journalists has been mixed. While some have enthusiastically adopted these norms as a way to secure their autonomy from political interference, others have defended their own journalistic culture against what they perceive as yet another example of cultural imperialism. The argument of the critics is that American-style journalism lacks sensitivity to the conditions of transitional democracies in the developing world where, in the face of poverty, the suppression of women and ecological disasters, journalistic neutrality and detachment appear impossible, if not irresponsible. Furthermore, it is argued that Western models of journalism contradict the indigenous cultural values of more traditional societies and would therefore, if fully adopted, cause more harm than good.

It is for these reasons that in many emerging democracies of the global South alternative models of journalism have gained wide popularity among news people. One of the most influential – and probably most controversial – models is that of development journalism, which states that journalism should play a constructive role in facilitating national development and contribute to nation-building. Having been utilized by the developmental dictatorships in Asia and Africa, development journalism is frequently criticized as a model that impedes journalistic autonomy because it subordinates journalism under the priorities of a certain policy agenda. And indeed, post-authoritarian governments still use development goals to muzzle journalists and to delegitimize critique as something harmful for social cohesion and progress (Xu 2009). However, the principles of development journalism also bear the seeds for professional emancipation. As Musa and Domatob (2007) point out, commitment to development goals really means putting the interests of the people first and acting as the people's advocate. Given the widespread corruption of political leaders and the inefficiency of governments in African countries, commitment to development involves oppositional journalism and fearless investigation. Thus, by combining elements of the ideology of development journalism with those of the adversary model, journalists in developing countries are constructing a professional role that incorporates democratic principles of checks and balances as well as responsiveness to the social problems that trouble their countries.

Other critics who argue against importing Anglo-American journalism models draw on the incompatibility of Western and non-Western cultures. The debate about Asian values is accompanied by propositions of a distinct Asian model of journalism that is sensitive to the local culture, which entails community-based notions of freedom, respect for elders and public authorities, the importance of face-saving in the public realm and social harmony (Romano 2005). A similar movement has emerged in Africa, called 'Afriethics' (Kasoma 1996), in an attempt to revitalize an Afro-centric approach to journalism. Central to this view is the notion of 'ubuntu' that emphasizes social belonging as the basis of individual identity. Both approaches can be read as anti-globalization and anti-Western discourses. Proponents of Asian values or a specific African ethics construct a sharp contrast between their own culture and the West by arguing that the excessive individualism and the celebration of conflict that characterize Western journalism are incompatible with the values and social norms that underlie their own culture. However, both forms of indigenous journalism have been widely criticized for essentializing culture as something homogenous and timeless (see Tomaselli 2003). This idealized view of culture disregards the diversity and complexity of cultural and journalistic practices within local cultures and the many ways in which Western and indigenous orientations have interpenetrated, merged and synthesized.

Like liberal democracy, Western-style journalism, with its emphasis on objectivity, detachment and adversarialism, goes through countless modifications and adaptations when it travels across cultural boundaries. Arguably, it is only through these alterations that democracy and a free press can put down roots in their new environments. Parallel to the emergence of hybrid forms of democracy (see Morlino 2009a; Voltmer 2012), a hybridity of journalistic role perceptions can be observed throughout the democratizing world, as Kanyegirire (2006: 163) notes: '[A]s journalism practices and assumptions travel in theory and practice from one context to another they mutate, stay the same and sometimes even reconstitute initial emphases to fit the specific local context.'

Democratizing journalism in a time of crisis

The multiplicity of models of 'good' journalism opens up new opportunities for journalists in emerging democracies to reinvent themselves as a profession independent from the prescriptions of political authorities about what journalists should and should not do. The expansion of media freedom allows journalists not only to cover a broader range of topics and opinions, but also to employ a more varied repertoire of professional skills. However, the diversity of models of what professional journalism entails in an emerging democracy comes with a great deal of uncertainty and conflict, frequently leaving journalists more exposed to manipulation by competing political and economic forces than ever before.

The transformation of journalism in 'third wave' democracies, with all its ambiguities and conflicts, coincides with a general crisis of journalism worldwide. Triggered by far-reaching economic and technological changes, the ethical and professional foundations of journalism are fundamentally challenged. Blumler (2010) identifies a 'two-legged crisis of journalism', one being the threat to its financial viability due to shrinking resources, the other the threat to its moral viability because of the inability of contemporary journalism to further democracy and citizenship. Of course, both crises are closely interconnected. Fierce competition unleashed by the proliferation of media channels and media formats over the past couple of decades has turned journalistic productivity into a commodity. Competition in a 24/7 newsreel increasingly puts winning the race for breaking news and maximizing audiences first, at the expense of ethical considerations, thorough investigation and commitment to the public interest. As a result of this, the autonomy of professional journalism and its normative foundations have effectively been diminished.

Moreover, it seems that the traditional journalistic media of press and broadcasting are losing their battle for audiences. This is not only because information is now available for free from the internet; it is also the case that audiences look out for different kinds of information that seem to them more relevant and authentic. More and more citizens mistrust mainstream media in the same way that they mistrust any other established authorities (Kiousis 2001). Platforms such as YouTube, Facebook and countless blogs have emerged as important sources of information that supplement and even replace mainstream media, thereby undermining the agenda-setting power of traditional journalism. With an increasing number of citizens themselves acting as journalists, the collection and interpretation of information is no longer regarded as the exclusive realm of professionals. Newspapers and broadcasters now encourage citizens to contribute to news content by submitting their personal accounts and images of events taken by mobile communication technologies. By including user-generated content in conventional news and related formats, such as talk radio, mainstream media hope to bridge the widening gap between what is perceived as elite-centred, top-down communication and the demands of ordinary citizens for participation and a more truthful representation of their experience in the public domain (Bakker and Paterson 2011). User-generated content probably has more influence on standard news than pervasive phone-in formats might imply, as a growing number of journalists use material from social media platforms as a seismograph for new trends and even as a source of information. However, the remedy might further exacerbate the disease. The accuracy and authenticity of this lay material is often difficult to establish. Uncritical and unaccounted use of user-generated information is therefore a potential threat to one of the cornerstones of journalistic professionalism: objectivity and factual accuracy, without which journalism would lose its moral authority (Tumber and Prentoulis 2012).

Arguably, the financial and credibility crisis of journalism hit media workers in transitional democracies even harder than it did their counterparts in established democracies. Ironically, the collapse of the old order can even have a detrimental effect on the cohesion and professional confidence of journalism in a post-authoritarian society. With the erosion of dominant doctrines of journalism in the aftermath of regime change, the journalistic field diversifies into multiple subcultures that compete with each other for influence, audience support and, ultimately, simple survival. For example, Roudakova (2009) describes the dramatic impact of privatization and the politicization of media ownership on the professional identity of Russian journalists. Based on ethnographic research in Nizhny Novgorod, a regional capital about 250 miles east of Moscow, she found a formerly unified field that was held together by a collective mission of moral and political leadership to be torn apart into 'fragmented alliances between journalists, politicians and money' (ibid.: 418). Especially during election campaigns, these 'centrifugal forces' unfold their destructive energies when journalists have to make tough decisions as to how far they allow themselves to become involved in the power struggles between different parties and candidates. As a consequence of media outlets becoming entrenched in partisan politics, the collective sense of solidarity between journalists broke up, leaving individual journalists exposed to the shifting power balance of the political and economic intrigues in their environment.

Another fault line running through the journalistic field is that between generations. While value conflicts between old and new generations are a fact of life, affecting professional groupings as much as families or communities, post-authoritarian generational frictions often allude to the role someone has played under the old regime, thus taking on a highly moralistic subtext. This division is particularly evident in post-communist countries where the past has created a new social cleavage, a central point of reference for identity formation and social judgements and an incredibly sharp weapon in the political power struggle. Yet conflicts over 'new' and 'old' journalism often run across generations (see Aumente et al. 1999; Dobreva et al. 2011; Pasti 2005). Some 'old' generation journalists who served the previous system remain committed to its ideology and the model of propagandist journalism. Others of the same generation, who were also loyal to the previous system, then changed their professional approach after the downfall of communism, partly as a result of a genuine revision in their way of thinking, partly out of opportunism so as to avoid being disadvantaged in the new environment. And there are also those who have worked in the underground. Their moral integrity can serve as a much-needed beacon of orientation in a world of uncertainty. But the moral high ground they frequently take on, their expressed disappointment, even disgust, with the new state of journalism can also invoke hostility among those who simply struggle to make ends meet. Meanwhile, most of the younger generation who entered journalism after the end of communism take a more pragmatic view and turn to Western role models for guidance. They want to free themselves from the burden of having to fulfil a mission in society and acknowledge that audiences want to be entertained rather than educated by a class of public mandarins.

Another dividing line within post-authoritarian journalism is the emergence of two classes of journalists who have little, if anything, in common. Their contradictory interests often turn journalism into a battlefield with the enemy not only outside (politicians, lobby groups, clerics, etc.), but also within. Coman (2004) distinguishes between an emerging 'media bourgeoisie' and a 'media proletariat'. Even though his analysis focuses on journalism in Romania, similar divisions can also be found in many other new democracies. The 'media bourgeoisie' consists of a small layer of leading journalists who have emerged as media entrepreneurs either by becoming the owners of their media outlets or by acquiring substantial shares therein. Ironically, members of this new class are often 'old' generation journalists who served the autocratic system. By utilizing their close networks with political decision-makers and by taking advantage of the legislative vacuum immediately following the demise of the old regime, they were able to re-establish themselves as part of the elite in the new order. This new media elite is mainly interested in maintaining good relationships with the political class and the corporate world rather than engaging in investigative journalism that is likely to disrupt the flow of influence and money within these elite circles.

In contrast, members of the 'media proletariat' find themselves at the bottom end of the new hierarchy of the journalistic field. They have hardly any say in the news decision process and have to do what they are told in terms of the kind of outputs they deliver, even if this violates their professional values. If members of the 'media proletariat' are lucky enough to secure a contract, the salary on offer is generally not sufficient to support themselves and their families. A growing number of journalists, however, have to work on a freelance basis, which often means accepting whatever commission is offered. Especially in Africa, poor work conditions, low salaries and insufficient professional training impede the work ethics of journalists and the quality of the information they provide. Nyamnjoh (2005: 73) talks about 'hand-to-mouth journalism, if not a journalism of misery'.

The proliferation of media outlets in the early years of the transition that occurred in many new democracies led to a huge growth in the journalistic workforce. In South Africa this was further promoted by various schemes of affirmative action to help a new generation of black journalists enter the profession. However, as the economic crisis of the industry set in, these numbers were no longer sustainable, thus putting further pressure on salaries, job security and working conditions of journalists. In many countries the economic transformations of the profession resulted in a 'juniorization' and feminization of the newsroom, while experienced male journalists were trying to move into more lucrative jobs like PR and political consultancy (for Taiwan, see Rawnsley and Gong 2011; for Africa, see Nyamnjoh 2005: 81–99; Wasserman 2011). Not surprisingly, the reality of working for the media has disillusioned many journalists. Moreover, there is often a marked discrepancy between the ideals of journalism and everyday practices. And instances of bravery and commitment to high-quality information are juxtaposed with unethical behaviour and corruption.

FOCUS: BROWN, RED AND OTHER ENVELOPES: THE HIDDEN STORY OF PAID JOURNALISM

The 'uneasy relationship between money and information' (Roudakova 2008: 51) has been largely overlooked in journalism research to date. Even though studies on media and politics and/or journalistic ethics regularly mention the problem of corruption in journalism, there is little empirical research that would provide a more systematic, let alone comparative, picture of the extent of the problem. Likewise, international NGOs have paid little attention to corruption in journalism. Organizations like Transparency International have mainly focused on state institutions and corrupt business practices, while media advocacy organizations, such as Freedom House, Reporters Without Borders or the Committee to Protect Journalists, see their main aim in the defence of media freedom, but shy away from exposing the wrongdoings of journalists. However, a recent report for the Center for International Media Assistance suggests that corruption in journalism is a pervasive problem worldwide and constitutes the 'dark side' of journalism (Ristow 2010; for Central America, see Rockwell and Janus 2003: 187–212; for Indonesia, see Romano 2003:

150–63; for East Asia, see Lo et al. 2005; for Russia, see Roudakova 2009; for Africa, see *African Communication Research* 2010). Almost all these countries can be categorized as transitional democracies that are in the process of transforming their political and media institutions into effective agents of democratic life.

It would be a mistake, however, to assume that corruption in journalism is a 'third world' problem. For example, the scandal that erupted around Rupert Murdoch's News Corporation revealed an alarming number of unethical activities amongst journalists, ranging from hacking the mobile phones of celebrities, politicians and crime victims to payments to police contacts, the latter leading to the arrest of several senior journalists from the *Sun* tabloid newspaper for alleged bribery (Batty 2012). In the US, Armstrong Williams, a columnist on a conservative newspaper and host of several radio and TV shows, was found to have been paid $240,000 by the Department of Education to regularly cover and promote an educational reform bill, called 'No child left behind', of the Bush government (Ristow 2010: 23). Less spectacular, but widely practised, are the free hotel stays and dinners (so-called 'freebies') offered to Brussels correspondents by the EU in an attempt to boost its notoriously meagre coverage (ibid.).

The examples illustrate different forms of cash flow between journalists and their sources. The News Corp scandal involves so-called 'chequebook journalism', or payments from journalists to public officials in order to obtain access to confidential information. There is a vast grey zone of media paying for leaked documents, exclusive interviews or other kinds of background information, which many editors defend as being necessary for effective investigative journalism. In this constellation it is the journalist or media organization that offers money in exchange for information that would otherwise not be accessible. The value of this information lies in its potential to maximize the economic power of a media organization – e.g., by boosting circulation rates – or to expand its power as a political player – e.g., by affecting the career of politicians or influencing policy decisions. Arguably, only rich media are able to get involved in this kind of collusive money-for-information exchange relationship. In the other examples given above, payments are offered by a source to a journalist with the – in some cases implicit, usually explicit – expectation of receiving favourable coverage in return. This exchange is often labelled 'envelope journalism', referring to the way in which the money is handed over. In this case, it is the source that exercises power through the transfer of money. Even though, as the examples illustrate, journalists in rich industrialized countries are not immune to the temptations of accepting payment for commissioned coverage, envelope journalism is particularly endemic in the developing and democratizing world. It is therefore this form of corruption of journalists that will be the focus of the following paragraphs.

Skjerdal (2010: 367) identifies three typical features of envelope journalism: it takes place on a personal level between source and journalist; it is confidential; and it constitutes an, often unspoken, informal contract that trades money or material goods for publicity. Envelope journalism has become a widespread practice whereby journalists attending press conferences are handed out envelopes containing cash, purportedly to cover their travelling expenses. The framing of the money transfer as acknowledgement of the time and effort journalists have invested to attend the event disguises the expectation of the donor to receive favourable publicity services in return. The word 'soli' that is used in Ghana is even more euphemistic. It derives from 'solidarity' and alludes to a sympathetic, caring gesture by the sponsor. Both the amount of money that is transferred and the degree to which a source can insist on the expected coverage vary across local cultures, and depend on the actors involved and, of course, the agreement that has been settled beforehand.

In many countries 'brown envelopes' ('red envelopes' in China) have become a customary part of source–media relationships. To the extent to which the bribery has lost much of its secrecy, it might well be that its effect has become diluted. Some journalists claim that they are not affected by the payments and still feel free to report issues in an objective way (Skjerdal 2010: 385). However, the cognitive dissonance experienced by individuals who receive bribes even as they attempt to consolidate their reputation as a professional makes it difficult for them to reflect on the real effect the acceptance of favours has on their behaviour. In communication research the third-person effect is a well-known phenomenon according to which people think that persuasive efforts of a communication source influence others, but not themselves. The real effects of envelope journalism are therefore likely to be much bigger than generally admitted. They are also difficult to investigate because bribery and corruption are sensitive issues that require subtle research techniques that allow respondents to save their face when talking about their experiences. In-depth interviews and field observation studies reveal that journalists do indeed feel that the money they have accepted puts pressure on them, and eventually, albeit grudgingly, they generally adhere to the expectations of the 'informal contract' to deliver in the interest of their sponsor. The rules of the 'informal contract' can also have the reverse effect. Journalists who have produced favourable news stories, sometimes even without being prompted by the person or organization covered, demand the payment to which they believe they are entitled, or complain about lower than expected 'remuneration'. In Cameroon, the conflicts over 'gombo' payments are even openly fought out in newspapers (Ndangam 2009: 820).

Whether it is large or small amounts of money that change hands, it is likely that the transaction will affect the content of coverage, if not with immediate effect, then in the long run as the collusive relationship between a source and a journalist or media outlet is established by regular money transfers. Since it is in the interest of the sponsor to preserve the impression that the news content is purely based on journalistic criteria, rather than external obligations created by payments, the source of the content remains obscure, thereby suggesting objectivity to the consumer of the 'news' where, in fact, there is none. Undeclared sponsorship has led to the genre of 'advertorials', a term that combines 'advertisement' and 'editorial', which are purposefully using journalistic style to promote the interests of a clandestine sponsor. The influence of payments can simply involve covering an event, for example a press conference, a speech or meeting, which otherwise, because of their minimal news value, would never make their way into the newspaper or news bulletin. Or the sponsor might be portrayed in a positive light and his or her achievements exaggerated. During election campaigns, in particular, this can become blatant propaganda when both news organizations and individual journalists sell their services to one of the competing candidates or parties.

For successful image management, control over negative information is at least as important as promoting a positive image. It is also more difficult, and hence more costly, to achieve. To avert looming investigations or to counter negative coverage, politicians are willing to pay large sums of money. The many instances of journalists who, in return for payment, have prevented stories of corruption from reaching the front pages sit side by side with instances of investigative reporting where journalists take great risks in order to expose the wrongdoings of powerful figures. An example that stands for many others are the Philippines, where an anti-corruption campaign led by investigative journalists brought down President Estrada and paved the way for democratization. But, as Florentino-Hofileña (2004) shows with regard to the 2004 general election, corruption and paid journalism have now entered democratic politics with particularly distorting consequences for the legitimacy of electoral outcomes.

Things get even nastier when powerful individuals decide that the best way to defend themselves is to damage their opponent. Smear campaigns go beyond giving a negative twist to a piece of information. They often resort to fabricated stories, unverified rumours and deliberately spread misinformation. Pasti (2005) finds that many Russian journalists regard lying as a tool of the trade that has to be accepted in order to remain in business. To get at the negative information needed to launch an attack, many of them are willing to employ all sorts of dubious methods, including hidden cameras or microphones to intrude into the private lives of their victims. Yet the threat posed by negative publicity can be an opportunity for journalists to turn against their sponsors and gain the upper hand in the relationship of mutual dependency. This happens when negative material is produced about powerful figures, like politicians or business leaders, and these people are then blackmailed by the media who offer payment for the story not to be published (Ristow 2010; Roudakova 2008). In Indonesia this has created a subculture of criminals who, by pretending to be journalists ready to publish a damaging story, try to extract money from people who they assume to be vulnerable and able to pay. Romano (2003: 154) notes that this criminal practice would not be possible without the existing unethical behaviour of journalists, because 'people of low moral integrity can infiltrate the arenas of professional practice and exploit the custom of envelope behaviour'.

It is easy to condemn practices of paid coverage, or what some authors have quite drastically called a form of 'prostitution' (Nyamnjoh 2005: 73; Roudakova 2009). However, it is important to understand why and under what circumstances journalists are prepared to accept favours and money in exchange for delivering commissioned content. Even though the transaction takes place between individuals, paid journalism is a structural problem that has to be understood within the cultural and economic contexts in which it occurs.

Evidently, the economic insecurity of members of the 'media proletariat' makes them particularly vulnerable to exploitation and corrupt practices. As with selling fake love, selling fake truth rarely happens voluntarily, but as a last resort when other options to survive fail. Where journalists are poorly paid or, even, do not see any salary for months, accepting envelopes is a way of generating income. Ndangam (2009) observes that a significant number of journalists in Cameroon live entirely on 'gombo' payments and have perfected their strategies to approach potential sponsors. Given the precarious economic situation of many journalists, it does not come as a surprise that initiatives to eradicate envelope journalism are often met with scepticism, even hostility. When, for example, the Indonesian journalists' association AJI launched its anti-bribery campaign, other organizations were reluctant to join and insisted on excluding small gifts and minor payments from the ban (Romano 2003: 160–3).

Poor journalists usually work for poor media. Quality journalism is expensive, whereas simply copying press releases or making up stories fills the news hole at no substantial cost. When facing the alternative of either closing down because of lack of profits or offering their 'advocacy skills' (Roudakova 2008: 44) to political or commercial sponsors, many media outlets choose the latter. However, corruption of journalism is not confined to floundering media enterprises and the poorly paid 'media proletariat'. Star journalists and influential editors with high-end salaries are equally involved, with even larger sums being exchanged. As part of a privileged 'media bourgeoisie', their interests are deeply entrenched with those of other elite groups, and they would go a long way to divert harm from those who are part of their own network of influence and with whom they have often become friendly. Journalists employed by media whose editors and/or owners are part of established elite networks are automatically drawn into the rules and constraints of these interdependencies. Thus, envelope journalism is not just an economic problem, but – like any other form of corruption – is rooted in the social fabric and the cultural values and customs of a society.

Corruption in journalism is particularly rife in societies that are built on strong patron–client relationships and where huge levels of income inequality leave large parts of the population, including well-educated and professional groups like journalists, but also white-collar civil servants and small traders, on the verge of poverty. Clientelistic social relationships constitute the primacy of vertical personal relationships over institutionalized procedures and horizontal, associational forms of collective action as a means of pursuing economic or political interests. They are based on the principle of reciprocity and individual dependency that provide the cement for the durability of social relationships. The exchange of money between a patron and a client-journalist can therefore be seen as part of this system of mutual responsibilities that is believed eventually to benefit both sides. As one Cameroonian journalist puts it, 'gombo means helping me to help you' (Ndangam 2009: 826).

Since bribes are framed as gifts, it would be seen as grossly impolite not to accept them. Thus, for a journalist to reject the money offered to him or her by a patron would not only violate the unwritten rules of reciprocity; it is also regarded as an open offence that challenges the status and assumed benevolent intentions of the patron. Especially in Asian societies that put much emphasis on face-saving social rituals, the refusal of a brown envelope 'gift' would most probably lead to a breakdown of the relationship, leaving the journalist without access to vital sources. Moreover, the refusal to accept the 'gift' signals moral superiority over all those who are taking part in the system of exchange and is therefore often greeted by fellow-journalists with hostility rather than admiration.

Nevertheless, many journalists would prefer to opt out of the system of 'brown envelopes' if they could count on support from their superiors and peers. This is because the purported benefits come at a price. For one, the relationship established by 'cash for coverage' exchanges is by no means one of equal give and take. It is a hierarchical relationship of dependency that puts the interests of the patron above accepted norms of journalistic truth. Bribes are therefore deeply humiliating for the journalist at the receiving end. Furthermore, even though individual journalists might live in a cultural context that is shaped by patronage, they also see themselves as members of a wider, even global, community of professionals. The transition to democratic rule and freedom of the press has instilled in them the hope that they can at last practise their profession without being pressurized by external powers. Being trapped in systems of deference and reciprocity, which forces them to produce dodgy news stories, leaves them in a permanent state of moral tension that eventually breeds disillusionment and cynicism.

Besides the obvious need to improve the material situation of journalists, press codes, ombudsmen in newsrooms and ethical training are important ways to overcome the entrenched culture of envelope journalism. But their effectiveness is bound to be limited because they focus on only one side of the exchange relationship. The donors of 'brown envelopes' are just as dependent on the collusive arrangements with journalists, even though they are usually the ones in control of the conditions. To address the problem of corruption in journalism, it is therefore important to also consider the reasons why powerful figures engage in bribery. Some observers suggest that envelope journalism has increased following the liberalization of markets and the introduction of electoral politics (Ristow 2010; Skjerdal 2010). The juxtaposition of liberal markets and democratization, both of which are regarded as processes of modernization, and the relapse into essentially pre-modern practices of patronage seem to be counterintuitive. However, several reasons might be responsible for these seemingly contradictory developments. Particularly in post-communist countries, the liberalization of markets had a massive, if not traumatic, impact on society. Since it was rarely supported by adequate legislation and law-enforcement mechanisms, the privatization of state assets and the introduction of competitive prices pushed large parts of the population into poverty, while others became incredibly rich within an incredibly short period of time, often by using dubious methods in the grey zones of legality. Not only did the post-communist *nouveaux riches* have a lot to hide, which makes them extremely vulnerable to the investigative activities of journalists; they also had a lot of money to spend on bribing journalists to stay away from their affairs. Many of the journalists killed in Russia over the past years by contract killers in the service of powerful business figures were engaged in uncovering their criminal activities. An easier and less risky way of controlling publicity is to buy individual journalists or entire media outlets.

For politicians, the uncertainties of democratic politics have also created an increased need for news management. In addition, many of the newly elected leaders have used their office to amass privileges and wealth. The list of corrupt, democratically elected leaders is depressingly long, ranging from provincial governors to heads of states. Like their counterparts in business, they have to fear a free and adversarial press. Yet with crude censorship no longer available, post-authoritarian politicians have to employ other methods to control the flow of information. Even if a politician does not have anything to hide, he or she depends on the media to create a favourable public image in order to be successful in the political arena. Some authors suggest that envelope journalism is used as a substitute by politicians who are unable, or unwilling, to invest in developing a professional communication strategy and in building sustainable relationships with the media (Ristow 2010; Romano 2003). In other words, paying journalists is seen as an easier and cheaper way of dealing with the media and influencing public opinion than investing in institutional communication capacity.

There is a third party involved in the relationship between politicians, or political institutions, and the media: public relations organizations. As intermediaries who manage the relationship with the media, they often handle the cash transfer between politicians or political organizations and journalists, thereby inevitably becoming part of the collusive relationship. In many cases this also involves dealing with the demands of journalists for their 'services' of producing favourable coverage or blocking negative information. It is probably for this reason that the initiative to address corruption in journalism worldwide came from an organization representing public relations professionals, IPRA (International Public Relations Association; www.ipra.org). In 2001 the organization launched a Campaign for Media Transparency. Fearing that corrupt practices of manipulating public communication would, arguably, eventually undermine their own reputation and professionalism, the PR industry decided to clean up its business. The IPRA Campaign for Media Transparency was later joined by major media development organizations, like the International Center for Journalists and Internews. However, as Ristow (2010: 24) observes, the initiative has, more recently, lost momentum and not much action has been taken. Meanwhile, two scholars of public relations developed indicators for measuring 'cash for news coverage' and ran the first survey among journalists cross-nationally to investigate the extent of paid journalism (Kruckeberg and Tsetsura 2003; Tsetsura and Kruckeberg 2012).

Corruption in the media has immense implications for both journalistic professionalism and the prospects of democratization. If professionalism in journalism is constituted by adherence to ethical norms of practice and autonomy from external powers, then it is obvious that 'cash for (non-)coverage' undermines both. As Coman (2004: 48) puts it with regard to the situation in Romania, the disrespect of professional standards has brought about 'journalists without journalism'. However, democracies, and even more so emerging democracies, need professional media. In order to prevent democracy from deteriorating into electoral authoritarianism, it depends on a multi-layered system of checks and balances that includes the media. Yet by engaging in collusive relationships with patrons seeking to manipulate public opinion, journalists lose their moral authority to scrutinize the dealings of those in power and to act as watchdogs on behalf of the citizens. Ultimately, weak media not only prevent democratic institutions from working properly, they also disempower citizens who do not receive the information they need to exercise their rights as voters in a meaningful way.

Another victim of envelope journalism is trust. While authoritarian regimes can rely on fear instilled by the brute force of power, democracy and the rule of law cannot work without a solid basis of trust when it comes to social, economic and political relationships: trust between citizens that everybody respects the needs and rights of others; trust of citizens in their representatives that they will use their office to the benefit of the country; and trust in the media that they provide a fair and reliable account of what is going on in politics. Broken trust is a major reason for cynicism and withdrawal from public life. The response of the Russian public to the murder of the journalist Anna Politkovskaya sheds some unsettling light on the consequences of lost trust in the media. Politkovskaya was shot dead on her doorstep on 7 October 2006, most probably because of her fearless investigations into the dirty politics of the Chechen War. Unlike in the West, there was very little public outcry about this crime in Russia. Roudakova (2009: 422) explains this silence by the bad image journalists have acquired in that country. With widespread corruption in journalism and most media outlets serving the interests of political or economic groups, citizens have grown used to a 'discourse of journalism as "prostitution" or "selling out"'. In the end they were unable to distinguish between those who sacrifice truth for material gains and those, like Politkovskaya, who had preserved her personal and professional integrity.

Conclusion

The wave of democratization that started at the end of the twentieth century and continues to unfold in the early decades of the twenty-first century takes place at a unique historical juncture of different global trends. Since the end of the Cold War new geopolitical constellations have been emerging that challenge the hegemony of the West in world politics. At the same time, democratic politics in established Western democracies is showing signs of fatigue and disorientation. Existing institutions of governance have repeatedly demonstrated their inability to solve the pressing problems of modern societies, like controlling financial markets, reversing global warming or reducing poverty. Large numbers of citizens in Western democracies have therefore turned their back on institutional politics to engage in new forms of political action outside the established channels of participation. Nevertheless, the democratic ideas of popular decision-making, individual freedom and a government that is accountable to its citizens continue to inspire people around the world, even though the role models for how to do democracy are no longer exclusively sought in Western democracies. As a consequence, it is not only world politics but also democracy itself that is likely to be less 'Western' in the future.

Coinciding with these trends, a communication revolution is taking place that fundamentally changes the way in which governments communicate with citizens, how citizens learn about and interpret politics and how political participation is organized. It started in the mid-1980s when the proliferation of audiovisual media outlets transformed a relatively static mediascape into a multi-channel environment. While this new plurality of channels increased the choice of citizens/consumers to select their sources of information – or to opt out of politics altogether – it also increased the uncertainty of political actors who were no longer able to target and control their messages as they had under the previous conditions of channel scarcity. An even more fundamental communication revolution was unleashed when in the mid-1990s the internet became available to the general public. The World Wide Web, especially Web 2.0 with its interactive tools and social networking software, created new spaces of communication and new opportunities for citizen empowerment and grassroot mobilization. Linking these devices with mobile communication technologies and smart phones then helped to spread the use of the internet even to regions where poor infrastructure had excluded large parts of the population from benefiting from the digital revolution. But amidst all the euphoria about these new communication technologies it must not be forgotten that they also provide authoritarian governments with new sophisticated tools of control and surveillance. The same technology that helps to mobilize resistance is also employed to suppress it.

These two phases of the communication revolution at the turn of the new millennium not only orchestrated the transitions of the new democracies that emerged during this time; they became an integral part of these transitions by shaping the behaviour of the actors involved and thus their eventual outcomes. Unlike the democracies of previous waves, the new democracies of the 'third wave' are directly leapfrogging into a condition of democratic politics that has been labelled 'media democracy', where political decision-making and democratic participation are inextricably intertwined with, and dependent on, the media of mass communication, both traditional and new.

This book provides a conceptual introduction to media and communication in processes of democratic transitions. By drawing on the experience of new democracies from around the world, the book takes a global perspective that allows for a more comparative understanding of the power, but also the limitations, of the media to serve as agents of democratization. Two major areas of inquiry guide the analysis of this book. The first is concerned with the impact of the media on the processes and outcomes of democratization. The second addresses the transformation of the media themselves and the question as to how successful the attempts are at recasting the media from servants of authoritarian power into independent democratic institutions.

Any discussion of media and democratization is embedded in a framework of norms and values that define our understanding of a functioning democracy and what kind of performance we expect from the media. Both politics and journalism are practices that are steeped in norms and ideals, and when either of them fails it is mostly because they fail to act according to these norms. Equally, the scholarly debate about democratization is guided by a set of normative assumptions that serve as a reference point when evaluating the quality and success of the newly emerging democracies. By and large, the verdict of the democratization literature on most new democracies is negative, which raises the question as to how valid the norms are that underlie these evaluations as universal standards for a functioning democracy. If, for example, liberal democracy as practised in established Western democracies is regarded as a yardstick, then the variations that can be observed across new democracies can only be interpreted as deviances. If press freedom is regarded as an absolute value that derives from other human rights such as freedom of expression, then any restrictions on the media must be regarded as a threat to the independence of the media. And if objectivity is seen as an indispensable ingredient of professional journalism, then surely the majority of media around the world fail to produce the desired quality of information.

In order to unpack these debates, Part I of this book set out to explore the norms that guide our understanding of a 'good' democracy and what we mean by media independence and media diversity. The two chapters of Part I aimed to challenge the norms of liberal democracy and unrestricted press freedom that dominate large parts of the literature in the field. However, the alternative to the hegemony of these discourses does not lie in proposing new normative models to replace the existing ones. Rather, it is argued that norms relating to democracy and the media are ambiguous, fluid and contextual. The chapters suggest understanding democracy and press freedom as social constructs that are interpreted in the contexts of existing cultural premises and values and hence take on very different meanings and forms. Even though norms of media independence and media diversity are the core of democratic media theories, these norms are practised in different ways depending on historical experiences, cultural traditions and – last, but not least – situational constraints that arise from the complexities of the transition itself.

The chapters of Part II introduced a set of conceptual tools that help to understand the way in which the media can play a democratizing role and under what circumstances this is likely to happen. One conceptual distinction we have to make is that between the media as communication technologies and the media as journalistic agency. Of course, these two dimensions are closely interrelated, but each of them – technologies and agency – can have independent and sometimes contradictory consequences for political and social developments. Communication technologies provide both opportunity structures and constraints for political actors. But they can also set in motion developments that are outside the intentions of their creators and those who are using them. One of the consequences of the innovations in communication technologies over the last couple of decades is the acceleration of political processes, which has increased the pressure on political decision-makers and activists to constantly readjust their actions to suit a 24/7 stream of information. Communication technologies have also been a driving force in the globalization of democratization that used to be a predominantly national affair. Thus, uprisings in one country quickly spread to others and capture the attention of a global audience. However, the 'demonstration effects' of transnational communication through broadcasting and the internet have different consequences in different situational constellations. In some cases, they have played out to the advantage of activist groups struggling for democratic change; in others, demonstration effects have hardened the determination of authoritarian leaders to cling on to power.

Journalistic agency dominates the operation of the traditional media press and broadcasting. The notion of media as journalistic agency suggests that the media are not, by nature, a democratic institution. Rather, it is the decisions of individual journalists or media organizations that make them either a mouthpiece of an authoritarian regime or a force for democratic change. Their decisions on what issues to cover and how to frame them have a significant impact on public opinion and the standing of a government. Political power struggles, whether in authoritarian or democratic systems, are therefore also always struggles for winning over the support of influential media.

Another argument made in Part II is that the role of the media during democratic transition is not uniform throughout the process. Even though democratization is not a one-way process and often resembles more of a circle than a straight line, the distinction between different phases of the transition is a useful heuristic to understand the interaction between media and democratic change over time. In particular, the struggle for democratic opening under an authoritarian regime and the period of consolidation after the fall of the old regime require the media to play different roles that require different journalistic practices.

Many authoritarian regimes – though not all – experience a certain level of liberalization and a relaxation of censorship, which tends to be initiated from above with the aim of stabilizing the system in the face of growing popular discontent. Top-down liberalization often triggers divisions amongst the ruling elites into hardliners and reformers. Some of the official media take the opportunity to side with the reformist course because it promises more journalistic and economic autonomy. However, others decide to support the conservative faction. Hence, the elite divisions are reflected and magnified by the media, thus opening a Pandora's box that can be difficult to control. Liberalization from below is driven by clandestine opposition movements that create their own media as a platform to express their ideas and to mobilize support. Even more important is the role of dissident media in strengthening the organizational ties of opposition groups. Like their mainstream counterparts, dissident media are highly partisan, one-sided and opinionated. In fact, in the struggle against the regime, objectivity as a journalistic norm would make little sense. In recent years social media like Facebook and Twitter have played a spectacular role in mobilizing anti-regime movements. These social network platforms allow large numbers of people to exchange ideas and to coordinate political action within very short periods of time. However, in spite of the central role that Web 2.0 technologies have played in recent democracy movements, internet-based mobilization seems to be less efficient when it comes to building sustainable organizational structures, effective leadership and a coherent policy agenda – all key elements for success in negotiating the transition with the old elites and leading the way after the demise of the old regime.

Even though the media are an indispensable part of a functioning democracy, their role in consolidating and deepening the young democracy can often be rather ambivalent. Democratic politics in a 'media democracy' opens up new opportunities, but also bears new risks. The expanded communication environment provides citizens with new channels to get their voices heard and to use their newly acquired participation rights. But the immediacy of citizen demands and the acceleration of political decision-making can also overstretch the capacities of the new post-authoritarian governments to manage change, thereby potentially increasing the fragility of transitional democracies. The omnipresence of the media can also be an obstacle for successful institution-building, in particular the development of political parties, which are crucial for a healthy democracy. In many new democracies, political leaders prefer to optimize their control over the media as a power resource in electoral contests rather than taking the long, but more sustainable, route towards building an effective party organization that can serve as a channel of communication between political leaders and constituencies. Media-centred politics in new democracies can result in a vicious circle, as governments and political parties that are dependent on the media for securing their power positions are unlikely to give up control over this precious power resource. As a consequence, 'media wars' between competing political camps over the control of the media, in particular the main television channels, are a notorious feature of new democracies and seriously undermine the independence of the media.

The final chapter of Part II compares the media's role in democratic transitions across four different regions of the world where the majority of the 'third wave' democratization movements took place: Latin America, Eastern Europe, East Asia and Africa. Each of these geopolitical regions was dominated by a particular type of authoritarianism (although there are, of course, overlaps), each of which created distinct pathways of democratic change. The theory of path dependency emphasizes continuity as a force that accompanies even the most dramatic regime changes. Thus, the particular features of the old regime still resonate in the democracies and the media systems that succeeded them. Revolutionary rhetoric frequently employed by democracy activists disguises the degree to which the old regime continues to shape the emerging democratic order: old elites reappear in new roles, democratic politics takes place within existing institutions that are rarely fundamentally restructured after regime change, often even simply left as they are, and the values and norms passed on by socialization continue to shape the behaviour and interactions of the individuals who are working in these institutions. Continuity in terms of institutional structure and professional performance also characterizes the transformation of the media. This is not to say that there is a deterministic relationship between the past and the present. Post-authoritarian actors who are involved in the transition process make decisions that break with the past and create political realities that are genuinely new. But they do not start from scratch. Rather, the emerging democratic order constitutes a unique juxtaposition of the old and the new. Hence, understanding the way in which the preceding old regime worked and the role the media were playing in its power structure helps to explain the vast variations between the new democracies of the 'third wave'.

The new democracies of the late twentieth and early twenty-first century emerged from four main authoritarian regime types: military dictatorship (dominant in Latin America), communist one-party rule (Eastern Europe), one-party rule in contexts of statism (East Asia), and personalized one-party rule in contexts of weak state institutions (sub-Saharan Africa). The media systems of these ideal-typical regimes differed significantly with regard to their relationship to political power, their ideological role and their economic resources. Depending on how important ideology was for the regime to legitimize itself, the degree to which the media were exploited as a propaganda tool varied and so, consequently, did the degree of censorship and control. This was particularly the case under communist rule, where the media were central to the regime's policy of mass mobilization and re-education of the masses. Censorship was less pressing where regimes built their power on demobilization and acquiescence of the masses, as in Latin America – at least as long as the media refrained from addressing sensitive issues that had the potential to challenge the existing power structure. The 'development dictatorships' of East Asia fall somewhere in between, as the media were expected to promote the ambitious development agenda of their governments. The media's role in the old regime often translates into a particular self-perception of journalists in the new democratic environment. For example, in post-communist Eastern Europe journalists still see themselves primarily as opinion leaders and ideological and moral guides in their country's journey towards democracy rather than as 'mere' chroniclers of events.

The degree to which the media benefited from the old regime as an industry also varied considerably. The authoritarian regimes in East Asia and many military dictatorships in Latin America invested large resources in their media industries and the communication infrastructures of their countries. As a consequence, the media industries of these regions are now characterized by strong oligopolistic conglomerates that dominate their national, frequently regional, in some cases even global, markets. But the media also inherited a close-knit network of relationships between media owners and political elites (Latin America) or the state bureaucracy (East Asia), which keeps them vulnerable to falling prey to the political and economic interests of powerful elites. Post-communist media industries and those in sub-Saharan Africa emerged from the authoritarian past considerably weakened, albeit for different reasons. Since communist regimes nationalized all privately owned assets, the media of these countries were under the direct economic control of the government or associated organizations. Thus, post-communist transformation of the media involved not only disentangling the relationship between state and the media, but also rebuilding an entire industry, which still remains relatively weak and, to a large extent, dependent on foreign investment. The economic weakness of African media today has its roots in the general underdevelopment of the region, which is further exacerbated by political mismanagement and widespread corruption. Due to the lack of sustainable revenues, many media organizations in Africa are still dependent on state subsidies and, as a result, are exposed to political instrumentalization and interference into editorial decision-making.

The four chapters that make up Part III of this book cover the main areas of transformation of the media after the end of authoritarian rule: (1) their relationship with the state, (2) the economy of the media industry, (3) the media's relationship with group interests and ideological divisions, and (4) journalistic professionalism itself. Based on Hallin and Mancini's (2004) models of media systems, these four dimensions capture the multiple challenges involved in transforming the media into democratic institutions. Since the media are embedded in a complex web of interdependencies with their environment, democratizing the media goes far beyond restructuring media organizations. It also requires the political, economic and societal environment to become more democratic. In other words, the media can only fulfil their democratic functions if the state is committed to democratic governance, if the markets are effective in providing the resources for quality journalism, and if citizens/audiences are willing to engage in an open and tolerant public debate. However, as the chapters of Part III demonstrate, there is a long way to go. And it should be emphasized that even in established democracies media systems expose many deficiencies which at times question their ability to fulfil their democratic functions.

The most contested relationship of the media in emerging democracies is that with the state. Given the experience of the past authoritarian regime, the state is seen as the main perpetrator and hence freedom of the press is mainly understood as freedom from state influence. However, democracy and a free press are only possible in a functioning state. For it is the key state institutions – government, parliament, judiciary – that have the power to implement and enforce an environment that enables the media to act as effective agenda-setters and watchdogs of political power. However, post-authoritarian governments are frequently unable or unwilling to provide this environment. In this respect, a weak state can be as much of a problem as a dominant state. In many new democracies the main threat to press freedom and to lives of journalists comes not from the state, but from mafia-like groups, drug cartels, militias or religious groups that operate outside the reach of the state. At the same time, many governments are tightening their grip on the media again by passing new restrictive laws or by interpreting existing legislation – most notably state security regulation and libel laws – in a way that works to the disadvantage of an open and critical public debate.

Commercialization of the media is widely regarded as a way of safeguarding their independence from state interference. In many instances it does. But the particular logic of the economy of the media invariably leads to high levels of concentration with only a few big companies controlling the market. Oligopolistic market structures, together with the media's dependence on advertising, systematically reduce the diversity of voices that are represented on the media agenda. Moreover, competition and price pressures frequently lead to media companies cutting down on investigative journalism that is essential for the media's role as watchdogs of political power. It needs political will – i.e., government action – to set up structures that shield some segments of the media from the detrimental forces of the market, for example public service broadcasting or community media. However, in many new democracies the state and the market are not two regulatory alternatives, but forces that have grown together into a politico-media oligopolistic power centre. Especially where the preceding authoritarian regime actively supported the growth of a strong media industry, political office and media ownership are frequently combined as mutually reinforcing resources of influence. Media ownership is used to exert pressure on government decision-making through the mobilization of public opinion, while politicians use the media they, or close allies or family members, own to exclude their opponents from the media agenda. Thus, commercial media are not necessarily independent media. What is needed are mechanisms of ownership transparency and rules to curb the political power of media ownership, which is far more difficult to achieve than simply privatizing the media industry.

In virtually all new democracies the majority of media, especially newspapers, endorse particular parties or group interests – be they ethnic, regional or religious – in their coverage of political matters. By reflecting and reinforcing these worldviews, alliances between individual media and particular groups establish patterns of 'parallelism' between the media and their social and political environment. Thus, while objective reporting is widely regarded as the professional model of journalism, partisanship is obviously the more common and more successful model. Partisanship and advocacy also dominate most political communication spaces on the internet. Hardly any blogger, discussion forum or Facebook group aims to be neutral. And this is what users seem to be looking out for. Partisan media – whether online or offline – can play an important role in strengthening civil society and in offering citizens guidance during the turbulences of transition. By presenting political information through the lens of a particular worldview, partisan media provide an interpretation of what is going on in politics that makes sense to their audience. Biased information is mobilizing information that can encourage citizens to get involved in politics and to establish durable ties with political parties or other civil society groups. But there is a dark side to it. In numerous cases partisan media have been one of the driving forces in the outbreak of interethnic or interreligious conflicts. In those new democracies that have emerged from violent group conflicts or that are struggling to keep existing conflicts under control, parallelism can be a destabilizing factor. The experience of divided societies raises fundamental questions about the boundaries of press freedom and freedom of expression in volatile situations. In these circumstances the notion of freedom of the press as a right that protects the whole communication process, i.e. both the speaker and the listener, is an important normative principle used to reflect on what can be said and what cannot be said in public. In order to maintain the inclusiveness of the public debate, political parallelism of the media has to be moderated by respect for the opponent, otherwise it can quickly become the breeding ground for group hostility, intolerance and even violence.

The dimension of political parallelism of the media is closely related to the fourth area of democratizing the media: the transformation of journalism itself. The consequences of the communication revolutions of past decades and the economic crises frequently following the breakdown of the authoritarian regime hit journalists and their work particularly hard. As media organizations cut down on staff and salaries, fewer resources are available for producing high-quality information. In these circumstances, partisanship is not so much a matter of choice, but of scarcity: opinion journalism is cheap; fact-based investigative journalism is expensive and time-consuming. Poor economic conditions are also one of the reasons why 'envelope journalism' is endemic in many new democracies, in particular, but not exclusively, in the developing world.

Essential to the transformation of journalism is the adoption of new professional ethics and performance norms to ensure that the media fulfil their democratic roles. Media assistance organizations usually expect journalists to adopt the Anglo-Saxon model of journalism that emphasizes political detachment and adversarialism. However, many journalists in emerging democracies argue that this model does not sufficiently take into account the particular social and political circumstances of their countries. As a response, various alternative models of journalism have emerged, amongst others so-called development journalism. Indigenous forms of journalism help the media to respond to audience needs, but they may also serve as an excuse for complacency about existing social hierarchies.

Overall, the 'third wave' of democratization has brought about not only a large 'divergence of democracy', but also a large divergence of media systems and forms of journalism. This new diversity poses a number of theoretical, empirical and normative challenges on future research on media and communication. More conceptual efforts of 'de-Westernizing' research are needed to understand the emerging hybridity of media practices in their specific political, social and cultural contexts. There is also need for more comparative research. Moving beyond single country or regional research will be important to a better understanding of the origins and forms of different media institutions and journalistic practices and their consequences for deepening democracy after the end of authoritarian rule.

Notes

Chapter 1 Democracy and Democratization: One Idea, Many Roads

1 I am referring here to the institutionalized democracy of the West, which has its origin in ancient Greece and later took on the form of representative liberal democracy that is now recognized as the standard model of democratic governance. Democratic forms of decision-making also developed outside this tradition, often referred to as 'primitive democracy', in virtually all regions of the world, including the Near East, India, Nordic and Slavic societies and tribal societies in Africa. However, in most cases these indigenous forms of democracy were overshadowed by autocratic forms of political power and never developed into institutional structures that were suitable for governing complex nation-states (Dahl 2000: 5–25; Robinson 1997).
2 For example, Lijphart (1984) distinguishes between 'majoritarian-' and 'consensus-'oriented forms of democratic government. While the former is generally characterized by centralized and effective power structures and a more competitive style of politics, the latter emphasizes power-sharing and the culture of compromise as principles of democratic decision-making. Depending on their preferences for one of the options on the majoritarian–consensus continuum, Western democracies have developed a wide scope of variation in their institutional and cultural pattern.
3 For a more detailed discussion of the problem of media pluralism and political parallelism in post-conflict societies, see the 'Focus' section in Chapter 8.

Chapter 2 Democratic Media: A Question of Means and Ends

1 This is not to say that Asian and African cultures are essentially collectivist and Western cultures essentially individualistic. Both elements exist in all these contexts. But the emphasis that is put on either the individual or the collective end of the dimension varies.
2 But see the problem of political ownership in the 'Focus' section of Chapter 7.
3 See the 'Focus' section in Chapter 8 for a more detailed discussion of media in post-conflict societies.
4 See Chapter 7 for a more detailed discussion of media markets.
5 See the 'Focus' section in Chapter 6 for a discussion of establishing public service broadcasting in Eastern Europe.

Chapter 3 Communication Technologies and Journalistic Agency: Mass Media and Political Change

1 For a detailed discussion of historical legacies and their impact on media systems emerging after the end of authoritarian rule, see Chapter 5.

Chapter 4 Complex Transitions and Uncertain Outcomes: The Media and Democratization Over Time

1 As noted in the introduction, the term 'transition' is used in this book in a broad way to encompass the whole process of change from authoritarian to democratic rule. Labels of different stages of the democratization process differ amongst authors. In the absence of terminological consensus, all that can be done is to make it clear what particular terms mean in the present context.
2 Based on round-table negotiations, the Polish government agreed on partially free parliamentary elections with two-thirds of the seats reserved for candidates of the Communist Party and its close allies. Solidarnosz candidates won all the remaining open seats, causing a political crisis that marked the end of communist rule in Poland.
3 For political ownership, see the 'Focus' section in Chapter 7; for the struggle of post-authoritarian journalism in Russia and elsewhere to establish independent professional standards, see Chapter 9.
4 Realizing that it was impossible to suppress the use of Western broadcasting, the main television channel of the GDR launched a weekly

programme, 'The Black Channel' ('Der schwarze Kanal') whose mission was to rebuke and challenge the daily news content of West German coverage. The programme attracted hardly any audience in the GDR, but was popular amongst students in the West – for entertainment purposes.

5 This assumption draws on social movement research and the concept of political opportunity structure that describes the preconditions that encourage participation in public protest (see Kitschelt 1986; McAdam et al. 2001). The theory suggests that political grievances have to be politicized – i.e., perceived as shared with others and mobilized by political entrepreneurs to develop into organized political action. Even though this research focuses on protest movements in established democracies, the assumptions can also be employed for understanding dissident movements in authoritarian regimes.

6 The text of the press release stated that the usual requirements for permission to travel to a Western country (e.g., being retired, family emergency, etc.) were no longer valid. However, the press release mentioned both 'permanent travel', which meant without return, and 'travel', which could be interpreted as permission to travel to a Western country without losing the right to come back to the GDR. Schabowski was also obviously confused about when this new regulation would become effective. The Politburo had scheduled it for 10 November after sufficient border controls had been put into place. But when Schabowski was asked at the press conference about the timing he responded that it would be with immediate effect ('nach meiner Kenntnis ist das sofort, unverzüglich'; see Hertle 1996: 145). An English transcript of this press conference can be found at the Cold War International History Project virtual archive (CWIHP).

7 For a detailed discussion of corruption in journalism, see the 'Focus' section in Chapter 9.

8 Existing large-scale comparative surveys, such as Afrobarometer (see www.afrobarometer.org), Latinobarometer (see www.latinobarometro.org) or the New Democracies Barometer (hosted by the Centre for the Study of Public Policy, University of Aberdeen, UK; see www.abdn.ac.uk/cspp) which focuses on post-communist countries in Eastern Europe, are primarily concerned with political attitudes and voting but do not include sufficient information about people's media use. The World Values Survey (see www.worldvaluessurvey.org) has only recently started also to include media variables (see Norris and Inglehart 2010).

Chapter 5 Emerging Media Systems and the Legacies of the Past

1 Conceptual elements of Hallin and Mancini's comparative framework will be used in Part III of this book to analyse emerging media systems in post-authoritarian democracies. Meanwhile, a follow-up edited volume focuses on democracies beyond the Western world (Hallin and Mancini 2012). While the volume includes a collection of analyses of mostly new democracies, it does not suggest a coherent typology.

2 Nepal and Bhutan are examples of the few cases where democracy emerged from monarchic rule, even though it has to be noted that in both cases the democratization process is still uncertain.

Chapter 6 Media and the State

1 The term 'state' is understood as the set of institutions through which power is exercised in a society. Even though the state is not the only source of power and social influence, in modern societies it is only the state that has the authority to make decisions that are binding on all members of a society. Most of the discussion here focuses on the national government as the most central institution of political power in modern societies.

2 It has to be noted that criminal libel and defamation laws are not the exclusive problem of authoritarian countries and new democracies. For example, the UK abolished its criminal libel law only in 2010, and France is presently in the process of reviewing the situation.

3 The government's ambitions go way beyond media policy. A new electoral law guarantees Fidesz's dominance in local elections, while the independence of the Hungarian central bank and the competencies of the constitutional court have been cut back.

4 In an article for *The European* Mong (2011) describes the chilling effect of the new media law that could already be felt in the newsrooms of both broadcasters and the printed press. He states that 'public media resemble more and more a propaganda machine, where loyalty to the government is a must'. Equally, editors of newspapers tell their staff to be extremely careful, i.e., to stay away from sensitive and risky issues, to avoid fines.

5 In this connection it is worth mentioning that in East Germany, too, public service broadcasting achieves significantly lower audience shares than commercial channels, while in the western part of the

country the two public channels attract the lion's share of viewers. In East Germany the former state television of the GDR was entirely dismantled and replaced by the West German public service channels ARD and ZDF. So their reputation is marred neither by their former role under dictatorship nor by a loss of credibility because of present politicization. It seems that all post-communist audiences share a certain dislike of any form of political education and use television primarily as a source of entertainment.

Chapter 7 Media Markets

1 See Chapter 5 for a more detailed discussion of path dependency and the transformation of the media.
2 For a non-market-based reading of Mill's metaphor of 'marketplace of ideas', see Chapter 2.
3 The military coup in March 2012 and the loss of control over large parts of its northern territory have plunged Mali into political instability that threatens its fragile democracy and, with it, the remarkable achievements in freedom of expression and the press of the last two decades.
4 For a more detailed discussion of corruption in journalism, see the 'Focus' section in Chapter 9.

References

Abbott, J.P. (2001) 'Democracy@internet.asia? The challenges to the emancipatory potential of the net: Lessons from China and Malaysia.' *Third World Quarterly* 22(1), 99–114.

Abts, K. and S. Rummens (2007) 'Populism versus democracy.' *Political Studies* 55(2), 405–424.

African Communication Research (2010) Special issue: 'Bribery and corruption in African journalism.' Available at: http://ccms.ukzn.ac.za/index.php?option=com_content&task=category§ionid=5&id=77&Itemid=103 (accessed October 2012).

Agh, A. (2001) 'Early consolidation and performance crisis: The majoritarian-consensus democracy debate in Hungary.' *West European Politics* 24(3), 89–112.

Albuquerque, A. de (2005) 'Another "Fourth Branch". Press and political culture in Brazil.' *Journalism* 6(4), 486–504.

Allen, T. and N. Stremlau (2005) 'Media policy, peace and state reconstruction.' Crisis States Discussion Paper #8. London: LSE Crisis States Development Research Centre. Available at: http://eprints.lse.ac.uk/28347/ (accessed October 2012).

Almond, G.A. and S. Verba (1963) *The Civic Culture: Political Attitudes and Democracy in Five Nations*. Princeton, NJ: Princeton University Press.

Amaral, R. (2002) 'Mass media in Brazil: Modernization to prevent change.' In E. Fox and S. Waisbord (eds), *Latin Politics, Global Media*. Austin: University of Texas Press, 38–46.

Anderson, B. (1983) *Imagined Communities. Reflections on the Origins and Spread of Nationalism*. London: Verso.

Anderson, C.J., A. Blais, S. Bowler, T. Donovan and O. Listhaug (2005) *Losers' Consent. Elections and Democratic Legitimacy*. Oxford: Oxford University Press.

Arblaster, A. (1994) *Democracy*, 2nd edn. Ballmoor: Open University Press.

Article 19: Global Campaign for Free Expression (2006) *The Impact of UK Anti-Terror Laws on Freedom of Expression*. Submission to ICJ Panel of eminent jurists on terrorism, counter-terrorism and human rights. London: Article 19. Available at: http://www.article19.org/data/files/pdfs/analysis/terrorism–submission–to–icj–panel.pdf (accessed 14 September 2012).

Aumente, J., P. Gross, R. Hiebert, O.V. Johnson and D. Mills (1999) *Eastern European Journalism. Before, During and After Communism*. Cresskill, NJ: Hampton Press.

Baker, E.C. (2007) *Media Concentration and Democracy: Why Ownership Matters*. Cambridge: Cambridge University Press.

Bakker, T. and C. Paterson (2011) 'The new frontiers of journalism: Citizen participation in the United Kingdom and the Netherlands.' In K. Brants and K. Voltmer (eds), *Political Communication in Postmodern Democracy. Challenging the Primacy of Politics*. Basingstoke: Palgrave Macmillan, 183–199.

Baldwin, T.F., D.S. McVoy and C. Steinfield (1996) *Convergence: Integrating Media, Information and Communication*. Thousand Oaks, CA: Sage.

Barbassa, J. (2012) 'Brazil freedom of information law passed.' *Huffington Post*, 17 May. Available at: http://www.huffingtonpost.com/2012/05/17/brazil–freedom–of–information_n_1525131.html (accessed October 2012).

Barendt, E. (2005) *Freedom of Speech*, 2nd edn. Oxford: Oxford University Press.

Barrera, C. and R. Zugasti (2006) 'The role of the press in times of transition: The building of the Spanish democracy.' In K. Voltmer (ed.), *Mass Media and Political Communication in New Democracies*. London: Routledge, 23–41.

Bartels, L.M. (1993) 'Message received: The political impact of media exposure.' *American Political Science Review* 87, 267–285.

Batty, D. (2012) 'Senior *Sun* journalists arrested in police payments probe.' *Guardian*, 11 February. Available at: http://www.guardian.co.uk/media/2012/feb/11/sun–journalists–arrested (accessed February 2012).

BBC News online (2011) 'Czech rally demands press freedom.' 4 January. Available at: http://news.bbc.co.uk/1/hi/world/europe/1099028.stm (accessed October 2012).

Bennett, W. L. (1998) 'The media and democratic development: The social basis of political communication.' In P.H. O'Neil (ed.), *Communicating Democracy. The Media and Political Transitions*. Boulder, CO: Lynne Rienner, 195–207.

Berman, B.J. (1998) 'Ethnicity, patronage and the African state: The politics of uncivil nationalism.' *African Affairs* 97(388), 305–341.

Bernhagen, P. (2009a) 'Measuring democracy and democratization.' In C.W. Haerpfer, P. Bernhagen, R.F. Inglehart and C. Welzel (eds), *Democratization*. Oxford: Oxford University Press, 24–40.

Bernhagen, P. (2009b) 'Democracy, business, and the economy.' In C.W. Haerpfer, P. Bernhagen, R.F. Inglehart and C. Welzel (eds), *Democratization*. Oxford: Oxford University Press, 107–125.

Besley, T. and A. Prat (2006) 'Handcuffs for the grabbing hand? Media capture and government accountability.' *American Economic Review* 96(3), 720–736.

Bird, K.L. (2000) 'Racist speech or free speech? A comparison of the law in France and the United States.' *Comparative Politics* 32(4), 399–418.

Blankson, I.A. (2007) 'Media independence and pluralism in Africa. Opportunities and challenges of democratization and liberalization.' In I.A. Blankson and P.D. Murphy (eds), *Negotiating Democracy. Media Transformations in Emerging Democracies.* Albany: State University of New York Press, 15–34.

Blokker, P. (2009) *Multiple Democracies in Europe. Political Culture in New Member States.* Abingdon: Routledge.

Blumler, J.G. (ed.) (1992) *Television and the Public Interest. Vulnerable Values in West European Broadcasting.* London: Sage.

Blumler, J.G. (2010) 'The two-legged crisis of journalism.' *Journalism Practice* 4(3), 243–245.

Blumler, J.G. and D. Kavanagh (1999) 'The Third Age of political communication: Influences and features.' *Political Communication* 16(3), 209–230.

Blumler, J.G. and M. Gurevitch (1995) *The Crisis of Public Communication.* London: Routledge.

Boas, T.C. (2005) 'Television and neo-populism in Latin America: Media effects in Brazil and Peru.' *Latin American Research Review* 40(2), 27–49.

Bohman, J. (2007) 'Political communication and the epistemic value of diversity: Deliberation and legitimation in media societies.' *Communication Theory* 17(4), 348–355.

Bohman, J. and W. Rehg (eds) (1997) *Deliberative Democracy. Essays on Reason and Politics.* Cambridge, MA: MIT Press.

Bourdieu, P. (1998) *On Television and Journalism.* London: Pluto Press.

Boyd-Barrett, O. and T. Rantanen (eds) (1998) *The Globalization of News.* London: Sage.

Brants, K. and H. van Kempen (2002) 'The ambivalent watchdog: The changing nature of political journalism and its effects.' In R. Kuhn and E. Neveu (eds), *Political Journalism. New Challenges, New Practices.* London: Routledge, 168–186.

Brants, K. and K. Voltmer (2011) 'Introduction: Mediatization and decentralization of political communication.' In K. Brants and K. Voltmer (eds), *Political Communication in Postmodern Democracy. Challenging the primacy of politics.* Basingstoke: Palgrave Macmillan, 1–16.

Bratton, M. (2009) 'Sub-Saharan Africa.' In C.W. Haerpfer, P. Bernhagen, R.F. Inglehart and C. Welzel (eds), *Democratization.* Oxford: Oxford University Press, 339–355.

Bratton, M. and N. van de Walle (1994) 'Neopatrimonial regimes and political transitions in Africa.' *World Politics* 46(4), 453–489.

Bratton, M., R.B. Mattes and E. Gyimah-Boadi (2005) *Public Opinion, Democracy, and Market Reform in Africa.* Cambridge: Cambridge University Press.

Brooker, P. (2009) *Non-Democratic Regimes*, 2nd edn. Basingstoke: Palgrave Macmillan.

Brunetti, A. and B. Weder (2003) 'A free press is bad news for corruption.' *Journal of Public Economics* 87, 1801–1824.

Bryant, J. and D. Zillmann (eds) (1991) *Responding to the Screen. Reception and Reaction Processes.* Hillsdale, NJ: Erlbaum.

Bryant, J. and D. Zillmann (eds) (2002) *Media Effects. Advances in Theory and Research*, 2nd edn. Mahwah: Erlbaum.

Canel, M.J. and K. Sanders (2012) *Government Communication: Cases and Challenges.* London: Bloomsbury.

Cappella, J. and K.H. Jamieson (1997) *Spiral of Cynicism. The Press and the Public Good.* Oxford: Oxford University Press.

Carothers, T. (2002) 'The end of the transition paradigm.' *Journal of Democracy* 13(1), 6–21.

Carothers, T. (2007) 'The "sequencing" fallacy.' *Journal of Democracy* 18(1), 12–27.

Carrington, T. and M. Nelson (2002) 'Media transition: The hegemony of economics.' In The World Bank (ed.), *The Right to Tell. The Role of Mass Media in Economic Development.* Washington, DC: World Bank, 225–245.

Catterberg, G. and A. Moreno (2006) 'The individual bases of political trust: Trends in new and established democracies.' *International Journal of Public Opinion Research* 18(1), 31–48.

Chaffee, S.H. and D.C. Mutz (1988) 'Comparing mediated and interpersonal communication data.' In R.P. Hawkins, J.M. Wiemann and S. Pingree (eds), *Advancing Communication Science: Merging Mass and Interpersonal Processes.* Newbury Park, CA: Sage, 19–43.

Chan, J.M. and J.L. Qiu (2002) 'China: Media liberalization under authoritarianism.' In M.E. Price, B. Rozumilowicz and S.G. Verhulst (eds), *Media Reform. Democratizing the Media, Democratizing the State.* London: Routledge, 27–47.

Cohen-Almagor, R. (2006) *The Scope of Tolerance. Studies on the Costs of Free Expression and Freedom of the Press.* Abingdon: Routledge.

Cold War International History Project (CWIHP) (2010) Available at: http://www.wilsoncenter.org/program/cold-war-international-history-project (accessed October 2010).

Coleman, S. and J.G. Blumler (2009) *The Internet and Democratic Citizenship: Theory, Practice and Policy.* Cambridge: Cambridge University Press.

Coleman, S., J. Taylor and W. van de Donk (1999) *Parliament in the Age of the Internet.* Oxford: Oxford University Press.

Collier, P. (2009) *Wars, Guns and Votes. Democracy in Dangerous Places.* London: The Bodley Head.

Coman, M. (2004) 'Media bourgeoisie and media proletariat in post-communist Romania.' *Journalism Studies* 5(1), 45–58.

Conway, M. (2006) 'Terrorism and the internet. New media – new threat?' *Parliamentary Affairs* 59(2), 283–298.

Cook, T.E. (2006) 'The news media as a political institution: Looking backward and looking forward.' *Political Communication* 23(2), 159–171.

Corner, J. (2004) 'Freedom, rights and regulations.' *Media, Culture & Society* 26(6), 893–899.

Coronel, S. (2010) 'Corruption and the watchdog role of the news media.' In P. Norris (ed.), *Public Sentinel. News Media and Governance Reform.* Washington, DC: The World Bank, 111–136.

Cotton, J. (1997) 'East Asian democracy: Progress and limits.' In L. Diamond, M.F. Plattner, Y.H. Chu and H.M. Tien (eds), *Consolidating the Third Wave Democracies. Regional Challenges.* Baltimore, MD: Johns Hopkins University Press, 95–119.

Couldry, N. (2010) *Why Voice Matters: Culture and Politics After Neoliberalism.* London: Sage.

Curran, J. and J. Seaton (1997) *Power Without Responsibility. The Press and Broadcasting in Britain*, 5th edn. London: Routledge.

Curran, J. and M.-J. Park (2000a) 'Beyond globalization theory.' In J. Curran and M.J. Park (eds), *De-Westernizing Media Studies.* London: Routledge, 2–15.

Curran, J. and M.-J. Park (eds) (2000b) *De-Westernizing Media Studies.* London: Routledge.

Dahl, R.A. (1971) *Polyarchy: Participation and Opposition.* New Haven, CT: Yale University Press.

Dahl, R.A. (1989) *Democracy and Its Critics.* New Haven, CT: Yale University Press.

Dahl, R.A. (2000) *On Democracy.* New Haven, CT: Yale University Press.

Dalton, R.J., P.A. Beck and R. Huckfeldt (1998) 'Partisan cues and the media: Information flows in the 1992 presidential election.' *American Political Science Review* 91(1), 111–126.

Dalton, R.J., D.C. Shin and Y.-H. Chu (eds) (2008) *Party Politics in East Asia. Citizens, Elections, and Democratic Development.* Boulder, CO: Lynne Rienner.

Darch, C. and P.G. Underwood (2005) 'Freedom of information legislation, state compliance and the discourse of knowledge: The case of South Africa.' *International Information and Library Review* 37(2), 77–86.

Darch, C. and P.G. Underwood (2009) 'Struggles for freedom of information in Africa.' In C. Darch and P.G. Underwood (eds), *Freedom of Information and the Developing World: The Citizens, the State and Models of Openness.* Oxford: Chandos Publishing. Available at: http://www.africafiles.org/article.asp?ID=22968 (accessed July 2011).

Dayan, D. and E. Katz (1992) *Media Events: The Live Broadcasting of History.* Cambridge, MA: Harvard University Press.

De Beer, A.S. and J. Merrill (2004) *Global Journalism: Survey of International Communication*, 4th edn. New York: Longman.

De Smaele, H. (2006) '"In the name of democracy". The paradox of democracy and press freedom in post-communist Russia.' In K. Voltmer (ed.),

Mass Media and Political Communication in New Democracies. London/New York: Routledge, 42–58.
De Zeeuw, J. and K. Kumar (eds) (2006) *Promoting Democracy in Postconflict Societies.* Boulder, CO: Lynne Rienner.
Dearing, J.W. and E.M. Rogers (1996) *Agenda Setting.* London: Sage.
Deasy, K. and H. Kaviani (2010) 'Iran's opposition abroad swells but lacks direction.' Radio Free Europe/Radio Liberty, 1 April. Available at: http://www.rferl.org/content/Irans_Opposition_Abroad_Swells_But_Lacks_Direction/1998665.html (accessed October 2010).
Deibert, R. and R. Rohozinski (2010) 'Liberation vs. control: The future of cyberspace.' *Journal of Democracy* 21(4), 43–57.
Deuze, M. (2005) 'What is journalism? Professional identity and ideology of journalists reconsidered.' *Journalism* 6(4), 442–464.
Deuze, M. (2007) *Media Work.* Cambridge: Polity.
Di Palma, G. (1990) *To Craft Democracies. An Essay on Democratic Transition.* Berkeley: University of California Press.
Diamond, L. (ed.) (1993) *Political Culture and Democracy in Developing Countries*. Boulder, CO: Lynne Rienner.
Diamond, L. (1996) 'Is the third wave over?' *Journal of Democracy* 7(3), 20–37.
Diamond, L. (1997) 'Introduction: In search of consolidation.' In L. Diamond, M.F. Plattner, Y.H. Chu and H.M. Tien (eds), *Consolidating the Third Wave Democracies. Regional Challenges.* Baltimore, MD: Johns Hopkins University Press, xiii–xlvii.
Diamond, L. (2010) 'Liberation technology.' *Journal of Democracy* 21(3), 69–83.
Diamond, L. and M.F. Plattner (eds) (2001) *The Global Divergence of Democracy.* Baltimore, MD: Johns Hopkins University Press.
Dobek-Ostrowska, B. and M. Glowacki (eds) (2011) *Making Democracy in 20 Years. Media and Politics in Central and Eastern Europe.* Wroclaw: University of Wroclaw Press.
Dobreva, A., B. Pfetsch and K. Voltmer (2011) 'Trust and mistrust on Yellow Brick Road. Political communication culture in post-communist Bulgaria.' In B. Dobek-Ostrowska and M. Glowacki (eds), *Making Democracy in 20 Years*. Wroclaw: University of Wroclaw Press, 171–192.
Donsbach, W. (2008) 'Journalists' role perceptions.' In W. Donsbach (ed.), *The International Encyclopedia of Communication*, vol. 6. Oxford: Wiley-Blackwell, 2605–2610.
Donsbach, W. and T.E. Patterson (2004) 'Political news journalists: Partisanship, professionalism, and political roles in five countries.' In F. Esser and B. Pfetsch (eds), *Comparing Political Communication. Theories, Cases, and Challenges.* Cambridge: Cambridge University Press, 251–270.
Doorenspleet, R. (2005) *Democratic Transitions: Exploring the Structural Sources of the Fourth Wave.* Boulder, CO: Lynne Rienner.
Doyle, G. (2002) *Understanding Media Economics.* London: Sage.
Dryzek, J.S. (2005) 'Deliberative democracy in divided societies. Alternatives to agonism and analgesia.' *Political Theory* 33(2), 218–242.

Dryzek, J.S. and L. Holmes (2002) *Post-Communist Democratization. Political Discourses across Thirteen Countries.* Cambridge: Cambridge University Press.

Eberts, M.W. (1998) 'The Roman Catholic Church and democracy in Poland.' *Europe-Asia Studies* 50(5), 817–842.

Elster, J., C. Offe, and U.K. Preuss (1998) *Institutional Design in Post-Communist Societies. Rebuilding the Ship at Sea.* Cambridge: Cambridge University Press.

Entman, R.M. (1993) 'Framing: Toward clarification of a fractured paradigm.' *Journal of Communication* 43(4), 51–58.

Entman, R.M. (2004) *Projections of Power: Framing News, Public Opinion and US Foreign Policy.* Chicago: Chicago University Press.

Entman, R.M. and S.S. Wildman (1992) 'Reconciling economic and non-economic perspectives on media policy: Transcending the "marketplace of ideas".' *Journal of Communication* 42(1), 5–19.

Fishkin, J.S. (1991) *Democracy and Deliberation. New Directions for Democratic Reform.* New Haven, CT: Yale University Press.

Festinger, L.A. (1962) *A Theory of Cognitive Dissonance.* Stanford: Stanford University Press.

Florentino Hofileña, C. (2004) *News for Sale. The Corruption and Commercialization of the Philippine Media.* Quezon City: Philippine Center for Investigative Journalism.

Forero, J. (2010) 'Venezuela President Chavez orders TV station off the air.' *Washington Post*, Monday, 25 January. Available at: http://www.washingtonpost.com/wp-dyn/content/article/2010/01/24/AR2010012402887.html (accessed October 2012).

Fossato, F. and J. Lloyd, with A. Verkhovsky (2008) *The Web That Failed. How Opposition Politics and Independent Initiatives are Failing on the Internet in Russia.* Oxford: Reuters Institute for the Study of Journalism.

Fox, E. and S. Waisbord (eds) (2002) *Latin Politics, Global Media.* Austin: University of Texas Press.

Fuenzalida, V. (2002) 'The reform of national television in Chile.' In E. Fox and S. Waisbord (eds), *Latin Politics, Global Media.* Austin: University of Texas Press, 69–88.

Fukuyama, F. (1991) 'Confucianism and democracy.' In L. Diamond and M.F. Plattner (eds), *The Global Divergence of Democracy.* Baltimore, MD: Johns Hopkins University Press, 23–36.

Fukuyama, F. (2004) 'The imperative of state building.' *Journal of Democracy* 15(2), 17–31.

Fuller, T. (2011) 'American arrested for insulting Thai King.' *New York Times*, 27 May. Available at: http://www.nytimes.com/2011/05/28/world/asia/28thai.html (accessed October 2012).

Gamson, W.A. and A. Modigliani (1989) 'Media discourse and public opinion on nuclear power: A constructionist approach.' *American Journal of Sociology* 95(1), 1–37.

Gehlbach, S. (2010) 'Reflections on Putin and the media.' *Post-Soviet Affairs* 26(1), 77–87.

Gibbs, J. (2000) *Gorbachev's Glasnost. The Soviet Media in the First Phase of Perestroika*. Tamu: Texas A&M University Press.
Giddens, A. (1984) *The Constitution of Society: Outline of the Theory of Structuration*. Cambridge: Polity.
Gilboa, E. (2005) 'The CNN effect: In search of a communication theory of international relations.' *Political Communication* 22(1), 27–44.
Gills, J. and S. Hughes (2005) 'Bureaucratic compliance with Mexico's new Access to Information Law.' *Critical Studies in Media Communication* 22(2), 121–137.
Goetz-Stankiewicz, M. (ed.) (1992) *Good-bye, Samizdat. Twenty years of Czechoslovak Underground Writing*. Evanston, IL: Northwestern University Press.
Goldstein, J. and J. Rotich (2008) *Digitally Networked Technology in Kenya's 2007–2008 Post-Election Crisis* (Internet and Democracy Case Study Series) Cambridge, MA: Harvard University, Berkman Center for Internet and Society. Available at: http://cyber.law.harvard.edu/sites/cyber.law.harvard.edu/files/Goldstein&Rotich_Digitally_Networked_Technology_Kenyas_Crisis.pdf.pdf (accessed October 2012).
Gordon, J. (1997) 'John Stuart Mill and the "marketplace of ideas".' *Social Theory and Practice* 23(2), 235–249.
Granovetter, M.S. (1973) 'The strength of weak ties.' *American Journal of Sociology* 78(6), 1360–1380.
Greener, I. (2005) 'The potential of path dependence in political studies.' *Politics* 25(1), 64–72.
Grugel, J. (2002) *Democratization. A Critical Introduction*. Basingstoke: Palgrave.
Gulyas, A. (1999) 'Structural changes and organisations in the print media markets of post-communist East-Central Europe.' *Javnost/The Public* 6(2), 61–74.
Gunther, A.C. and K. Schmitt (2004) 'Mapping boundaries of the hostile media effect.' *Journal of Communication* 54(1), 55–70.
Gunther, R. and A. Mughan (eds) (2000) *Democracy and the Media. A Comparative Perspective*. Cambridge: Cambridge University Press.
Gunther, R., J.R. Montero and M. Torcal (2007) 'Democracy and intermediation: Some attitudinal and behavioural dimensions.' In R. Gunther, J.R. Montero and H.J. Puhle (eds), *Democracy, Intermediation, and Voting on Four Continents*. Oxford: Oxford University Press, 29–74.
Gutmann, A. and D. Thompson (1996) *Democracy and Disagreement*. Cambridge: Cambridge University Press.
Habermas, J. (1984) *The Theory of Communicative Action: Reason and Rationalization of Society*. Cambridge: Polity.
Hacker, K.L. and J. Van Dijk (eds) (2001) *Digital Democracy. Issues of Theory and Practice*. London: Sage.
Hackett, R.A. and W.K. Caroll (2006) *Remaking Media. The Struggle to Democratize Public Communication*. Abingdon: Routledge.
Haerpfer, C.W., P. Bernhagen, R.F. Inglehart and C. Welzel (eds) (2009) *Democratization*. Oxford: Oxford University Press.

Hague, B.N. and B.D. Loader (eds) (1999) *Digital Democracy*. London: Routledge.

Hall, R.A. and P.H. O'Neil (1998) 'Institutions, transitions, and the media: A comparison of Hungary and Romania.' In P.H. O'Neil (ed.), *Communicating Democracy. The Media and Political Transitions.* Boulder, CO: Lynne Rienner, 125–145.

Hallin, D.C. and P. Mancini (2004) *Comparing Media Systems. Three Models of Media and Politics.* Cambridge: Cambridge University Press.

Hallin, D.C. and P. Mancini (eds) (2012) *Comparing Media Systems Beyond the Western World.* Cambridge: Cambridge University Press.

Hallin, D. and S. Papathanassopoulos (2002) 'Political clientelism and the media: Southern Europe and Latin America in comparative perspective.' *Media, Culture and Society* 24(2), 175–195.

Hanitzsch, T. (2011) 'Populist disseminators, detached watchdogs, critical change agents and opportunist facilitators: Professional milieus, the journalistic field and autonomy in 18 countries.' *International Communication Gazette* 73(6), 477–494.

Hankiss, E. (1994) 'The Hungarian media's war of independence.' *Media, Culture and Society* 16(3), 293–312.

Harcourt, A. (2003) 'The regulation of media markets in selected EU accession states in Central and Eastern Europe.' *European Law Journal* 9(3), 316–340.

Harcourt, A. (2004) *The European Union and the Regulation of Media Markets.* Manchester: Manchester University Press.

He, B. (2001) 'The national identity problem and democratization: Rustow's theory of sequence.' *Government and Opposition* 36(1), 97–119.

Heinzelman, J., R. Brown and P. Meier (2011) 'Mobile technology, crowdsourcing and peace mapping: New theory and applications for conflict management.' In M. Poblet (ed.), *Mobile Technologies for Conflict Management. Online Dispute Resolution, Governance, Participation.* Heidelberg: Springer, 39–54.

Held, D. (1996) *Models of Democracy*, 2nd edn. Cambridge: Polity.

Hellman, J.S., G. Jones and D. Kaufmann (2003) 'Seizing the state, seizing the day. State capture, corruption and influence in transition economies.' *Journal of Comparative Economics* 31(4), 751–773.

Hertle, H.H. (1996) *Die Chronik des Mauerfalls. Die dramatischen Ereignisse um den 9. November 1989.* Berlin: C. Links.

Hesmondhalgh, D. (2005) 'Media and cultural policy as public policy.' *International Journal of Cultural Policy* 11(1), 95–109.

Hesse, K. (1990) 'Cross-border mass communication from West to East Germany.' *European Journal of Communication* 5, 355–371.

Hollifield, J.F. and C. Jillson (eds) (2000) *Pathways to Democracy. The Political Economy of Democratic Transitions.* New York/London: Routledge.

Hong, J. (1999) 'Globalization and change in Taiwan's media. The interplay of political and economic forces.' *Asian Journal of Communication* 9(2), 39–59.

Howard, P.N. (2010) *The Digital Origins of Dictatorship and Democracy. Information Technology and Political Islam.* Oxford: Oxford University Press.

Huckfeldt, R. and J. Sprague (1987) 'Networks in context. The social flow of political information.' *American Political Science Review* 81(4), 1197–1216.

Hughes, S. and C.H. Lawson (2004) 'Propaganda and crony capitalism: Partisan bias in Mexican television news.' *Latin American Research Review* 39(3), 81–105.

Huntington, S.P. (1991) *The Third Wave. Democratization in the Late Twentieth Century.* Norman/London: University of Oklahoma Press.

Hyden, G. and M. Leslie (2002) 'Communications and democratization in Africa.' In G. Hyden, M. Leslie and F.F. Ogundimu (eds), *Media and Democracy in Africa.* New Brunswick, NJ: Transaction Publishers, 1–27.

Hyden, G., M. Leslie and F. Ogundimu (eds) (2003) *Media and Democracy in Africa.* New Brunswick, NJ: Transaction Publishers.

Index of Censorship (2011) 'Tens of thousands protest Hungarian media law', 17 March. Available at: http://www.indexoncensorship.org/2011/03/tens-of-thousands-protest-hungarian-media-law/ (accessed October 2012).

Inkeles, A. (1951) *Public Opinion in Soviet Russia. A Study in Mass Persuasion.* Cambridge, MA: Harvard University Press.

Ismail, J.A. and J. Deane (2008) 'The 2007 General Election in Kenya and its aftermath: The role of local language media.' *International Journal of Press/Politics* 13(3), 319–327.

Iyengar, S. and D.R. Kinder (1987) *News That Matters. Television and American Opinion.* Chicago: University of Chicago Press.

Jakubowicz, K. (2002) 'Media in transition. The case of Poland.' In M.E. Price, B. Rozumilowicz and S.G. Verhulst (eds), *Media Reform. Democratizing the Media, Democratizing the State.* London: Routledge, 203–231.

Jakubowicz, K. (2004) 'Ideas in our heads. Introduction of PSB as part of media system change in Central and Eastern Europe.' *European Journal of Communication* 19(1), 53–74.

Jakubowicz, K. and M. Sükösd (2008) 'Twelve concepts regarding media system evolution and democratization in post-communist societies.' In K. Jakubowicz and M. Sükösd (eds), *Finding the Right Place on the Map. Central and Eastern European Media Change in Global Perspective.* Bristol: Intellect, 9–40.

Janowitz, M. (1975) 'Professional models in journalism: The gatekeeper and the advocate.' *Journalism Quarterly* 52, 618–626.

Jenkins, H. (2006) *Convergence Culture. Where Old and New Media Collide.* New York: New York University Press.

Johnson, O.V. (1998) 'The media and democracy in Eastern Europe.' In P.H. O'Neil (ed.), *Communicating Democracy. The Media and Political Transitions.* Boulder, CO: Lynne Rienner, 103–124.

Johnson-Cartee, K. (2005) *News Narratives and News Framing: Constructing Political Reality.* Lanham, MD: Rowman & Littlefield.

Johnston, G. (1999) 'What is the history of samizdat?' *Social History* 24(2), 115–133.

Kalathil, S. (2011) *Developing Independent Media as an Institution of Accountable Governance. A How-to Guide.* Washington, DC: The World Bank.

Kang, D.C. (2002) *Crony Capitalism: Corruption and Development in South Korea and the Philippines.* Cambridge: Cambridge University Press.

Kanyegirire, A. (2006) 'Hybrid journalistic identities? Journalisms and NEPAD.' *Ecquid Novi* 27(2), 159–178.

Karl, T.L. and P.C. Schmitter (1991) 'Modes of transition in Latin America, Southern and Eastern Europe.' *International Social Science Journal* 127, 269–284.

Kasoma, F.P. (1996) 'The foundations of African ethics (Afriethics) and the professional practice of journalism: The case of society-centred media morality.' *Africa Media Review* 10(3), 93–116.

Keane, J. (1991) *The Media and Democracy*. Cambridge: Polity.

Kelley, D. and R. Donway (1990) 'Liberalism and free speech.' In J. Lichtenberg (ed.), *Democracy and the Mass Media*. Cambridge: Cambridge University Press, 66–101.

Kern, H.L. and J. Hainmueller (2009) 'Opium for the masses: How foreign media can stabilize authoritarian regimes.' *Political Analysis* 17, 377–399.

Kinzer, S. (2010) 'The limits of free speech in Rwanda. The country's president claims that laws against disseminating "genocide ideology" are necessary to stop a return to violence.' *Guardian*, 2 March. Available at: http://www.guardian.co.uk/commentisfree/libertycentral/2010/mar/02/rwanda-free-speech-genocide (accessed October 2012).

Kiousis, S. (2001) 'Public trust or mistrust? Perceptions of media credibility in the information age.' *Mass Communication and Society* 4(4), 381–403.

Kirschke, L. (2000) 'Informal repression, zero-sum politics and late third wave transitions.' *Journal of Modern African Studies* 38(3), 383–405.

Kitschelt, H.P. (1986) 'Political opportunity structures and political protest: Anti-nuclear movements in four democracies.' *British Journal of Political Science* 16(1), 57–85.

Klingemann, H.D. (1999) 'Mapping political support in the 1990s: A global analysis.' In P. Norris (ed.), *Critical Citizens. Global Support for Democratic Governance*. Oxford: Oxford University Press, 31–56.

Klingemann, H.D., D. Fuchs and J. Zielonka (eds) (2006) *Democracy and Political Culture in Eastern Europe.* London: Routledge.

Koch-Baumgarten, S. and K. Voltmer (eds) (2010) *Public Policy and the Mass Media. The Interplay of Mass Communication and Political Decision Making.* Abingdon: Routledge.

Koecher, R. (1986) 'Bloodhounds or missionaries: Role definitions of German and British journalists.' *European Journal of Communication* 1(1), 43–64.

Koltsova, O. (2006) *New Media and Power in Russia.* Abingdon: Routledge.

Krabill, R. (2001) 'Symbiosis: Mass media and the Truth and Reconciliation Commission of South Africa.' *Media, Culture and Society* 23(5), 567–585.

Kruckeberg, D. and K. Tsetsura (2003) 'A composite index by country of variables related to the likelihood of the existence of "cash for news coverage".' Institute for Public Relations/International Public Relations Association. Available at: http://banners.noticiasdot.com/termometro/boletines/docs/marcom/comunicacion/ipr/2003/index-cash-for-news-2003-final.pdf (accessed October 2012).
Krug, P. and M.E. Price (2002) 'The legal environment for news media.' In The World Bank (ed.), *The Right to Tell. The Role of Mass Media in Economic Development.* Washington, DC: World Bank, 187–205.
Kubicek, P. (1994) 'Delegative democracy in Russia and Ukraine.' *Communist and Post-Communist Studies* 27(4), 423–441.
Kumar, K. (2006) *Promoting Independent Media. Strategies for Democracy Assistance.* Boulder, CO: Lynne Rienner.
LaMay, C.L. (2009) *Exporting Press Freedom. Economic and Editorial Dilemmas in International Media Assistance.* New Brunswick, NJ: Transaction Publishers.
Lampert, N. (1988) 'The dilemmas of glasnost.' *Journal of Communist Studies* 4, 48–63.
Lauria, C. and M. O'Connor (2010) *Silence or Death in Mexico's Press. Crime, Violence and Corruption Are Destroying the Country's Journalism*, New York: Committee to Protect Journalists. Available at: http://cpj.org/reports/cpj_mexico_english.pdf (accessed October 2012).
Lawrence, R.G. (2000) 'Game-framing the issues: Tracking the strategy frame in public policy news.' *Political Communication* 17(2), 93–114.
Lazarsfeld, P.F., B. Berelson and H. Gaudet (1968) *The People's Choice: How the Voter Makes Up His Mind in a Presidential Campaign*, 3rd edn. New York: Columbia University Press.
Lee, C.C. (2000) 'State, capital, and media: The case of Taiwan.' In J. Curran and M.-J. Park (eds), *De-Westernizing Media Studies.* London: Routledge, 124–138.
Lees-Marshment, J., J. Strömbäck and C. Rudd (eds) (2010) *Global Political Marketing.* Abingdon: Routledge.
Lerner, D. (1958) *The Passing of Traditional Society: Modernizing the Middle East.* New York: Free Press.
Levitsky, S. and L.A. Way (2010) *Competitive Authoritarianism. Hybrid Regimes After the Cold War.* Cambridge: Cambridge University Press.
Levy, L.W. (1985) *Emergence of a Free Press.* Oxford: Oxford University Press.
Lichtenberg, J. (ed.) (1990a) *Democracy and the Mass Media.* Cambridge: Cambridge University Press.
Lichtenberg, J. (1990b) 'Foundations and limits of freedom of the press.' In J. Lichtenberg (ed.), *Democracy and the Mass Media.* Cambridge: Cambridge University Press, 102–135.
Lijphart, A. (1984) *Democracies: Patterns of Majoritarian and Consensus Government in Twenty-One Countries.* New Haven, CT: Yale University Press.

Lijphart, A. and C.H. Waisman (eds) (1996) *Institutional Design in New Democracies. Eastern Europe and Latin America*. Boulder, CO: Westview.

Linz, J. (1975) 'Totalitarian and authoritarian regimes.' In F.I. Greenstein and N.W. Polsby (eds), *Macropolitical Theory: Handbook of Political Science*, vol. 3. Reading: Addison-Wesley, 175–411.

Linz, J. (2000) *Totalitarian and Authoritarian Regimes*. Boulder, CO: Lynne Rienner.

Linz, J. and A. Stepan (1996) *Problems of Democratic Transition and Consolidation. South Europe, South America, and Post-Communist Europe*. Baltimore, MD: Johns Hopkins University Press.

Lipset, S.M. (1959) 'Some social requisites of democracy: economic development and political legitimacy.' *American Political Science Review* 53(1), 69–105.

Lipset, S.M. and S. Rokkan (1967) 'Cleavage structure, party systems and voter alignments.' In S.M. Lipset and S. Rokkan (eds), *Party Systems and Voter Alignments: Cross-national Perspectives*. New York: Free Press, 1–67.

Livingston, S. and T. Eachus (1995) 'Humanitarian crises and US foreign policy. Somalia and the CNN effect reconsidered.' *Political Communication* 12(4), 413–429.

Lloyd, J. (2004) *What the Media are Doing to Our Politics*. London: Constable.

Lo, V., J.N. Chan and Z. Pan (2005) 'Ethical attitudes and perceived practice: A comparative study of journalists in China, Hong Kong and Taiwan.' *Asian Journal of Communication* 15(2), 154–172.

Lohmann, S. (1994) 'The dynamics of informational cascades. The Monday Demonstrations in Leipzig, East Germany, 1989–91.' *World Politics* 47(1), 42–101.

Loveless, M. (2008) 'Media dependency: Mass media as sources of information in the democratizing countries of Central and Eastern Europe.' *Democratization* 15(1), 162–183.

Ma, E.K.W. (2000) 'Rethinking media studies: The case of China.' In J. Curran and M.-J. Park (eds), *De-Westernizing Media Studies*. London: Routledge, 21–34.

MacKinnon, R. (2008) 'Flatter world and thicker walls? Blogs, censorship and civic discourse in China.' *Public Choice* 134(1–2), 31–46.

Marcus, J. (2011) 'Hungary: Media law row overshadows EU presidency.' BBC News online, 7 January. Available at: http://www.bbc.co.uk/news/world-europe-12140395 (accessed October 2012).

Margolis, M. (1979) *Viable Democracy*. London: Macmillan.

Markowski, R. (1997) 'Political parties and ideological spaces in East Central Europe.' *Communist and Post-Communist Studies* 30(3), 221–254.

Mattes, R. and M. Bratton (2007) 'Learning about democracy in Africa: Awareness, performance, and experience.' *American Journal of Political Science* 51, 192–217.

Mayr, W. (2010) 'The monster at our door. Hungary prepares for shift in power.' Spiegel Online International, 9 April. Available at: http://www.spiegel.de/international/europe/0,1518,687921,00.html (accessed October 2012).

Mazzoleni, G. (2003) 'The media and the growth of neo-populism in contemporary democracies.' In G. Mazzoleni, J. Stewart and B. Horsfield (eds), *The Media and Neo-Populism. A Contemporary Comparative Analysis*. Westport, CT: Praeger, 1–20.

Mazzoleni, G. and W. Schulz (1999) '"Mediatization" of politics: A challenge for democracy?' *Political Communication* 16(3), 247–261.

McAdam, D., S. Tarrow and C. Tilly (2001) *Dynamics of Contention*. Cambridge: Cambridge University Press.

McCargo, D. (2003) *Media and Politics in Pacific Asia*. London: Routledge.

McCargo, D. (2012) 'Partisan polyvalence: Characterising the political role of Asian media.' In D. Hallin and P. Mancini (eds), *Comparing Media Systems Beyond the Western World*. Cambridge: Cambridge University Press, 201–223.

McChesney, R.W. (1999) *Rich Media, Poor Democracy. Communication Politics in Dubious Times*. Urbana: University of Illinois Press.

McCombs, M., D.L. Shaw and D. Weaver (eds) (1997) *Communication and Democracy. Exploring the Intellectual Frontiers of Agenda-Setting Theory*. Mahwah: Erlbaum.

McLoughlin, B. (2011) 'How Brazil is opening up access to official information.' BBC News, 31 December. Available at: http://www.bbc.co.uk/news/world-latin-america-16292843 (accessed October 2012).

McLuhan, M. (1964) *Understanding Media. The Extensions of Man*. Cambridge, MA: MIT Press.

McNair, B. (2000) 'Power, profit, corruption and lies: The Russian media in the 1990s.' In J. Curran and M.-J. Park (eds), *De-Westernizing Media Studies*. London: Routledge, 69–83.

McQuail, D. (1992) *Media Performance. Mass Communication and the Public Interest*. London: Sage.

McQuail, D. (1994) *McQuail's Mass Communication Theory*, 2nd edn. London: Sage.

McQuail, D. (2003) *Media Accountability and Freedom of Publication*. Oxford: Oxford University Press.

McQuail, D. and K. Siune (eds) (1998) *Media Policy. Convergence, Concentration and Commerce*. London: Sage.

Merkel, W. (1998) 'The consolidation of post-autocratic democracies.' *Democratization* 5(3), 33–67.

Meyer, T., with L. Hinchman (2002) *Media Democracy: How the Media Colonize Politics*. Cambridge: Polity.

Michener, G. (2011) 'FOI laws around the world.' *Journal of Democracy* 22(2), 145–159.

Mickiewicz, E. (1999) *Changing Channels. Television and the Struggle for Power in Russia*, rev. and exp. edn. Durham, NC: Duke University Press.

Mickiewicz, E. (2008) *Television, Power, and the Public in Russia*. Cambridge: Cambridge University Press.
Mill, J.S. (1972/1859) *On Liberty*. London: Penguin.
Milton, A.K. (2000) *The Rational Politician. Exploiting the Media in New Democracies*. Aldershot: Ashgate.
Mishler, W. and R. Rose (2001) 'What are the origins of political trust? Testing institutional and cultural theories in post-communist societies.' *Comparative Political Studies* 34(1), 30–62.
Mong, A. (2011) 'The price tag of a better life?' *The European*, 21 July. Available at: http://theeuropean-magazine.com/310-mong-attila/311-hungarys-media-law (accessed October 2012).
Moore, B. (1966) *Social Origins of Democracy and Dictatorship*. Boston, MA: Beacon Press.
Morlino, L. (2009a) 'Are there hybrid regimes? Or are they just an optical illusion?' *European Political Science Review* 1(2), 273–296.
Morlino, L. (2009b) 'Political parties.' In C.W. Haerpfer, P. Bernhagen, R.F. Inglehart and C. Welzel (eds), *Democratization*. Oxford: Oxford University Press, 201–218.
Morlino, L. (2012) *Changes for Democracy. Actors, Structures, Processes*. Oxford: Oxford University Press.
Mughan, A. and R. Gunther (2000) 'The media in democratic and nondemocratic regimes: A multilevel perspective.' In R. Gunther and A. Mughan (eds), *Democracy and the Media. A Comparative Perspective*. Cambridge: Cambridge University Press, 1–27.
Mungiu-Pippidi, A. (2003) 'From state to public service. The failed reform of state television in Central Eastern Europe.' In M. Sükösd and P. Bajomi-Lazar (eds), *Reinventing Media: Media Policy Reform in East-Central Europe*. Budapest: Central European University Press, 31–62.
Musa, B.A. and J.K. Domatob (2007) 'Who is a development journalist? Perspectives on media ethics and professionalism in post-colonial societies.' *Journals of Mass Media Ethics* 22(4), 315–331.
Mutz, D.C. (2002) 'Cross-cutting social networks: Testing democratic theory in practice.' *American Political Science Review* 96, 111–126.
Mutz, D.C. (2006) *Hearing the Other Side. Deliberative Versus Participatory Democracy*. Cambridge: Cambridge University Press.
Mutz, D.C. and P.S. Martin (2001) 'Facilitating communication across lines of political difference: The role of mass media.' *American Political Science Review* 95, 97–114.
Myers, M. (1998) 'The promotion of democracy at the grassroots: The example of radio in Mali.' *Democratization* 5(2), 200–216.
Nacos, B.L. (2002) *Mass-mediated Terrorism: The Central Role of the Media in Terrorism and Counterterrorism*. Lanham, MD: Rowman & Littlefield.
Napoli, P.M. (1999a) 'Deconstructing the diversity principle.' *Journal of Communication* 49(4), 7–34.
Napoli, P.M. (1999b) 'The marketplace of ideas metaphor in communications regulation.' *Journal of Communication* 49(4), 151–169.

Ndangam, L.N. (2009) '"All of us have taken Gombo". Media pluralism and patronage in Cameroonian journalism.' *Journalism* 10(6), 819–842.

Nerone, J. (2004) 'Four Theories of the Press in hindsight: Reflections on a popular model.' In M. Semati (ed.), *New Frontiers in International Communication Theory.* Lanham, MD: Rowman & Littlefield, 21–32.

Neuman, L. and R. Calland (2007) 'Making the access to information law work. The challenges of implementation.' In A. Florini (ed.), *The Right to Know*. New York: Columbia University Press, 179–213.

Neuman, R.W. (1986) *The Paradox of Mass Politics. Knowledge and Opinion in the American Electorate*. Cambridge, MA: Harvard University Press.

Newton, K. (1999) 'Mass media effects: Mobilization or media malaise.' *British Journal of Political Science* 29, 577–599.

Nisbet, E.C. (2008) 'Media use, democratic citizenship, and communication gaps in a developing democracy.' *International Journal of Public Opinion Research* 20(4), 454–482.

Nkosi, M. (2011) 'Will South Africa's "secrecy bill" become law?' BBC News, 23 November. Available at: http://www.guardian.co.uk/world/2012/jun/13/south-africa-secrecy-bill-un-condemnation (accessed October 2012).

Noorlander, P. (2011) *Media and the Law: An Overview of Legal Issues and Challenges.* Washington, DC: Center for International Media Assistance. Available at: http://cima.ned.org/publications/media-and-law-overview-legal-issues-and-challenges (accessed October 2011).

Norris, P. (2000) *A Virtuous Circle. Political Communication in Post-Industrial Democracies*. Cambridge: Cambridge University Press.

Norris, P. (2004) 'Global political communication.' In F. Esser and B. Pfetsch (eds), *Comparing Political Communication. Theories, Cases, and Challenges*. Cambridge: Cambridge University Press, 115–150.

Norris, P. and R. Inglehart (2010) 'Limits on press freedom and regime support.' In P. Norris (ed.), *Public Sentinel: New Media and the Governance Agenda*. Washington, DC: The World Bank, 193–220.

Norris, P. and S. Odugbemi (2009) 'Evaluating media performance.' In P. Norris (ed.), *Public Sentinel: New Media and the Governance Agenda*. Washington, DC: The World Bank, 3–29.

Nyamnjoh, F.B. (2004) 'Media ownership and control in Africa in the age of globalization.' In P.N. Thomas and Z. Nain (eds), *Who Owns the Media. Global Trends and Local Resistances.* Penang (Malaysia): Southbound, 119–134.

Nyamnjoh, F.B. (2005) *Africa's Media. Democracy and the Politics of Belonging.* London: Zed Books.

Nyman-Metcalf, K. (2011) *Analysis of the Hungarian Media Legislation.* Report commissioned by the Office of the OSCE Representative on Freedom of the Media. Available at: http://www.osce.org/fom/75990 (accessed October 2012).

Oates, S. (2006) 'Where's the party? Television and election campaigns in Russia.' In K. Voltmer (ed.), *Mass Media and Political Communication in New Democracies.* London: Routledge, 152–167.

Oates, S. and L. Roselle (2000) 'Russian elections and TV news: Comparison of campaign news on state-controlled and commercial television channels.' *International Journal of Press/Politics* 5(2), 30–51.

Obe, A. (2007) 'The challenging case of Nigeria.' In A. Florini (ed.), *The Right to Know*. New York: Columbia University Press, 143–178.

O'Donnell, G. (1994) 'Delegative democracy.' *Journal of Democracy* 5(1), 55–69.

O'Donnell, G. (2003) 'Horizontal accountability: The legal institutionalization of mistrust.' In S. Mainwaring and C. Welna (eds), *Democratic Accountability in Latin America*. Oxford: Oxford University Press, 34–54.

O'Donnell, G. and P.C. Schmitter (1986) *Transitions from Authoritarian Rule. Tentative Conclusions about Uncertain Democracies*. Baltimore, MD: Johns Hopkins University Press.

O'Flynn, I. (2006) *Deliberative Democracy and Divided Societies*. Edinburgh: Edinburgh University Press.

Okara, A. (2007) 'Sovereign democracy: A new Russian idea or a PR project?' *Russia in Global Affairs* 5(3), 8–20.

Olukotun, A. (2002) 'Authoritarian state, crisis of democratization and the underground media in Nigeria.' *African Affairs* 101, 317–342.

O'Neill, O. (1990) 'Practices of toleration.' In J. Lichtenberg (ed.), *Democracy and the Mass Media*. Cambridge: Cambridge University Press, 155–185.

Open Society Institute (2005) *Television Across Europe: Regulation, Policy and Independence*. Budapest: Open Society Institute.

Open Society Institute (2008) *Television Across Europe. More Channels, Less Independence*. Budapest: Open Society Institute.

Open Society Justice Initiative (2008) *The Price of Silence. The Growing Threat of Soft Censorship in Latin America*. New York: Open Society Institute.

Osa, M. and C. Corduneanu-Huci (2003) 'Running uphill: Political opportunity in non-democracies.' *Comparative Sociology* 2(4), 605–629.

Owusu, M. (1997) 'Domesticating democracy: Culture, civil society, and constitutionalism in Africa.' *Comparative Studies in Society and History* 39(1), 120–152.

Paletz, D., K. Jakubowicz and P. Novosel (eds) (1995) *Glasnost and After. Media and Change in Central and Eastern Europe*. Cresskill, NJ: Hampton Press.

Paletz, D.L. and K. Jakubowicz (eds) (2003) *Business as Usual. Continuity and Change in Central and Eastern Europe*. Cresskill, NJ: Hampton Press.

Paley, J. (2002) 'Toward an anthropology of democracy.' *Annual Review of Anthropology* 31, 469–496.

Parenti, M. (1993) *Inventing Reality. The Politics of News Media*, 2nd edn. New York: St Martin's Press.

Park, M.J., C.N. Kim and B.W. Sohn (2000) 'Modernization, globalization, and the powerful state: The Korean media.' In J. Curran and M.-J. Park (eds), *De-Westernizing Media Studies*. London: Routledge, 111–123.

Pasti, S. (2005) 'Two generations of Russian journalists.' *European Journal of Communication* 20(1), 89–115.

Patterson, T.E. (1993) *Out of Order.* New York: Knopf.

PEN International (2011) 'Rwanda: Long prison sentences for two journalists.' 14 February. Available at: http://www.internationalpen.org.uk/go/news/rwanda-long-prison-sentences-for-two-journalists (accessed October 2012).

Petrova, M. (2008) 'Inequality and media capture.' *Journal of Public Economics* 92(1–2), 183–212.

Pfetsch, B. and K. Voltmer (2012) 'Negotiating control: Political communication cultures in Bulgaria and Poland.' *International Journal of Press/Politics* 17(4), 388–406.

Pharr, S.J. and R.D. Putnam (eds) (2000) *Disaffected Democracies: What's Troubling the Trilateral Countries?* Princeton, NJ: Princeton University Press.

Picard, R.G. (1985) *The Press and the Decline of Democracy.* Westport, CT: Greenwood Press.

Picard, R.G. (1989) *Media Economics: Concepts and Issues.* London: Sage.

Plasser, F. and A. Pribersky (eds) (1996) *Political Culture in East Central Europe.* Aldershot: Avebury.

Potter, D., D. Goldblatt, M. Kiloh and P. Lewis (eds) (1997) *Democratization.* Cambridge: Polity.

Press Reference (2010) 'Poland.' Available at: http://www.pressreference.com/No-Sa/Poland.html (accessed October 2012).

Price, M.E. and M. Thompson (eds) (2002) *Forging Peace. Intervention, Human Rights and the Management of Media Space.* Edinburgh: Edinburgh University Press.

Price, M.E., B. Rozumilowicz and S.G. Verhulst (eds) (2002) *Media Reform. Democratizing the Media, Democratizing the State.* London: Routledge.

Pridham, G. (ed.) (1991) *Encouraging Democracy: The International Context of Regime Transition in Southern Europe.* London: Routledge.

Przeworski, A. (1991) *Democracy and the Market. Political and Economic Reforms in Eastern Europe and Latin America.* Cambridge: Cambridge University Press.

Przeworski, A. et al. (1995) *Sustainable Democracy.* Cambridge: Cambridge University Press.

Przeworski, A., M. Alvarez, J. Cheibub and F. Limongi (1996) 'What makes democracies endure?' *Journal of Democracy* 7(1), 39–55.

Puddington, A. (2000) *Broadcasting Freedom. The Cold War Triumph of Radio Free Europe and Radio Liberty.* Lexington: University of Kentucky Press.

Puddington, A., A. Piano, E. Young and T. Roylance (eds) (2010) *Freedom in the World 2010. The Annual Survey of Political Rights and Civil Liberties.* Washington, DC: Freedom House.

Putnam, R.D. (1993) *Making Democracy Work. Civic Traditions in Modern Italy.* Princeton, NJ: Princeton University Press.

Putnam, R.D. (2000) *Bowling Alone: The Collapse and Revival of American Community.* New York: Simon & Schuster.

Putzel, J. and J. Van der Zwan (2006) *Why Templates for Media Development Do Not Work in Crisis States. Defining and Understanding Media Development Strategies in Post-War and Crisis States.* London: LSE Research Online. Available at: http://eprints.lse.ac.uk/archive/00000837 (accessed October 2012).

Pye, L.W. (ed.) (1963) *Communications and Political Development.* Princeton, NJ: Princeton University Press.

Raboy, M. (1998) 'Public broadcasting and the global framework of media democratization.' *International Communication Gazette* 60(2), 167–180.

Rawnsley, G. (1996) *Radio Diplomacy and Propaganda.* London: Macmillan.

Rawnsley, G. (2006) 'Democratization and election campaigning in Taiwan: Professionalizing the professionals.' In K. Voltmer (ed.), *Mass Media and Political Communication in New Democracies.* Abingdon: Routledge, 133–151.

Rawnsley, G. and Q. Gong (2011) 'Political communications in democratic Taiwan. The relationship between politicians and journalists.' *Political Communication* 28(3), 323–340.

Reisinger, W.N. (1995) 'The renaissance of a rubric. Political culture as concept and theory.' *International Journal of Public Opinion Research* 7, 328–352.

Reporters Without Borders (2011) 'Fourth netizen murdered in two months in Nuevo Laredo, cartels feared.' Press release 14 November. Available at: http://en.rsf.org/mexique-fourth-netizen-murdered-in-two-14-11-2011,41385.html (accessed October 2012).

Rheingold, H. (1995) *The Virtual Community: Finding Connection in a Computerized World.* London: Minerva.

Ricchiardi, S. (2011) *Iraq's News Media After Saddam: Liberation, Repression, and Future Prospects.* Washington, DC: Center for International Media Assistance/National Endowment for Democracy. Available at: http://cima.ned.org/publications (accessed October 2012).

Ristow, B. (2010) *Cash for Coverage: Bribery of Journalists Around the World.* Washington, DC: Center for International Media Assistance. Available at: http://cima.ned.org/publications/research-reports/cash-coverage-bribery-journalists-around-world (accessed October 2010).

Robinson, E.W. (1997) *The First Democracies. Early Popular Government Outside Athens.* Stuttgart: Steiner.

Robinson, P. (2002) *The CNN Effect. The Myth of News, Foreign Policy and Intervention.* London: Routledge.

Rockwell, R. (2002) 'Mexico: The Fox factor.' In E. Fox and S. Waisbord (eds), *Latin Politics, Global Media.* Austin: University of Texas Press, 107–122.

Rockwell, R.J. and N. Janus (2003) *Media Power in Central America.* Urbana: University of Illinois Press.

Rodan, G. (1998) 'The Internet and political control in Singapore.' *Political Science Quarterly* 113(1), 63–89.

Romano, A. (2003) *Politics and the Press in Indonesia. Understanding an Evolving Political Culture.* London: Routledge.

Romano, A. (2005) 'Asian journalism, news, development and the tides of liberalization and technology.' In A. Romano and M. Bromley (eds), *Journalism and Democracy in Asia.* London/New York: Routledge, 1–14.

Roudakova, N. (2008) 'Media-political clientelism: lessons from anthropology.' *Media, Culture and Society* 30(1), 41–59.

Roudakova, N. (2009) 'Journalism as "Prostitution": Understanding Russia's reactions to Anna Politkovskaya's murder.' *Political Communication* 26(4), 412–429.

Rozumilowicz, B. (2002) 'Democratic change: A theoretical perspective.' In M.E. Price, B. Rozumilowicz and S.G. Verhulst (eds), *Media Reform. Democratizing the Media, Democratizing the State.* London: Routledge, 9–26.

Ryfe, D.M. (2001) 'History and political communication: An introduction.' *Political Communication* 18(4), 407–420.

Sartori, G. (2001) 'How far can free government travel?' In L. Diamond and M.F. Plattner (eds), *The Global Divergence of Democracy.* Baltimore, MD: Johns Hopkins University Press, 52–62.

Schaffer, F. (1998) *Democracy in Translation. Understanding Politics in an Unfamiliar Culture.* Ithaca, NY: Cornell University Press.

Schedler, A., L. Diamond and M.F. Plattner (eds) (1999) *The Self-restraining State. Power and Accountability in New Democracies.* Boulder, CO: Lynne Rienner.

Schlesinger, P. (1978) *Putting Reality Together.* London: Constable.

Schmitt-Beck, R. and K. Voltmer (2007) 'The mass media in third-wave democracies: Gravediggers or seedsmen of democratic consolidation?' In R. Gunther, J.R. Montero and H.J. Puhle (eds), *Democracy, Intermediation, and Voting in Four Continents*. Oxford: Oxford University Press, 75–134.

Schneider, C.Q. and P.C. Schmitter (2004) 'Liberalization, transition and consolidation. Measuring the components of democratization.' *Democratization* 11(5), 59–90.

Schudson, M. (1978) *Discovering the News. A Social History of American Newspapers.* New York: Basic Books.

Schudson, M. (2002) 'The news media as political institutions.' *Annual Review of Political Science* 5, 249–269.

Schumpeter, J.A. (1954) *Capitalism, Socialism and Democracy*, 4th edn. London: Allen and Unwin.

Schwartz, B. (ed.) (1971) *The Bill of Rights. A Documentary History.* New York: Chelsea House.

Seib, P. (2002) *The Global Journalist. News and Conscience in a World of Conflict.* Lanham, MD: Rowman & Littlefield.

Seligson, M.A. (2007) 'The rise of populism and the left in Latin America.' *Journal of Democracy* 18(3), 81–95.

Sen, A. (2001) *Development as Freedom.* Oxford: Oxford University Press.

Seymour-Ure, C. (1974) *The Political Impact of Mass Media.* London: Constable.

Siebert, F.S., T. Peterson and W. Schramm (1956) *Four Theories of the Press.* Urbana: University of Illinois Press.

Sigal, I. (2009) *Digital Media in Conflict-Prone Societies.* Washington, DC: Center for International Media Assistance. Available at: http://cima.ned.org/publications/research-reports/digital-media-conflict-prone-societies (accessed October 2011).

Simons, G. and D. Strovsky (2006) 'Censorship and contemporary Russian journalism in the age of the war against terrorism.' *European Journal of Communication* 21(2), 189–211.

Skidmore, T.E. (ed.) (2001) *Television, Politics, and the Transition to Democracy in Latin America.* Baltimore, MD: Johns Hopkins University Press.

Skilling, G.H. (1989) *Samizdat and an Independent Society in Central and Eastern Europe.* Basingstoke: Macmillan.

Skjerdal, T.S. (2010) 'Research on brown envelope journalism in the African media.' *African Communication Research* 3(3), 367–406. Available at: http://ccms.ukzn.ac.za/index.php?option=com_content&task=view&id=1057&Itemid=103 (accessed October 2012).

Smith, D. (2010) 'South African journalists condemn efforts to silence them.' *Guardian*, 15 August. Available at: http://www.guardian.co.uk/world/2010/aug/15/south-africa-media-censorship (accessed October 2012).

Smith, D. (2012) 'South Africa's "secrecy bill" attracts international condemnation.' *Guardian*, 13 June. Available at: http://www.guardian.co.uk/world/2012/jun/13/south-africa-secrecy-bill-un-condemnation (accessed October 2012).

Sparks, C. (2008) 'Media systems in transition: Poland, Russia, China.' *Chinese Journal of Communication* 1(1), 7–24.

Splichal, S. (2001) 'Imitative revolutions: Changes in the media and journalism in East-Central Europe.' *Javnost/The Public* 4, 31–58.

Stanford Encyclopedia of Philosophy (2007) 'Prisoner's dilemma.' Available at: http://plato.stanford.edu/entries/prisoner-dilemma (accessed October 2012).

Stiglitz, J. (2002) 'Transparency in government.' In The World Bank (ed.), *The Right to Tell. The Role of Mass Media in Economic Development.* Washington, DC: The World Bank, 27–44.

Street, J. (2011) *Mass Media, Politics and Democracy*, 2nd edn. Basingstoke: Palgrave.

Strömbäck, J. (2005) 'In search of a standard: Four models of democracy and their normative implications for journalism.' *Journalism Studies* 6, 331–345.

Sükösd, M. (2000) 'Democratic transformation and the mass media in Hungary: From Stalinism to democratic consolidation.' In R. Gunther and A. Mughan (eds), *Democracy and the Media. A Comparative Perspective.* Cambridge: Cambridge University Press, 122–164.

Sunstein, C.R. (2001) *Republic.com.* Princeton, NJ: Princeton University Press.

Sunstein, C.R. (2002) 'The law of group polarization.' *Journal of Political Philosophy* 10(2), 175–195.

Switzer, L. (2000) 'Introduction. South Africa's resistance press in perspective.' In L. Switzer and M. Adhikari (eds), *South Africa's Resistance Press: Alternative Voices in the Last Generation under Apartheid.* Athens: Ohio State University Press, 1–75.

Switzer, L. and M. Adhikari (eds) (2000) *South Africa's Resistance Press: Alternative Voices in the Last Generation under Apartheid.* Athens: Ohio State University Press.

Taylor, R.H. (ed.) (2002) *The Idea of Freedom in Asia and Africa.* Stanford: Stanford University Press.

Theiss-More, E. and J.R. Hibbing (2005) 'Citizenship and civic engagement.' *American Review of Political Science* 8, 227–249.

Thompson, J.B. (1995) *The Media and Modernity. A Social Theory of the Media.* Cambridge: Polity.

Thompson, M. and D. De Luce (2002) 'Escalating to success? The media intervention in Bosnia and Herzegovina.' In M.E. Price and M. Thompson (eds), *Forging Peace. Intervention, Human Rights and the Management of Media Space.* Edinburgh: Edinburgh University Press, 201–235.

Tironi, E. and G. Sunkel (2000) 'The modernization of communications: The media in the transition to democracy in Chile.' In R. Gunther and A. Mughan (eds), *Democracy and the Media: A Comparative Perspective.* Cambridge: Cambridge University Press, 165–194.

Tomaselli, K.G. (2000) 'Faulting faultiness: Racism in the South African media.' *Ecquid Novi* 21(2), 157–174.

Tomaselli, K.G. (2003) 'Our culture vs. foreign culture. An essay on ontological and professional issues in African journalism.' *International Communication Gazette* 65(6), 427–444.

Tomaselli, K.G. and R.E. Teer-Tomaselli (2008) 'Exogenous and endogenous democracy: South African politics and media.' *International Journal of Press/Politics* 13(2), 171–180.

Tracey, M. (2002) *The Decline and Fall of Public Service Broadcasting.* Oxford: Oxford University Press.

Tremewan, C. (1994) *The Political Economy of Social Control in Singapore.* Basingstoke: Macmillan.

Tsfati, Y. (2002) 'www.terror.com: Terror on the Internet.' *Studies in Conflict and Terrorism* 25(5), 317–332.

Tsetsura, K. and D. Kruckeberg (2012) *Transparency, Public Relations and the Mass Media. Combating Media Bribery Worldwide.* New York: Routledge.

Tuchman, G. (1972) 'Objectivity as strategic ritual: An examination of newsmen's notions of objectivity.' *American Journal of Sociology* 77, 660–679.

Tumber, H. and M. Prentoulis (2012) *Journalism and the End of Objectivity.* New York: Bloomsbury.

Van Dijk, J. (2006) *The Network Society: Social Aspects of New Media*, 2nd edn. Thousand Oaks, CA: Sage.

Vanhanen, T. (1997) *Prospects of Democracy. A Study of 172 Countries.* London: Routledge.

Verseck, K. (2011) 'Press freedom in Hungary. Prime Minister launches new offensive against journalists.' *Spiegel Online International*, 14 July. Available at: http://www.spiegel.de/international/europe/0,1518,774480,00.html (accessed October 2012).

Voltmer, K. (2010) 'The media, government accountability and citizen engagement.' In P. Norris (ed.), *Public Sentinel: New Media and the Governance Agenda*. Washington, DC: The World Bank, 137–159.

Voltmer, K. (2012) 'How far can media systems travel? Applying Hallin and Mancini's comparative framework outside the Western world.' In D. Hallin and P. Mancini (eds), *Comparing Media Systems Beyond the Western World*. Cambridge: Cambridge University Press, 224–245.

Voltmer, K. and G. Rawnsley (2009) 'The media.' In C.W. Haerpfer, P. Bernhagen, R.F. Inglehart and C. Welzel (eds), *Democratization*. Oxford: Oxford University Press, 234–248.

Voltmer, K. and M. Lalljee (2007) 'Agree to disagree: Respect for political opponents.' In A. Park et al. (eds), *British Social Attitudes. The 23rd Report*. London: Sage, 95–118.

Wahl-Jorgensen, K. and T. Hanitzsch (2009) 'Introduction: On why and how we should do journalism studies.' In K. Wahl-Jorgensen and T. Hanitzsch (eds), *The Handbook of Journalism Studies.* New York: Routledge, 3–16.

Waisbord, S. (1995) 'The mass media and consolidation of democracy in South America.' *Research in Political Sociology* 7, 207–227.

Waisbord, S. (2000a) 'Media in South America: Between the rock of the state and the hard place of the market.' In J. Curran and M.-J. Park (eds), *De-Westernizing Media Studies.* London: Routledge, 43–53.

Waisbord, S. (2000b) *Watchdog Journalism in South America. News, Accountability, and Democracy.* New York: Columbia University Press.

Waisbord, S. (2003) 'Media populism: Neo-populism in Latin America.' In G. Mazzoleni, J. Stewart and B. Horsfield (eds), *The Media and Neo-Populism. A Contemporary Comparative Analysis*. Westport, CT: Praeger, 197–216.

Waisbord, S. (2006) 'In journalism we trust? Credibility and fragmented journalism in Latin America.' In K. Voltmer (ed.), *Mass Media and Political Communication in New Democracies.* Abingdon: Routledge, 76–91.

Waisbord, S. (2007) 'Democratic journalism and "statelessness".' *Political Communication* 24(2), 115–129.

Walden, R. (2002) 'Insult laws.' In The World Bank (ed.), *The Right to Tell. The Role of Mass Media in Economic Development.* Washington, DC: World Bank, 206–224.

WAN – World Association of Newspapers (2007) *Declaration of Table Mountain. Abolishing 'Insult Laws' in Africa and Setting Free Press Higher on the Agenda.* Cape Town. Available at: http://www.wan-press.org/IMG/pdf/TableMountainDeclaration.pdf (accessed October 2012).

WAN – World Association of Newspapers (2010) *Repealing Insult Laws and Criminal Defamation Across Africa*. Available at: http://www.wan-press.org/article18638.html (accessed October 2012).

Ward, D. (2001) 'The democratic deficit and European Union communication policy. An evaluation of the Commission's approach to broadcasting.' *Javnost/The Public* 8(1), 75–94.

Wasserman, H. (2011) 'Towards a global journalism ethics via local narratives. Southern African perspectives.' *Journalism Studies* 12(6), 791–803.

Wasserman, H. and A.S. de Beer (2006) 'Conflicts of interest? Debating the media's role in post-Apartheid South Africa.' In K. Voltmer (ed.), *Mass Media and Political Communication in New Democracies*. London: Routledge, 59–75.

Wattenberg, M.P. (1998) *The Decline of American Political Parties, 1952–1996.* Cambridge, MA: Harvard University Press.

Weaver, D.H. (1998) *The Global Journalist: News People Around the World.* Cresskill, NJ: Hampton Press.

Weaver, D.H. and G.C. Wilhoit (1986) *The American Journalist.* Bloomington: Indiana University Press.

Weinthal, B. (2010) 'EU must forgo commercial interests to help Iran's Green movement.' *Guardian*, 18 June. Available at: http://www.guardian.co.uk/commentisfree/2010/jun/18/eu-iran-green-revolution-sanctions (accessed October 2012).

Welzel, C. and R. Inglehart (2008) 'Democratization as human empowerment.' *Journal of Democracy* 19(1), 126–140.

Wendell, C.R. (2009) *The Right to Offend, Shock or Disturb. A Guide to Evolution of Insult Laws in 2007 and 2008.* World Press Freedom Committee. Available at: http://www.wpfc.org (accessed October 2011).

White, S. (ed.) (2008) *Media, Culture and Society in Putin's Russia.* Basingstoke: Palgrave Macmillan.

Whitehead, L. (2002) *Democratization: Theory and Experience.* Oxford: Oxford University Press.

Willnat, L. and A. Aw (eds) (2008) *Political Communication in Asia.* London: Routledge.

World Bank (2009) *The Contribution of Government Communication Capacity to Achieving Good Governance Outcomes.* Communication for Governance and Accountability Programme. Rapporteurs' report on roundtable discussion, 19 February. Available at: http://siteresources.worldbank.org/EXTGOVACC/Resources/GWCommGAProundtablerapporteursreport.pdf (accessed October 2012).

World Bank (2012) *South Africa Economic Update: Focus on Inequality of Opportunity.* Washington, DC: The World Bank. Available at: http://siteresources.worldbank.org/INTAFRICA/Resources/257994-1342195607215/SAEU-July_2012_Full_Report.pdf (accessed October 2012).

Wright, S. and J. Street (2007) 'Democracy, deliberation and design: The case of online discussion forums.' *New Media and Society* 9(5), 849–869.

Xu, X. (2009) 'Development journalism.' In K. Wahl-Jorgensen and T. Hanitzsch (eds), *The Handbook of Journalism Studies.* New York: Routledge, 357–370.

Yordan, C.L. (2009) 'Towards deliberative peace: A Habermasian critique of contemporary peace operations.' *Journal of International Relations and Development* 12, 58–89.

Zakaria, F. (1997) 'The rise of illiberal democracy.' *Foreign Affairs* 76(6), 22–43.

Zaller, J. (2003) 'A new standard for news quality: Burglar alarms for the monitorial citizen.' *Political Communication* 20(2), 109–130.

Zassoursky, I. (2004) *Media and Power in Post-Soviet Russia.* New York: Sharpe.

Zhao, Y. (1998) *Media, Markets, and Democracy in China.* Urbana: University of Illinois Press.

Zhao, Y. and R.A. Hackett (2005) 'Media globalization, media democratization: Challenges, issues, paradoxes.' In R.A. Hackett and Y. Zhao (eds), *Democratizing Global Media. One World, Many Struggles.* Lanham, MD: Rowman & Littlefield, 1–34.

Index